SCRAP SAVER'S
101
GREAT
LITTLE
GIFTS

Sandra Lounsbury Foose

Oxmoor House®

Library of Congress Catalog Number: 94-65474
Hardcover ISBN: 0-8487-1127-0
Softcover ISBN: 0-8487-1419-9
Manufactured in the United States of America
First Printing 1994

Editor-in-Chief: Nancy Janice Fitzpatrick
Senior Crafts Editor: Susan Ramey Wright
Senior Editor, Editorial Services: Olivia Kindig Wells
Art Director: James Boone

Scrap Saver's 101 Great Little Gifts

Editor: Catherine S. Corbett
Assistant Art Director: Cynthia R. Cooper
Editorial Assistants: Catherine Barnhart Pewitt,
Wendy L. Wolford
Senior Photographer: John O'Hagan
Photostylist: Connie Formby
Copy Editor: L. Amanda Owens
Copy Assistants: Leslee Rester Johnson,
Jennifer K. Mathews
Production and Distribution Director: Phillip Lee
Production Manager: Gail Morris
Associate Production Manager: Theresa L. Beste
Production Assistant: Marianne Jordan
Computer Artist: Carol Loria
Senior Production Designer: Larry Hunter
Publishing Systems Administrator: Rick Tucker

To my husband,
Dean,
for 101 great
little reasons.

Contents

INTRODUCTION

Right in the heart of my hometown, on a welcoming patch of green, stands a weathered, old inn. On this historic square, edged with flowers and surrounded by shade trees, a border of quaint brick storefronts provides the frame around a picture-perfect scene. The charm of the shops and the quality of the merchandise within are matched by the warmth of the proprietors, making the square a gift-shopper's paradise. I know you would love it!

This wonderful place was the inspiration for *101 Great Little Gifts*. As I completed the projects, I sorted them into different chapters, much like the various shops around the square. So now a trip into town is just as close as your bookshelf. For early birds and night owls, the doors are always open, 24 hours a day, 7 days a week. You are cordially invited to come in and spend a few minutes browsing for ideas. Or sit for hours selecting patterns. With an emphasis on quick and easy designs, each shop offers a collection of gifts to make for any reason, in every season. But before you begin, please turn to page 168 and look over the suggestions for Supplies and Techniques; then be sure to read every step of the instructions for the gift you are making.

You can make most of the designs in this book with ease at those times when you need both the perfect gift and the pleasure of a few creative moments. Some of the projects can involve the whole family, and a few might even be simple enough to make with the littlest person in your home. On those occasions, you'll be sharing the best gifts of your time, attention, wisdom, and skill.

Surely the best gifts of all are love and friendship, but next in line, I think, are the little surprises and gestures of kindness that come our way when we least expect them. Remember some of the gifts you've received from the hands of children...a bunch of wilting dandelions, a blue jay feather, a macaroni necklace, and all those rocks! These gifts were so precious because they came straight from loving hearts that expected nothing in return.

Gifts from the heart, especially the handmade ones, are my favorites to give and receive. When I receive a handmade present, it becomes a part of my life. Each time I see it, I appreciate the gift as well as the love, the thought, and the time that went into making it.

This book is my handmade gift to you. I hope it will become a part of your life, offering inspiration and encouragement as you plan surprises for your loved ones. And you can start now, because the Lollipop Shop is right next door.

Sandy

6

Lollipop Shop

To snuggle a newborn or tickle a toddler, visit the Lollipop Shop for gifts of every flavor. Several ideas were inspired by classic toys of long ago and will encourage hours of creative play.

Drop in the Bucket Game

Materials
Pattern on page 126
Tracing paper
12 (9") squares scrap fabric (4
   each of different colors)
Black embroidery floss
Thread to match fabrics
Extra-fine unwaxed dental floss
1 (2-pound) bag of plastic
   stuffing pellets*
1 clean gallon paint can
   (available at paint stores)
*See Resources, page 173.
Note: Because of stuffing pellets,
this game is not intended for
very young children. (Pellet
packaging suggests use for children over 7 years of age.) For
optional scorecards, use color
coding labels available at
stationery stores and unruled
3" x 5" index cards. Match label
colors to fabric colors.

*A dozen "drips" fill a new paint
can to make this colorful version
of the classic beanbag toss. Many
paint stores will supply a painter's
cap or two for the players.*

Instructions
Note: Seam allowances are ¼"
and are included in pattern.
1. On folded tracing paper, trace
paint drip pattern, transferring
markings and face details. Cut
out eyes and along mouth line.
Unfold pattern.
2. Trace pattern on bias on right
side of each fabric square.
Transfer face details. Using 1
strand of black floss, satin-stitch
eyes and backstitch mouths. Cut
out drips.
3. For each drip, with right sides
facing and raw edges aligned,
fold drip in half along center
front. Stitch center back seam,
leaving 2" opening. Using dental
floss, run gathering stitches along
lower curved raw edge. Pull
tightly to gather. Wrap dental
floss around gathered edge; then
stitch back and forth through
seam allowance to secure. Tie
off. Turn right side out. Fill with
½ cup plus 1 tablespoon of
pellets. (For easier filling, make
funnel from piece of paper rolled
and taped to form open-ended
cone.) Securely slipstitch
opening closed.

To play the game:
   Mark a line one foot
away from the empty, new
paint can. Continue mark-
ing lines one foot apart
until you reach five feet.
   Give each player a different color set of beanbags.
From the one-foot line, let
each player toss the paint
drips, one at a time, into
the bucket. On the score-
cards, record the number of
drips that each player lands
in the bucket. Once all
players have tossed from
the one-foot line, move
back to the two-foot line.
Continue in this manner
until all players have tossed
their beanbags from each of
the lines.
   Total the scorecards. The
player who tossed the most
paint drips into the bucket
wins.

Paper Mice

Materials for one mouse

Patterns on page 126
Tracing paper
Craft knife
⅛" paper punch
3" x 6½" scrap art paper in
    desired color for mouse
Fine-tip permanent black
    marker
1½" square yellow art paper
White glue

Instructions

1. Trace mouse body, ear, and cheese patterns onto tracing paper, transferring markings. Cut out, using craft knife. Cut eyes, mouth, and ear slits on mouse body. Punch holes in cheese.
2. Trace 1 mouse body and 2 ears onto 3" x 6½" scrap of art paper. Transfer details, lightly marking glue tab and transferring dot for tail to wrong side. Draw small eyes with marker. Cut out mouse body, making slits for mouth and ears. Cut out ears, making slits. To make tail, cut 5½"-long strip from remaining paper, tapering it from ⅛" wide at 1 end to point at other end.
Trace cheese pattern onto yellow art paper. Cut out and punch holes as indicated.
3. Gently pull mouse body over scissors blade to curl slightly and begin to form cone shape. Spread thin layer of glue on top of glue tab. Overlap opposite side, shaping mouse body into cone. Insert blunt pencil into nose of cone to help with shaping and gluing. Hold in place until dry. Add more glue with pin if necessary.
4. Place dot of glue on 1 ear near base. Overlap edges along slit to form slightly concave ear. Insert ear into 1 slit on body. Repeat to make and attach other ear.
Gently pull tail over scissors blade to curl. Glue tail inside mouse at center back seam. Insert cheese into mouth.

Crayon Container

Materials

2¾" x 8¼" piece posterboard
8-ounce tomato sauce can, empty and clean (approximately 2⅝" x 3")
Craft glue
Rubber bands
28 standard-size crayons*
*Note: Be *sure* crayons are non-toxic and contain no lead.

Due to variations in sizes of crayons and containers, you may need to adjust measurements and quantities.

Use these mini mice as place cards, package toppers, or decorations for a playroom bookshelf.

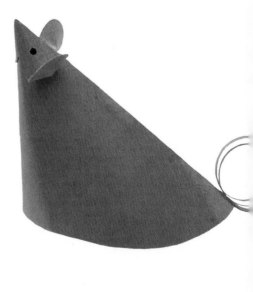

Instructions

1. On each end of posterboard, draw several parallel lines perpendicular to long edges. These lines will be used for aligning crayons.
2. Wrap posterboard around can, overlapping ends. Glue in place. Hold posterboard in place with rubber bands until dry.
3. Glue crayons around can, aligning them between drawn lines. Hold in place with rubber bands until dry.

Crayon Frame

Materials

Pattern on page 127
Tracing paper
4⅜" square thick cardboard
⅛" paper punch
Craft knife
2"-square piece artwork
5" length jute cord
4⅜" square thin cardboard
Craft glue
Duct tape *or* mailing tape
16 standard-size crayons*
Note: Be *sure* crayons are non-toxic and contain no lead.

Instructions

1. Trace pattern onto tracing paper, transferring markings. Cut out.
2. To make frame back, place pattern on top of thick cardboard, aligning edges. Transfer numbered dots and center square to cardboard. Punch out dots, using paper punch. Glue artwork in place in center square.
3. To make hanging loop, knot 1 end of jute cord once or twice so that knot is larger than punched-out holes. Working from back, pass unknotted end of cord through hole No. 1 to artwork side and then through hole No. 2

This colorful set is ideal for a budding young artist.

to back. Leaving small loop at center top of frame, pass cord through hole No. 3 to artwork side and then through hole No. 4 to back. Knot cord end so loop won't show when frame is hung.
4. To make frame front, place pattern on top of thin cardboard, aligning edges. Transfer center square and placement lines to cardboard. Using craft knife, cut out center square. Glue frame front on top of frame back, aligning edges and centering artwork in opening. Secure edges with duct tape.

5. Referring to placement lines and photo, glue crayons in groups of 4 to front of frame.

Reversible Play Capes

Materials for one cape
1 yard 42"- to 45"-wide fabric
   for cape
1 yard 42"- to 45"-wide fabric
   for lining
Vanishing fabric marker
Thread to match
18" length ¼"-wide elastic
Small safety pin
54" length velvet tubing
   or cording

Instructions
Note: Seam allowances are ½"
and are included in fabric measurements. Neckline of cape is
elastic so, once it is tied, the
child can easily slip it on and off
without retying it. Cape measures approximately 35" from
hood peak to hem and is a good
length for 3- to 6-year-old magicians and royalty.
1. Referring to Diagram 1,
measure and cut out cape and
hood. (Use full width of fabric for
cape.) Repeat to cut same size
lining pieces for cape and hood.
2. Referring to Diagram 2, with
right sides facing and raw edges
aligned, pin cape and lining
together. Using ½" seam and
beginning and ending stitches
1⅛" from top raw edge, stitch
sides and bottom of cape. Then
stitch across top raw edge,
leaving 22" opening in center for
hood. Turn cape right side out.
Press so that seams are exactly
on edge. Press lining seam
allowance along opening to
wrong side of cape.
3. To make hood, referring to
Diagram 3 and with right sides
facing, fold 11" x 23" hood piece,
short edges together, to measure
11" x 11½". Position fold at top.
Stitch center back seam as
indicated. Press seam as open as
possible. Leave wrong side out.
Repeat to make hood lining. Turn
hood lining right side out. With
right sides facing, insert lining
into hood, aligning seams and
raw edges. Stitch front opening
seam. Turn unit right side out.
Align and baste raw edges
together, ½" from edge. Press
front opening so that seam is
exactly on edge. Tack hood and
lining layers together at peak.
4. Referring to Diagram 4, with
right sides facing and raw edges
aligned, pin hood to cape neck
edge opening (*do not pin to cape
lining*). Machine-stitch hood unit
to cape.

Pin cape lining over hood
seam allowance and slipstitch,
catching only hood and cape
lining fabrics with stitches.
Machine-topstitch along cape
neck edge, 1/16" from edge. Make
another line of stitches ½" from
neck edge to form casing.

Using small safety pin, insert
elastic into casing. Adjust
gathers. Fold elastic under ¼" at
each end of casing. Tack elastic
securely to lining part of casing.
Cut tubing in half; insert 1 piece
½" into 1 casing opening. Tack
tubing securely to casing. Repeat
with remaining piece. Knot ends
of tubing.

Diagram 1: Cutting Cape and Hood

Approximately 44"

Scrap

11" x 23" Hood

36"

Cape

25" x 44"
(or width of fabric)

Diagram 2: Stitching Cape and Lining

Stitching begins 1⅛" from top raw edge.

Neck edge
22" Opening

Cape

Stitching begins 1⅛" from top raw edge.

Diagram 3: Stitching Hood

Folded top edge

Center back seam

Hood

Front opening

Neck edge

Diagram 4: Stitching Hood to Cape

Open →

← Open

Magic Wands

Materials for one wand

Pattern on page 126
Tracing paper
5" x 10½" piece lamé
Thread to match
Pinking shears
Polyester stuffing
12" length ¼"-diameter dowel
   (painted, if desired)
Craft glue
Matching wooden bead with
   ¼" opening
Narrow satin ribbons in various
   colors *or* ¼"-wide gold
   metallic paper ribbon
   (optional)

Instructions

Note: Broken pattern line is stitching line. Add ¼" seam allowance when cutting fabric.

1. Trace pattern onto tracing paper and cut out.

2. Cut lamé into 1 (5") square and 2 (2¾" x 5") rectangles. To make back, with right sides facing and raw edges aligned, stitch rectangles together along 1 long edge. Press seam open.

3. Center and trace star on wrong side of 5" square. With right sides facing and raw edges aligned, pin marked square to seamed back (seam should run from top to bottom). Stitch along entire star outline and cut out. For best results, trim seam to ⅛" using pinking shears.

Clip into crevices. Clip a few threads at base of back seam for opening. Turn star right side out.

4. Stuff star, maintaining flatness. Slipstitch all except end of opening closed. Cover 1" of 1 end of dowel with glue. Insert glued portion into opening. When dry, stitch opening, if necessary, for secure fit. Apply glue to opposite end of dowel and fit bead in place.

5. Tie ribbon streamers to dowel below star or wrap dowel with paper ribbon.

Fairy godmothers and magicians over the age of three can spend many enchanting afternoons with these fanciful ensembles.

Little Sweetheart Receiving Blanket

Materials
Pattern on page 127
Tracing paper
6" square acetate
Craft glue
2 (35") squares flannel
Vanishing fabric marker
Thread to match flannel

Instructions
Note: Seam allowances are ¼" and are included in fabric measurements.

1. Trace heart pattern onto tracing paper, transferring markings. Glue to acetate and cut out.

2. On wrong side of 1 flannel square, use vanishing fabric marker to draw seam line around square, ¼" from edge.

3. To make curved corners, place heart pattern in 1 corner of marked flannel square, aligning outside side edges of heart with marked seam lines. Using vanishing fabric marker, trace around bottom outside curved edge of heart. Repeat with remaining corners. With right sides facing and raw edges aligned, layer marked flannel

These handmade gifts cost a fraction of purchased ones.

square on top of unmarked flannel square.

4. Stitch around blanket along seam line, following marked curves at corners and leaving 4" opening along 1 straight edge. Trim each corner to within ¼" of curve. Clip curves. Turn blanket right side out. Lightly press so that seam is exactly on edge. Slipstitch opening closed.

5. Using vanishing fabric marker, mark topstitching line ½" from edges of blanket. With marked side up, fold blanket in half, top to bottom; finger-press and unfold. Then fold blanket in half, left to right; finger-press and unfold. Using vanishing fabric marker, mark these horizontal

and vertical lines to indicate quarter sections of blanket.

Using pattern and referring to Diagram, trace 1 heart in each outer corner, aligning bottom outside curved edge of heart with edges of blanket. At midpoint along each edge, mark 2 adjacent hearts, aligning 1 edge of heart with edge of blanket and dotted placement line of other edge of heart with marked quarter section line. At center of blanket, mark 4 hearts, aligning dotted placement lines on pattern with quarter section lines on blanket.

Referring to Diagram, machine-topstitch around hearts and perimeter of blanket.

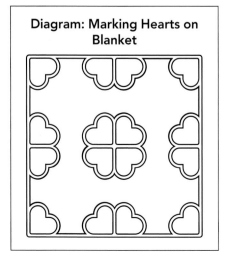

Diagram: Marking Hearts on Blanket

Playful Pentagon Ball

Materials

Pattern on page 128
Craft glue
4" square sandpaper
8" x 12" piece crisp fusible
   interfacing
12 (3¼") squares different
   print cotton fabrics
Thread to match
Polyester stuffing

Instructions

1. For best results, photocopy pattern. Glue pattern to smooth side of sandpaper. Cut out.
2. Place rough side of pattern on interfacing and, using sharp pencil, trace 12 accurate pentagons (edges can be adjacent). Cut out along outlines. Following manufacturer's instructions, center and fuse 1 pentagon to wrong side of each fabric square. Cut out fabric pentagons, adding ¼" seam allowance beyond interfacing edges.
3. Fold, finger-press, and baste seam allowance to interfacing side of each pentagon. (In order for all pentagons to fit together perfectly, fabric must be folded *exactly* along edges of interfacing. As you work, hold up unit to light to check edges.)
4. Referring to Diagram, place 6 pentagons right side down on work surface. Label center pentagon. With right sides facing and edges aligned, join side pentagons 1 at a time to center pentagon by whipstitching adjoining edges together. Knot thread securely at beginning and end of each line of stitches. Keep closely placed, shallow stitches exactly on edges of fabric. Finished unit will resemble flower with 5 "petals" around center.
5. Noting arrows on Diagram, use whipstitches to join adjacent edges of 5 pentagon petals. The resulting bowl-like unit is half of ball. Repeat with remaining 6 pentagons to make other half of ball.
6. Turn both "bowl" units inside out. Bring 2 units together to form ball, fitting "peaks" of 1 into "valleys" of other. Whipstitch edges together, knotting thread securely at beginning and end of each line of stitches and leaving 2 edges of 1 pentagon open for turning.
7. Turn ball right side out and stuff. Slipstitch opening tightly closed.

Diagram: Joining Pentagons

Half of unit

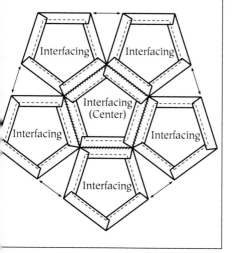

Pentagon Play Shirt

Materials

Pattern on page 128
Sandpaper scrap
5 (3") squares different color
   cotton fabrics
Vanishing fabric marker
Thread to match
Purchased baby play shirt

Instructions

Note: Broken pattern line is stitching line. Add ¼" seam allowance when cutting fabrics.
1. For best results, photocopy pattern. Glue pattern to smooth side of sandpaper. Cut out.
2. Place rough side of pattern on right side of 1 fabric square. Using vanishing fabric marker, trace pattern. Repeat with remaining fabric squares. Cut out 5 pentagons, adding ¼" seam allowance.
3. Fold, finger-press, and baste seam allowance to wrong side of each pentagon.
4. Referring to photo, place 5 pentagon patches together on shirt so that center area forms star. Pin patches in place. Tack edges together at star points. Slipstitch patches to shirt. (Bury knots under patches on front of shirt so that inside of shirt is smooth.)

Child's Pleated Eyelet Apron

Materials

Pattern on page 128
Tracing paper
Vanishing fabric marker
10" x 18" piece fabric for facings (eyelet or similar fabric)
Thread to match fabrics
1¼ yard scallop-bordered eyelet fabric for apron, approximately 24" wide
2⅔ yards ⅞"-wide double-face satin ribbon for ties

Instructions

Note: Seam allowances are ¼" and are included in pattern and fabric measurements.

1. On folded tracing paper, trace apron arm facing pattern, transferring markings. Cut out.

2. From facing fabric, cut 2½" x 10" piece for bib facing. Along 1 long edge of bib facing, press under ¼" and stitch. Set aside.

On remaining facing fabric, trace 1 arm facing; reverse pattern and trace 1 arm facing. Transfer markings and cut out. Along outer curved edge of each arm facing, press under ¼" and stitch. Along each short end, press under ¾"; stitch. Set aside.

3. Center and mark 42" along scalloped edge of eyelet. (Make sure this measurement is centered on scallops so that when side edges are hemmed, scallops will match at sides.) Trim excess fabric from sides.

Referring to Diagram 1 (see page 21) and working on wrong side of eyelet fabric, measure and mark 7¾" down from top raw edge. Draw horizontal line across apron at this mark. Fold fabric in half, short edges together, and mark center top.

Measure and mark ½" on each side of center, drawing vertical lines to meet horizontal line drawn across apron. Then mark vertical lines at 1" intervals across apron to within 2½" of each cut end of eyelet. (If eyelet is transparent, this can be done quickly by taping fabric in place on 1" gridded board.)

4. To pleat apron top, with right sides facing and raw edges aligned, fold apron along center line. Backstitching at beginning and end, stitch along marked lines on each side of center fold to horizonal line to make first tuck. Continue folding and stitching to make pleats across apron. On wrong side, press center tuck flat; then press all other tucks toward center.

5. With right sides facing and raw edges aligned, center and stitch bib facing along top pleated edge of apron. (Facing will not match apron width.) Press facing to wrong side so that seam is exactly on edge. Tack facing to pleats.

6. Referring to Diagram 2 (see page 21), with right sides facing, align 1 folded end of 1 arm facing with faced top edge of apron, 4" from center pleat seam. If pleats are exactly 1" wide, top dot on arm facing should align with pleat seam. Other dot on facing should be 6½" from top *raw* edge of apron (portion that isn't faced). Securely pin arm facing in place. Repeat with remaining facing on other side of apron. Before stitching facings or trimming apron fabric, fold each apron side edge under ¼"; press. Then turn edges under again to match edge of each facing. Lift arm facings and stitch side hems. Trim apron to match raw edge of facings.

Stitch arm seam along curved raw edge of 1 facing, beginning and ending with backstitches. Clip seam allowance along curves. Repeat with remaining facing. Press facings to wrong side of apron so that seams are exactly on edge.

7. Cut ribbon into 4 (24") lengths. Place 1 end of 1 ribbon approximately ¾" inside arm facing at bib top; slipstitch side edges of ribbon to bib facing. Place 1 edge of another ribbon approximately ¾" inside arm facing at apron side; slipstitch side edges of ribbon to apron side hem. Refold and flatten arm facing over ribbons. Slipstitch curved hemmed edge of facing to bib facing, pleats, and apron side hem. Repeat with remaining ribbons on other side of apron. Fold cut ends of ribbons under and hem by hand.

Child's Pleated Striped Apron

Materials

Pattern on page 128
Tracing paper
Vanishing fabric marker
10" x 18" piece fabric for facings
Thread to match fabrics
26" x 42" piece fabric with 1"-wide stripes for apron, cut so that stripes run parallel to 26" edge and light stripe runs down center of fabric
3 (3¼" x 24") strips fabric for ties, cut so that 1 edge of each strip aligns with 1 edge of 1 stripe *or* 3 (24") lengths ⅞"-wide grosgrain ribbon

Instructions

Note: Seam allowances are ¼" and are included in pattern and fabric measurements.

These instructions are for

Mother's little helper needs an apron just her size.

stripes that are exactly 1" wide. If stripes are slightly more or less than 1" wide, the fabric can be used, but pleats will not be centered on bib and top dot on arm facing won't align with pleat seam. Make apron ties to equal the width of stripes.

1. Complete steps 1 and 2 of Child's Pleated Eyelet Apron.

2. Referring to Diagram 1 (see page 21) and working on wrong side of fabric, measure and mark

7¾" down from top raw edge. Draw horizontal line across apron at this mark. Fold fabric in half, short edges together, and mark center top. Mark should align with center light stripe. There is no need to draw 1" pleats across apron, as with Child's Pleated Eyelet Apron, since stripes will provide guidelines.

3. To pleat apron top, with right sides facing and raw edges

aligned, fold apron along center line. Backstitching at beginning and end, stitch along edge of stripe at center fold to horizontal line to make first tuck. Continue to make pleats across apron, leaving 2½" in from each side unpleated. On wrong side, press center tuck flat; then press all other tucks toward center.

4. Complete steps 5 and 6 of Child's Pleated Eyelet Apron.

(Continued on page 20)

(Continued from page 19)

5. Fold each tie strip under ¼" along 1 short edge and press. Referring to Diagram 3, fold long edge that is not aligned with stripe under ¼". Then fold remaining fabric in thirds to make 1"-wide strap. Machine-stitch around ties, close to folded edges. For waist ties, place raw end of 1 tie approximately 1" inside 1 arm facing at apron side edge; securely slipstitch in place. Repeat on other side of apron.

6. For neck strap, attach remaining tie strap to 1 side of bib top as in Step 5 above. To make adjustable neck strap loop,

cut 1" x 3" piece from facing fabric scraps. Fold in half, long edges together; press. Open and fold raw edges to center fold line. Refold to make ¼"-wide strip, aligning long folded edges. Press. Stitch close to folded edges. Place raw ends of loop under right arm facing at bib top. Tack securely along edges to bib facing. Refold and flatten arm facings over ties and loop ends. Slipstitch ends of facings closed. Slipstitch curved hemmed edge of each facing to bib facing, pleats, and apron side hem. Thread other end of neck strap through loop and tie in knot.

7. To hem apron, fold bottom raw edge under ¼" and press. Then fold under 1¾" (adjust hem depth, if necessary); hem.

Child's Straight Apron

Materials

Pattern on page 128
Tracing paper
Vanishing fabric marker
10" x 18" piece fabric for facings
Thread to match fabrics
22" x 26" piece sturdy fabric for apron (lightweight fabric can be reinforced with fusible interfacing)
2 yards ⅞"-wide coordinating ribbon for ties (optional)
3" length ¼"-wide coordinating ribbon for loop
3 (¾") flat buttons

Instructions

Note: Seam allowances are ¼" and are included in pattern and fabric measurements

1. On folded tracing paper, trace apron arm facing pattern, transferring markings. Cut out.

2. On facing fabric, trace 1 arm facing; reverse pattern and trace 1 arm facing. Transfer markings and cut out. Along outer curved edge of each arm facing, press under ¼" and stitch. Along each short end, press under ¾" and stitch. Set aside.

3. To hem sides of apron, fold each long end under ¼" and press. Then fold under ½". Press and machine-stitch.

To hem top of apron, fold 1 short raw edge under ¼" and press. Then fold under 1⅛". Press and machine-stitch. To hem bottom, fold remaining short raw edge under ¼" and press. Then fold under 2" (adjust hem according to child's size). Press and machine-stitch.

4. Referring to Diagram 4, with right sides facing, align folded ends of 1 facing with top and side of apron. Dots on facing should be 6¼" from top corner. Pin securely; trim apron fabric to match raw edge of facing. Beginning and ending with backstitches, stitch seam along curved raw edge of facing. Clip seam allowance along curve. Repeat with remaining facing. Press facings to wrong side of apron so that seams are exactly on edge.

5. Cut ribbon into 3 (24") lengths. Hem ends of ribbon. Place cut end of 1 ribbon approximately ¾" inside facing at 1 apron side; slipstitch side edges of ribbon to apron side hem. Repeat on other side. Attach remaining ribbon in same way on 1 side of bib top. Stitch buttons 3½", 5", and 6½" from free end of tie. To make button loop, insert raw ends of ¼"-wide ribbon under arm facing at other side of bib top. Tack ends securely to bib hem. Refold and flatten arm facings over ribbons. Machine-stitch edges of facings to apron.

Diagram 1: Marking Pleat Lines

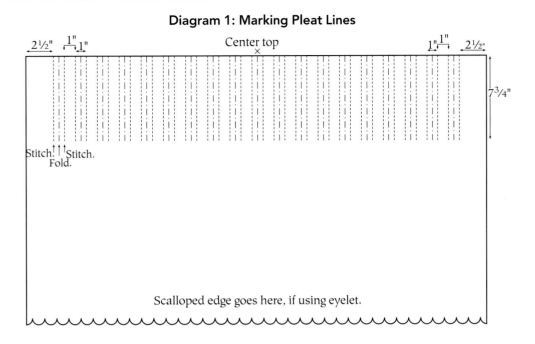

2½" 1" 1" Center top 1" 1" 2½"
×

7¾"

Stitch. ↑↑ Stitch.
Fold.

Scalloped edge goes here, if using eyelet.

Diagram 2: Stitching Arm Facings on Pleated Aprons

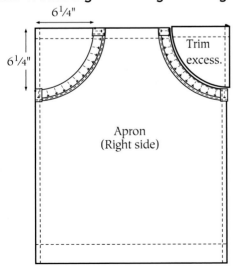

Raw edge Faced top edge Trim excess.
4" × 4"

Hem edge to match facing.

Place dot on facing 6½" from raw edge.

Apron
(Right side)

Hem edge to match facing.

Diagram 3: Folding Ties

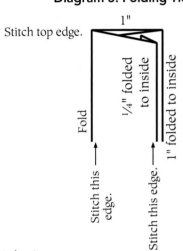

Stitch top edge.
1"

Fold

Stitch this edge.

¼" folded to inside

Stitch this edge.

1" folded to inside

Diagram 4: Stitching Arm Facings on Straight Apron

6¼"

6¼"

Trim excess.

Apron
(Right side)

Newborn Booties

Materials
Pattern on page 129
Tracing paper
9" x 14" piece fabric for booties
9" x 14" piece flannel for lining
Thread to match
Pinking shears
2 (8") pieces ⅛" corded piping
1 yard ¼"-wide coordinating
    double-face satin ribbon
Small safety pin

Instructions
Note: Broken pattern line is stitching line. Add ¼" seam allowances when cutting fabrics.

1. On folded tracing paper, trace bootie pattern, transferring markings. Cut out. Unfold pattern.

2. On wrong side of bootie fabric, place pattern pieces ½" apart. Trace 2 booties. Cut out, adding ¼" seam allowances. Using basting stitches, transfer casing line to right side of each piece.

3. Repeat Step 2 with lining fabric, omitting casing line.

4. With right sides facing and raw edges aligned, fold 1 bootie fabric piece in half along center bottom. Pin and stitch center front seam, leaving open between large dots for casing. Clip seam allowance once above casing. Clip entire stitched curved seam allowance below casing. Open seam allowance and finger-press flat. If fabric is thick, whipstitch seam allowance to wrong side of bootie, as invisibly as possible. If fabric is thin, baste seam allowance to wrong side of bootie. (Leave in basting stitches until ribbon is pulled through casing in Step 8.) Use tiny stitches to anchor seam allowance around casing. Stitch center back seam. Open seam allowance and

These soft gifts are sure to be treasured additions to a newborn's layette.

finger-press flat. Whipstitch or baste to bootie.

5. With right sides facing, fold bootie, aligning dots on sole with dots at center front and center back seams. Pin and stitch A edges together to form heel and B edges together to form toe. Trim seam allowances with pinking shears. Leave wrong side out. Trim piping seam allowance to ¼" if necessary. Aligning raw edges, baste and stitch piping to right side of bootie along top edge, tapering cut ends into seam allowance at back. Turn right side out. To reduce bulk, trim approximately half of piping seam allowance *only*. Repeat to assemble other bootie fabric piece.

6. To make lining, repeat steps 4 and 5, omitting piping and

leaving 1½" opening along center back seam for turning. Leave wrong side out.

7. With right sides facing and raw edges aligned, fit 1 bootie fabric piece inside 1 lining piece. Pin and machine-stitch together along top edge. Trim 1 layer of seam allowance to ⅛" to reduce bulk; clip seam allowance. Turn right side out through opening. Slipstitch opening closed. Tuck lining into bootie. Smooth wrinkles. Tack bootie and lining together at toe and heel seams, as invisibly as possible.

8. Turn bootie inside out and stitch casing. Turn right side out. Using small safety pin, insert ribbon through casing. Tack ribbon to bootie at center back. Repeat to complete other bootie.

Newborn Cap

Materials

Patterns on page 129
Tracing paper
8" x 19" piece fabric for cap
8" x 19" piece fabric for lining
Thread to match
1 yard ⅛" corded piping
28" length ⅜"-wide
    coordinating double-face
    satin ribbon

Instructions

Note: Broken pattern lines are stitching lines. Add ¼" seam allowance when cutting fabrics.

1. On folded tracing paper, trace cap side and back patterns, transferring markings. Cut out. Unfold patterns.

2. Working on wrong side of cap fabric and placing pattern pieces ½" apart, trace 1 side and 1 back. Cut out, adding ¼" seam allowances. With right sides facing and raw edges aligned, stitch side piece together along short center back seam. Press open. Turn right side out.

3. Repeat Step 2 with lining fabric, leaving wrong side out.

4. Trim piping seam allowance to ¼" if necessary. Aligning raw edges and clipping piping seam allowance, baste and stitch piping to right side of cap back circle, tapering cut ends into seam allowance.

   Aligning raw edges, stitch remaining piping in continuous line along neck and front edges on right side of cap side piece. Clip seam allowance of piping at curves and taper cut ends of piping into cap seam allowance at center back.

5. Make row of large machine stitches along seam line on back edge of cap side piece. Pull threads to gather. With right

sides facing and raw edges aligned, pin cap side and back pieces together, matching dots and adjusting gathers evenly. Stitch. Trim 1 layer of back seam allowance to ⅛" to reduce bulk. Clip seam allowances. Press and baste seam allowances to cap back or, if fabric is thick, whip-stitch seam allowances to wrong side of cap back, as invisibly as possible. Turn right side out.

6. To make lining, repeat Step 5, leaving wrong side out.

7. Use basting stitches to transfer ribbon placement line to right side of cap. Cut ribbon in half. Pin and baste each piece in place, extending 1 cut end ½" beyond curved seam allowance and leaving long end against cap (tucked and pinned out of way of seams). With right sides facing and raw edges aligned, pin cap and lining together. Machine-stitch, leaving 3" opening along front edge. Layer seam allowance (except at opening) to reduce bulk. Clip all stitched seam allowances. Turn cap right side out. Slipstitch opening closed. Tack lining to cap at top and bottom of cap back. Knot ends of ribbon and trim.

Scalloped Heart Bib

Materials

Pattern on page 130
Tracing paper
Darning needle
2 (9½") squares cream flannel
Vanishing fabric marker
Thread to match
Pastel embroidery floss
28" length ¼"-wide pastel
    satin ribbon

Instructions

Note: Broken pattern line is stitching line. Add ¼" seam allowance when cutting fabric.

1. On folded tracing paper, trace pattern, transferring all markings. Cut out. Unfold pattern. Use darning needle to pierce dotted quilting lines at ¼" intervals.

2. Using vanishing fabric marker, trace bib shape and transfer quilting lines to right side of 1 flannel piece. Transfer stitching line to wrong side of fabric with basting stitches or hold piece against sunlit window and trace.

   With right sides facing and raw edges aligned, pin marked square to unmarked square. Stitch seam line, leaving 2" opening on 1 scallop. Cut out, adding ¼" seam allowance. Trim 1 layer of seam allowance to ⅛" (except at opening). Clip into crevices and around curves; omit clipping around opening.

3. Turn bib right side out. Tuck in seam allowance at opening and slipstitch closed. Flatten bib; baste around edges so that seam is exactly on edge. Using embroidery floss, quilt along design lines around bib.

4. Cut ribbon in half. Tuck under 1 raw end of 1 length and stitch securely to wrong side of bib (see Diagram). Knot other end of ribbon. Repeat with remaining ribbon piece to make other tie.

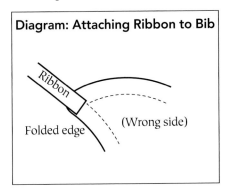

Diagram: Attaching Ribbon to Bib

Ribbon
Folded edge
(Wrong side)

Gentle Giraffes

Materials for one giraffe

Patterns on page 131
Tracing paper
9½" x 18" piece print fabric
Thread to match
Polyester stuffing
2 (⅛") black buttons *or* black
  embroidery floss for eyes
1¾ yards pearl cotton for
  mane and tail

Instructions

Note: Seam allowances are ¼"
and are included in patterns. For
best results, use tightly woven
fabric and small machine
stitches. Backstitch at beginning
and end of all seams.

1. Trace pattern pieces onto
tracing paper, transferring
markings. Cut out.

2. With right sides facing and
raw edges aligned, fold fabric in
half, short ends together. Trace 1
body, 1 underbody, and 2 ears
onto folded fabric, transferring
markings. Cut out. On wrong side
of single layer of remaining
fabric, trace 1 head top, transferring markings, including seam
lines. Cut out.

3. With right sides facing, raw
edges aligned, and dots matching, pin body pieces together.
Stitch back seam from rear dot to
horn dot. Stitch front seam from
chin dot to leg dot. Clip curves
around stitching.

4. With right sides facing, fold
head top and stitch dart. Clip
seam allowance at ⅛" intervals
below horns where shaded on
head top pattern. With right sides
facing and raw edges aligned, fit
head top between body pieces,
with point of head top piece
following curve of body nose.
Working on 1 side of head at a
time, baste along seam line; then
stitch from horn dot around and
down to chin dot. Avoid catching
dart seam allowance in stitching.
Trim and clip stitched seam
allowances.

5. With right sides facing, stitch
underbody pieces together from
each small dot toward center,
leaving open between large dots.
Trim and clip stitched seam
allowances. Turn under and
baste seam allowance at opening. With right sides facing and
working on 1 side at a time, pin
and stitch underbody to body
from front dot around legs to rear
dot. Turn right side out through
opening and stuff, filling head,
neck, legs, and then body. Slipstitch opening closed.

6. On each ear piece, fold under
seam allowance along straight
edge. With right sides facing and
raw and folded edges aligned, pin
pairs of ears together and stitch
each curved seam. Trim and clip
stitched seam allowances. Turn
each ear right side out. Slipstitch
openings closed. Fold sides of
each ear toward center.

Whipstitch overlapping edges
together along base of each ear.
Pin and slipstitch each ear in
place on head. Stitch on button
eyes or use 1 strand of floss to
satin-stitch eyes.

7. To make tail, cut 27" piece of
pearl cotton. Thread needle but
do not knot. Take small stitch
through back of giraffe, entering
and exiting just above seam at
back where body joins underbody. Leave 3" lengths and cut off
needle. Repeat 2 more times to
make 6 tail pieces. Divide lengths
evenly and loosely braid pearl
cotton pieces to make 1⅛" tail.
Knot ends together and trim pearl
cotton below knot to ⅞".

8. To make mane, use remaining
1 yard piece of pearl cotton.
Thread needle but do not knot.
Beginning at crest on head top
where horns meet, mark 17 to 18
dots approximately ¼" apart
down neck center back seam.
Take small stitch, entering at
front of horns and exiting at first
dot. Leave tail of thread at point
of entry. Referring to Diagram,
take tiny stitch, leaving small
loop. Pass needle through loop to
form knot. Take tiny stitch at next
dot, leaving ¼" to ⅜" loop. Take
tiny stitch again at this point,
leaving small loop to pass needle
through and form knot. Continue
in this manner down center back.
Exit approximately ½" from last
stitch. Trim pearl cotton ends at
beginning and end of mane.

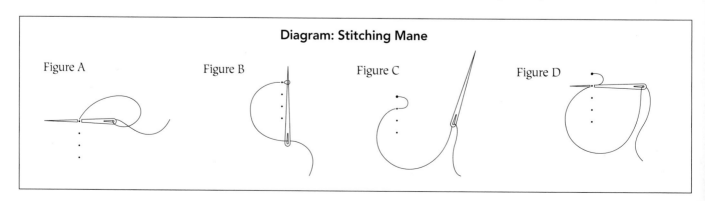

Diagram: Stitching Mane

Figure A Figure B Figure C Figure D

These delightful companions will win the heart of any child.

25

Hooded
Bath Towel

Materials

Pattern on page 132
Tracing paper
1 (13" x 13" x 17") triangle
  corner of bandanna *or* 13"
  square scrap fabric
Vanishing fabric marker
1 yard terry cloth
Thread to match
4½ yards ½"-wide double-fold
  bias tape*
*Note: To make your own
double-fold bias tape, cut 2"-
wide bias strips of fabric. Join together to form continuous bias
strip. One yard of 44"-wide fabric
will yield enough bias striping
for both Hooded Bath Towel and
Pullover Bath Duty Smock.

Instructions

Note: Seam allowances are ½"
and are included in pattern and
fabric measurements.
1. On folded tracing paper, trace
hood pattern, transferring
markings. Cut out.
2. On bandanna fabric, trace 1
hood, transferring markings. Cut
out and set aside. From terry
cloth, cut 1 (35") square for towel
and 1 hood, transferring
markings.
3. With bandanna fabric right
side up and raw edges aligned,
pin and baste hood pieces
together. Encase longest straight
edge in bias tape.
4. Place hood pattern on 1
corner of towel square. Mark
curved edge. Repeat for
remaining corners. Trim curved
edges. Pin hood in place at 1
corner, aligning raw edges. Stitch
around outer curved edge.
5. Encase all edges of towel in
bias tape.

*Wrap your little bather
from head to toe in this
towel. The smock has deep
pockets to hold shampoo
bottles and tub toys.*

Pullover Bath Duty Smock

Materials

Pattern on page 132
Tracing paper
1 large bandanna *or* 10¼" x 19½" scrap fabric for pocket
1¼ yard terry cloth
Vanishing fabric marker
Thread to match
6¾ yards ½"-wide coordinating double-fold bias tape*
1 bandanna *or* 56" of bias tape for ties

*Note: To make your own double-fold bias tape, cut 2"-wide bias strips of fabric. Join together to form continuous bias strip. One yard of 44"-wide fabric will yield enough bias striping for both Pullover Bath Duty Smock and Hooded Bath Towel.

Instructions

Note: Seam allowances are ½" and are included in pattern and fabric measurements.

1. Fold tracing paper into quarters. Trace neckline pattern guide onto folded tracing paper. Cut out. Unfold pattern.

2. Cut large bandanna in half lengthwise; reserve 1 piece for pocket. From terry cloth, cut 2 (19½" x 35") pieces for smock and 1 (10¼" x 19½") piece for pocket.

3. Join smock pieces together along 1 short edge. Press seam open and stitch seam allowance flat against unit, approximately ⅛" from seam. Trim seam allowance close to this stitching.

With seam allowance to the outside, fold smock along seam line. Pin fabric layers together along seam line. Center neckline guide on seam line. Trace neckline and cut out opening for head. Staystitch neckline edge, making 2 rows of stitches ¼" apart. Stitch 6" length of bias tape on each smock shoulder to cover raw edges of seam allowances (making this the right side of smock). Bind neck edge.

4. With bandanna fabric right side up, pin to terry cloth pocket piece. (If bandanna piece is too wide, make seam at center to narrow fabric.)

Using neckline pattern, trace rounded corners on lower edge of pocket. Trim along outline and baste edges together. Bind top long edge of pocket.

5. Using neckline pattern, trace rounded corners on lower edges of smock front and back; trim. Place pocket, bandanna side up, on right side of smock front, aligning side and bottom edges. Pin and baste pocket on smock. Machine-topstitch center of pocket to create 2 compartments.

6. To make bandanna ties, refer to Figure A and cut 4 (4" x 12½") bias ties from corners of remaining bandanna. Referring to Figure B, with right sides facing and raw edges aligned, stitch 1 tie together along long raw edges. Turn right side out. Referring to Figure C, with seam at center back, stitch raw edges together. Press flat. Repeat to complete 4 ties. Referring to photo for placement, with raw edges aligned, pin and securely stitch ties to wrong side of smock, 15" below shoulder seams.

If substituting bias tape ties for bandanna ties, cut bias tape into 4 (14") lengths and stitch open edges closed. Stitch ties to smock as above, knotting free ends.

7. Bind edges of smock with bias tape. Fold ties over bias binding, bringing them from behind smock. Slipstitch ties to edge of bias binding.

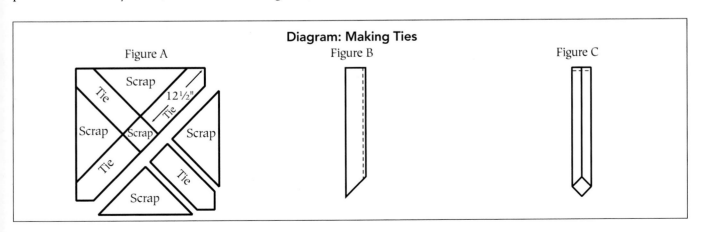

Diagram: Making Ties

Figure A   Figure B   Figure C

Quilt Scrap Teddy Bear

Materials for one bear
Patterns on pages 133–134
Tracing paper
8" x 29" piece lightweight old
    quilt for bear
4" x 5" piece contrasting fabric
    for muzzle and inner ears
Thread to match
2 (¼") buttons with low shanks
    or dark embroidery thread for
    eyes*
Polyester stuffing
24" length ½"-wide coordi-
    nating ribbon
Tracing paper
*Note: If teddy bear is for a child
younger than 3 years of age, use
embroidery floss for eyes.

Instructions
Note: Seam allowances are ¼"
and are included in patterns.
1. Trace ear and muzzle patterns
onto tracing paper. On folded
tracing paper, trace remaining
patterns. Transfer all markings.
Cut out. Unfold patterns.
2. Trace patterns (except muzzle)
on wrong side of quilt piece,
transferring markings and seam
lines. Then reverse ear pattern
and trace 1. Cut out. Trace
muzzle and ear patterns on
wrong side of contrasting fabric,
transferring markings and seam
lines. Reverse ear pattern and
trace 1. Cut out. Do not cut darts
or between legs at this time. Use
running stitches to transfer eyes
and topstitching lines for arms to
right side of head front, upper
body back, and body front.
3. Staystitch (make small
machine stitches along seam
line) shaded areas of patterns in
following manner: On head front,
staystitch around muzzle, on dart

*Make sure there is no way to mend a quilt and keep it intact
before cutting it to make the bear.*

lines, and along neck edge. On
lower body back, staystitch seat
line. On muzzle, staystitch curved edge that will be joined to
head. On upper body back, staystitch seat line, neck crevices,
and underarm crevices. On body
front, stitch at underarm crevices
and neck dart.
4. With right sides facing and
raw edges aligned, pin 1 quilted
ear piece to 1 contrasting inner
ear piece. Use small machine
stitches to stitch curved seam
only. Trim and clip stitched seam
allowance. Turn right side out.
Referring to Diagram 1 and with
raw edges aligned, pin straight
edges together. Machine-stitch
along longer straight seam line.
Clip this seam allowance at ¼"
intervals. Run tiny gathering
stitches along remaining straight

seam line between dots; pull to
gather to ¾". Tie off. Repeat to
make other ear.
5. On head front, carefully clip
⅞" into center of each dart
between staystitching lines.
Referring to Diagram 2, place
lining side of 1 ear facedown on
right side of head front, covering
1 dart as shown. Referring to
Diagram 3, fold head piece along
dart, placing right sides together
and exposing wrong side. Pull
seam allowance of gathered edge
of ear into head dart. Use pins to
match dots on ear with dots on
dart (edges will not align). Ease
in fullness of ear. Baste and stitch
dart along staystitching line,
catching ear in seam. Unfold
head and, referring to Diagram 4,
pin and stitch long edge of ear to
right side of head, spreading

clipped seam allowance and matching end of ear with dot on head. Repeat for other ear.

6. On head front, clip seam allowance to staystitching around muzzle. On muzzle piece, clip seam allowance to staystitching. With right sides facing and raw edges aligned, match center dots on muzzle and head front. Pin pieces together, spreading seam allowance of head front and easing in seam allowance of muzzle. Baste securely. (This step is a must!)

With muzzle piece on top, machine-stitch. Trim and clip seam allowance. With right sides facing and raw edges aligned, fold head and stitch muzzle curved center seam. Clip and trim seam allowance.

7. On body front, clip approximately ½" into center of dart. Stitch dart. With right sides facing, pin head front to body front, aligning muzzle seam with dart as well as matching dots at neck and sides of head. Ease head fullness into neck edge.

Baste and stitch between dots, backstitching at beginning and end. Clip neck. Set aside.

8. Stitch dart on upper body back. Clip dart as indicated on pattern. Trim dart seam allowance to ⅛". Also clip into neck crevices at sides of piece. With right sides facing and raw seatline edges aligned, pin and stitch upper body back and lower body back together, easing in fullness of upper body and leaving open between large dots. Clip stitched seam allowance (but not between opening dots). At neck, clip almost to dot.

9. With right sides facing and raw edges aligned, pin body front and body back together, matching dots at center top, neck, and under arms. Ease in fullness. Stitch around bear, lifting seam allowance at neck to stitch to dot and leaving entire bottom edge open. Clip into crevices under arms. Trim and clip all curved seams.

10. Stitch seam between legs (avoid catching seat of bear). Cut straight up between legs to split seam allowance. Clip curve between legs. Referring to Diagram 5, open 1 leg bottom and rotate and align seams; finger-press seam allowances. Stitch. Trim and clip curved seam. Repeat for other leg.

11. Turn bear right side out through seat opening. Fold under and baste seam allowance at opening. Stuff. Slipstitch opening closed. Handstitch arm lines. Stitch button eyes in place or, using 1 strand of floss, satin-stitch eyes. Tie ribbon into bow around neck. Head and body can be molded to be rounded or flattened.

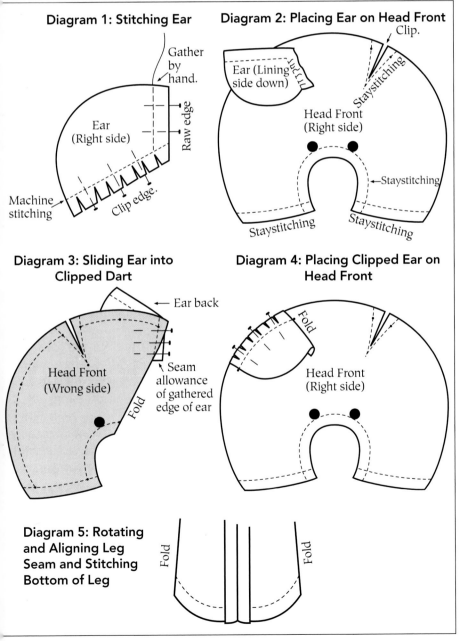

Diagram 1: Stitching Ear

Diagram 2: Placing Ear on Head Front

Diagram 3: Sliding Ear into Clipped Dart

Diagram 4: Placing Clipped Ear on Head Front

Diagram 5: Rotating and Aligning Leg Seam and Stitching Bottom of Leg

Baby Shoe Package Toppers

Materials for one shoe

Patterns on page 134
Tracing paper
1/8" paper punch
Acetate scrap (optional)
5½" square sturdy white paper
Craft knife
White glue
11" length 1/8"-wide pastel
   satin ribbon

Instructions

1. Trace patterns onto tracing paper, transferring markings. Cut out, using craft knife. Punch out holes on shoe. If desired, glue patterns to acetate for added stability. Cut out.
2. Trace 1 shoe and 1 sole onto white paper, transferring markings. Before cutting out, lightly score around shoe outline at base of tabs. Cut out area between each tab. Cut out remainder of shoe and sole. Fold tabs under. Punch out holes on shoe.
3. Apply glue to tab at back of shoe. Overlap tab at center back. Hold in place with paper clip until dry. Working from bottom, gently insert sole inside shoe, aligning center back mark on sole with center back seam of shoe and leaving tabs outside shoe. Add dot of glue to each tab and press to sole (glue works best if slightly tacky). Place shoe on flat surface. Put fingers inside shoe and press against sole. Let dry. For more finished appearance, cut second sole and glue it over tabbed bottom.
4. Thread ribbon through holes on top of shoe and tie into bow.

These little shoes are ideal package toppers or mint cups.

Scrubby Monkey Mitts

Materials for one mitt (either size)

Patterns on pages 135–136
Tracing paper
2 colored washcloths
Vanishing fabric marker
Thread: to match washcloths, white
8" square white terry cloth
Embroidery floss in contrasting color
4" square minicheck or minidot fabric for inner ears

Instructions

Note: Broken pattern lines are stitching lines. Add ¼" seam allowances when cutting fabrics.
1. On folded tracing paper, trace mitt and face in desired size. On unfolded paper, trace ear and inner ear in desired size. Transfer markings. Cut out.
2. Pin unfolded mitt pattern to 1 washcloth, aligning bottom edge of pattern with finished edge of cloth. With vanishing fabric marker, trace around pattern and transfer placement lines for ears and face. Transfer markings to other side of cloth with basting stitches or hold marker against fabric so that it soaks through. *Do not cut out yet.*
3. With finished edges aligned, place marked washcloth facedown on remaining washcloth. Following outline, stitch washcloths together along sides and top, leaving bottom edge open. Cut out mitt, adding ¼" seam allowance. Clip curves and into crevices at paws. Turn right side out.

Using matching thread, topstitch ¼" from seamed edge of mitt, leaving bottom open.

Playful washcloth pals make a little one's bath time more enjoyable.

4. Using vanishing fabric marker, trace face pattern onto white terry cloth, transferring features. *Do not cut out yet.* Using 2 strands of floss, chainstitch nose line and mouth; satin-stitch eyes and nose. Using 1 strand of thread, backstitch around eyes and nose, if desired. Cut out face, adding ¼" seam allowance. Clip into crevices at sides but do not clip curves. Turn under seam allowance and baste. Set aside.

5. Using vanishing fabric marker, trace ear pattern onto white terry cloth scrap. *Do not cut out yet.* Place marked terry cloth scrap faceup on unmarked terry cloth scrap. Stitch together along outer curved edge only. Cut out ear. Turn ear right side out and hand-press flat. Topstitch ¼" from curved edge of ear. Baste open raw edge closed. Repeat for other ear.

On right side of printed fabric, trace 2 inner ears. Cut out, adding ¼" seam allowance. For each, turn under and baste seam allowance of outer curved edge only. Pin in place and slipstitch 1 inner ear to 1 ear. Pin ears to mitt front, aligning dots. Securely handstitch ears in place on head, catching only fabric of mitt front.

6. Baste face in place on mitt front, covering raw edges of ears. Using white thread, securely appliqué face in place. For best results, slide your hand or thin piece of cardboard into mitt so that stitches won't go through to mitt back. Remove all basting stitches.

31

Lazy Lion Toy

Materials

Patterns on page 136
Tracing paper
6¼" x 24" piece beige soft
  cotton fabric
Vanishing fabric marker
Embroidery floss: brown,
  peach, cream, coordinating
  color for tail
Thread to match fabric and bow
Polyester stuffing
2" length ⅜"-wide cream
  grosgrain ribbon
Small embroidery hoop
12" length 1¼"-wide
  pregathered Cluny lace *or*
  2¾" x 18" strip of contrasting
  fabric for mane
Squeaker (optional)*
Small safety pin
22" length ¼"-wide
  coordinating satin ribbon
See Resources, page 173.
Note: If lace is not full and ruffly,
purchase an additional 6" to 8"
of lace and gather it to 12".

Instructions

Note: Broken pattern lines are
stitching lines. Add ¼" seam allowances when cutting fabric.
Use small machine stitches,
backstitching at beginning and
end of all seams.
1. Trace pattern pieces onto
tracing paper, transferring
markings. Cut out.

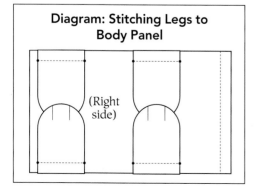

Diagram: Stitching Legs to
Body Panel

(Right
side)

2. Cut 6¼" x 10" rectangle from
beige fabric. With right sides
facing and raw edges aligned,
fold in half, long edges together.
Place patterns on fabric ½" apart
and trace 4 legs and 2 ears. *Do
not cut out.* Unfold rectangle.
Holding fabric against sunlit
window, use vanishing fabric
marker to trace paw lines onto
right side of each leg. Backstitch
lines using 1 strand of brown
floss. Refold fabric as before and
pin. Stitch seams, leaving top of
each leg and bottom of each ear
open. Cut out, adding ¼" seam
allowance. Trim stitched seam
allowances to ⅛"; clip curves.
Turn pieces right side out. Leaving raw edges of seam allowances
outside, machine-stitch open
edges of ears closed; clip almost
to stitching. Push a little stuffing
into paw area and stitch open
edges closed, leaving raw edges
of seam allowances outside.
3. On right side of remaining
beige fabric, center and trace 1
head, transferring features. *Do
not cut out yet.* To make nose
strip, fold 1 end of grosgrain
ribbon under ¼". Baste in place
so that folded edge rests on nose
top and cut end overlaps seam
allowance at head top. Stitch
finished edges of ribbon to head.

Use embroidery hoop and 1
strand of floss for all embroidery.
Using brown, backstitch eyes
and mouth, satin-stitch nose,
and straight-stitch eyelashes and
eyebrows. Satin-stitch cheeks
with peach. Chainstitch whiskers
with cream. Cut out face, adding
¼" seam allowance.
4. Place 1 ear between dots on
right side of head. Align raw
edges. Pin, baste, and machine-
stitch in place. Repeat with other
ear. Aligning gathered edge of
lace with raw edge of head, pin,
baste, and stitch lace to right side

of head, folding lace back ¼" at
each cut end. Slipstitch folded
edges together.

If making fabric mane, with
right sides facing and raw edges
aligned, stitch short edges together to form ring. Turn right
side out. With wrong sides facing, fold ring in half, aligning
long raw edges. Run gathering
threads along long raw edge
through both layers of fabric.
Pull to gather tightly. Aligning
gathered edge of mane with raw
edge of head, pin and stitch
mane to right side of head.
Temporarily baste finished edge
of mane to face to keep it from
catching in head seam.
5. From remaining fabric, cut 3
body panels, transferring dots
onto 1 panel. Referring to
Diagram, along 1 long edge on
right side of marked panel, (this
will be bottom panel) pin and
stitch 2 legs (paw lines up)
between dots. Pin and stitch
remaining 2 legs to opposite
edge. Paws will overlap at center.

With right sides facing and
raw edges aligned, stitch remaining panels to leg panel along
long edges to form tube. With
right sides facing, raw edges
aligned, and stars on head
matched with body seams, pin
and stitch head circle to body
tube where indicated. Clip
around head seam allowance.
6. Turn right side out and press
under ½" along open end of tube
(this fold will not be along seam
line traced on fabric). Stitch
casing ⅜" from folded edge. Clip
a few stitches at center top seam
to make small opening.

Stuff body, maintaining soft-
ness and squeezability. (If desired, bury squeaker in stuffing
in middle of body.)
7. Cut 3 (30") lengths from floss
for lion tail. Pass 1 end of each

6-strand length through loop at base of safety pin and align ends of doubled floss. Work safety pin and floss through casing. Pull floss tightly. Tie and knot together. Cut pin free. Divide lengths evenly and braid together. Knot ends together and trim to resemble tassel.

8. Tie ribbon into bow behind mane. Tack in place.

Lion Hanger

Materials

Patterns on page 136
Tracing paper
6¼" x 16" piece beige cotton fabric
Vanishing fabric marker
Embroidery floss: brown, peach, cream
Thread to match fabric and bow
Polyester stuffing
2" length ⅜"-wide piece tan grosgrain ribbon
Small embroidery hoop
2¾" x 18" strip of contrasting fabric *or* 12" length 1¼"-wide pregathered Cluny lace for mane*
Small safety pin
Purchased child's plastic tube clothes hanger
15" length ¼"-wide satin ribbon
*Note: If lace is not full and ruffly, purchase an additional 6" to 8" of lace and gather it to 12".

Instructions

Note: Broken pattern lines are stitching lines. Add ¼" seam allowances when cutting fabric.
1. Complete steps 1–4 of Lazy Lion Toy, cutting 6¼" square from beige fabric and tracing 2 legs instead of 4. Cut out.
2. From remaining fabric, cut 2 (2" x 3½") pieces for back. With

Whether hanging clothes or taking a nap, your child will have a roaring good time with these lazy lions.

right sides facing and raw edges aligned, stitch pieces together along 1 long edge, leaving 1½" opening at center. Press seam open. With right sides facing, center and pin lion head on prepared back (seam should run from top to bottom). Stitch together along stitching line on lion head. Cut out. Trim and clip

seam allowance. Turn right side out through opening. Stuff and slipstitch opening closed. Fold raw seam allowance on legs to front. Referring to photo for placement, slipstitch legs to back of head. Tack lion to hanger.
3. Tie ribbon into bow on hanger at top of lion's head and tack.

Dress-up Doll

Materials

Patterns on page 137
Tracing paper
4½" x 31" piece cotton fabric for body
Thread to match
Polyester stuffing
White or silver fabric marking pencil
Embroidery floss: black, red
3" x 4¾" piece cotton fabric to match hair
10 yards 3-ply crewel yarn for hair
Large-eyed needle
Note: Use tightly woven cotton fabric for doll and set sewing machine for tiny stitches.

Instructions

Note: Broken pattern lines are stitching lines. Add ¼" seam allowances when cutting fabrics.

1. Trace patterns onto tracing paper, transferring markings. Cut out.

2. Cut 4½" x 9" piece from body fabric. With right sides facing and raw edges aligned, fold piece in half, short edges together, to measure 4½" square. Baste open edges closed. Place pattern pieces ½" apart on fabric and trace 2 legs. Machine-stitch along outlines, leaving tops open as indicated. Cut out, adding ¼" seam allowances. Trim stitched seam allowances to ⅛" and clip curves. Turn right side out and firmly stuff each to within ½" of opening. Rotate so that seams are along center front and center back of each leg. Baste open edges closed. Set aside.

Cut 4½" x 8" piece from remaining body fabric. With right sides facing and raw edges aligned, fold in half, long edges together, to measure 2¼" x 8".

This doll is perfect for an overnight trip to grandmother's house. The doll and her clothes tuck into the tote, which also serves as the doll's bed.

Baste open edges closed. Trace 1 arms piece onto fabric. Machine-stitch along outline, leaving area between dots open as indicated. (Hand-turn machine around thumb.) Trim seam allowance at opening to ¼". Trim stitched seam allowance to ⅛" and clip curves. Turn right side out and lightly stuff each arm up to opening, leaving approximately 1½" unstuffed between arms. Slipstitch opening closed. Run gathering stitches where indicated on pattern. Pull to gather fabric across arms to ½" width. Set aside.

3. On remaining body fabric, use marking pencil to trace 1 face, 1 lower head side, and 1 body. Before cutting out face, use 1 strand of black floss to satin-stitch eyes; use 1 strand of red floss to backstitch mouth. Cut out pieces, adding ¼" seam allowance. From hair-colored fabric, cut 1 upper head side.

Aligning raw edges, pin and baste legs (toes against body) in place between dots on right side of body piece. With right sides facing, raw edges aligned, and legs inside, pin and stitch body center back seam. Then flatten and stitch seam across top of legs. Turn right side out. Fold top raw edge of body top under ¼". Using 4 strands of thread, run gathering stitches along folded edge of body top. Pull to gather slightly. Stuff. Pull tightly and tie off. Place arm unit, thumbs facing forward, across top of body. Securely stitch arms to body at center top. To form shoulders, lift each arm and slipstitch underarm to body where indicated. (No stuffing should be in shoulder area.)

4. To make head, with right sides facing and raw edges aligned, form ring by joining upper (hair color) and lower (body color) head side pieces. Clip seam allowance at ¼" intervals along edge that will be joined to face. With right sides facing and raw edges aligned, pin and stitch head side unit to face, matching center top and center bottom dots. Trim and clip stitched seam allowance. Turn right side out. Fold raw edge under ¼". Using 4 strands of thread, run gathering stitches along open edge close to fold. Pull to gather slightly. Stuff firmly. Pull thread tightly and tie off. (There will probably be ¼"-diameter circular opening remaining. If so, add more stuffing.) Whipstitch opening closed. Securely slipstitch head to body.

5. For curly hair, separate crewel yarn into strands and use single pieces. Knot thread and take small stitch on head. Make loop and then take another small stitch to anchor loop. Repeat, alternating loops and stitches to make cap of curls. (Loops need not all be even.) Make stitches along top and side of face line and over entire back of head, including body-colored area of head. Add extra stitches around face if hairline seems too high.

Dress-up Doll Clothing

Materials for all clothing
Patterns on page 137–138
Tracing paper
Vanishing fabric marker
White or silver fabric marking pencil
Threads to match fabrics and trims
Small safety pin

For Pantie
2 (4" x 2¾") pieces knit T-shirt fabric
11" length ⅛"-wide elastic

For Nightgown
7" x 21" piece flannel
5½" length ⅛"-wide elastic
20" length narrow lace
14" length ⅛"-wide coordinating satin ribbon

For Dress
6" x 21" piece print cotton fabric
5½" length ⅛"-wide elastic
20" length narrow lace
20" length ⅛"-wide coordinating satin ribbon
Tiny buttons*

For Blouse
4½" x 20" piece cotton fabric *or* ⅝ yard 3½"-wide eyelet edging
5½" length ⅛"-wide elastic

For Skirt
3⅝" x 11¼" piece cotton fabric
5½" length ⅛"-wide elastic

For Pants
6" x 11" piece fabric
5½" length ⅛"-wide elastic

For Shoes or Slippers
Tiny scissors
5" x 6½" scrap felt
Embroidery floss
Small scrap stuffing (optional)
2 (½") pom-poms for slippers
*See Resources, page 173.
Note: Doll is not intended for children under 3 years of age.

(Continued on page 36)

(Continued from page 35)

Instructions

Note: Broken pattern lines are stitching lines. Add ¼" seam allowances when cutting fabrics, unless otherwise noted.

Some pattern shapes are similar. Label to avoid confusion.

Place safety pin across end of elastic to make "brake" for elastic. Try clothing items on doll and adjust elastic before stitching it and closing casing.

Pantie

Stitch knit fabric pieces together along short edges to form tube. To make casings, fold each long edge under ¼" and baste. Then fold each long edge under ⅜" and baste. Stitch casings ¼" from folded edges. Clip a few stitches of 1 seam on wrong side of each casing. Cut elastic in half. Using safety pin, insert 1 piece of elastic through each casing. Overlap elastic ends ½" and whipstitch together. Work elastic back inside each casing. Slipstitch casings closed. To form leg openings along 1 long edge, securely tack layers together at center on wrong side of pantie.

Nightgown

1. Trace nightgown front/back and long sleeve patterns onto tracing paper, transferring markings. Cut out.
2. On wrong side of nightgown fabric, trace 2 front/back pieces and 2 sleeves, transferring markings. Cut out, adding ¼" seam allowance.
3. Referring to Diagram 1, with right sides facing and raw edges and dots aligned, pin and stitch 1 side edge of 1 sleeve to 1 front/back piece from neck edge to dot. Backstitch at beginning

and end. Repeat to stitch remaining sleeve to remaining front/back piece. With right sides facing and raw edges aligned, place unit as in Diagram 2. Pin and stitch remaining side edge of

1 sleeve to remaining side edge of other front/back piece from neck edge to dot. Repeat to join pieces to form front/back unit.
4. Referring to Diagram 3, stitch each sleeve seam from wrist to

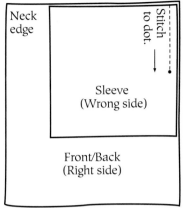

Diagram 1: Stitching Sleeves

Neck edge · Stitch to dot. · Sleeve (Wrong side) · Front/Back (Right side)

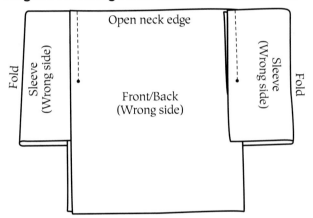

Diagram 2: Joining Front/Back Units with Sleeves

Open neck edge · Fold · Sleeve (Wrong side) · Sleeve (Wrong side) · Fold · Front/Back (Wrong side)

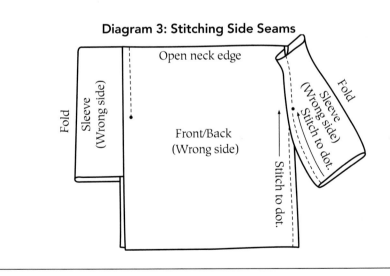

Diagram 3: Stitching Side Seams

Open neck edge · Fold · Sleeve (Wrong side) · Front/Back (Wrong side) · Stitch to dot. · Fold · Sleeve (Wrong side) · Stitch to dot.

underarm dot. Stitch each garment side seam from lower edge to underarm dot. Press seam allowances flat. Check underarm seams at dot and handstitch to reinforce if necessary.

5. To make casing, fold raw neck edge under ¼". Then fold under ⅜" and stitch ¼" from top edge. Clip a few stitches of seam on wrong side of 1 sleeve top. Using safety pin, insert elastic through casing and gather neck edge. Pull 1 end of elastic 1" outside casing; trim and discard. Overlap elastic ends ½" and whipstitch together. Work elastic back inside casing. Slipstitch casing closed.

6. Fold raw bottom edge under ¼". Then fold under ⅜" and hem. In same manner, hem sleeves, making second fold ½" and slipstitching bound edge of lace to wrong side of hemmed edges. Tie ribbon into bow and tack to top center front.

Dress

1. Trace dress front/back and long sleeve patterns onto tracing paper. Transfer markings. Cut out.

2. On wrong side of dress fabric, trace 2 front/back pieces and 2 sleeves, transferring markings. Cut out, adding ¼" seam allowance. Complete steps 3–6 of Nightgown. Stitch satin ribbon around sleeves and hem where lace and fabric meet. Stitch small buttons down center front of dress, if desired.

Blouse

1. For cotton blouse, trace blouse front/back and long sleeve patterns onto tracing paper, transferring markings. Cut out.

2. On wrong side of fabric, trace 2 front/back pieces and 2 sleeves, transferring markings. Cut out, adding ¼" seam allowance.

Complete steps 3–5 of Nightgown. (Sleeve pieces are longer than blouse front/back pieces.) For rolled sleeve cuffs, fold raw sleeve edges under ¾" and hem. Then fold ⅜" of each hem back to right side and tack. Fold raw bottom edge of blouse under ¼". Then fold under ⅜" and hem.

For eyelet blouse, use eyelet blouse front/back and eyelet sleeve patterns. Complete as above, omitting references to rolled sleeve cuffs and bottom hem. Tack eyelet seam allowances inside garment.

Skirt

Note: Seam allowances are ¼" and are included in fabric measurements.

1. With right sides facing and raw edges aligned, fold skirt fabric in half, short edges together. Stitch center back seam. To make casing, fold raw edge under ¼" at waist. Then fold under ⅜" and stitch casing ¼" from top folded edge.

2. Clip a few stitches of casing seam on wrong side of skirt. Using safety pin, pull elastic through casing. Overlap ends ½" and whipstitch together. Work elastic back inside casing. Slipstitch casing closed.

3. Fold skirt bottom under ¼". Then fold under ⅜" and hem.

Pants

1. Trace pants pattern onto tracing paper, transferring markings. Cut out.

2. Fold fabric in half, long edges together. Trace 2 pants pieces, transferring markings. Cut out, adding ¼" seam allowances. Unfold pieces. With right sides facing and raw edges aligned, stitch curved seams. Clip curves. Rotate seams and align at center front and center back. To make

legs, stitch 1 seam at a time from bottom of leg to dot. Check seams at dot and handstitch to reinforce if necessary. Turn right side out.

3. To make casing, fold raw edge under ¼" at waist. Then fold under ⅜" and stitch casing ¼" from edge.

4. Clip a few stitches of casing seam on wrong side of pants. Using safety pin, pull elastic through casing. Overlap ends ½" and whipstitch together. Work elastic back inside casing. Slipstitch casing closed.

5. Fold raw bottom edge of each leg under ¼". Then fold each under ⅝" and hem. For cuffed pants, hem lower portion of inseam seam allowances by tucking under ⅛" and slipstitching to legs. Fold raw bottom edge of each leg ¼" to right side of pants and baste. Then fold each leg 2 more times to the right side and tack cuffs securely to pants.

Shoes

1. Trace shoe and sole patterns onto tracing paper, transferring markings. Cut out pattern and vamp opening.

2. On felt, trace 2 shoes and 2 soles. *Add ⅛" seam allowance to short center back edges of shoes*

(Continued on page 38)

(Continued from page 37)

only. Elsewhere, cut out along pattern line. Cut out vamp.

3. Machine-stitch center back seams. Flatten seams; blanket-stitch edges of seam allowances to inside of each shoe, as invisibly as possible on outside.

4. Using 2 strands of embroidery floss, make tiny blanket stitches along top edge and vamp opening of each shoe.

5. Aligning edges and matching dots, baste soles to shoes and then edge with blanket stitches.

Slippers

Follow steps 1–5 of Shoes, omitting vamp opening. Trace pattern for bunny head onto tracing paper and cut out. On doubled felt, trace 2 heads. Cut out. Stack 2 bunny heads and edge with blanket stitches, tucking a little stuffing between layers, if desired. Make French knots for eyes. Repeat for other bunny head. Securely tack heads and pom-pom tails to slippers.

Dress-up Doll Bed Tote

Materials

Vanishing fabric marker
Solid color cotton flannel:
   9½" x 31¼" piece for bag,
   4½" x 13" piece for pillowcase
9½" x 29¾" piece cotton fabric
Thread to match fabrics and lace
20" length ¾"-wide crochet-look
   lace (optional)
20" length ½"-wide grosgrain
   ribbon for bag handle
5½" x 7½" piece lightweight
   ticking for pillow
Polyester stuffing
Note: All pieces must be cut to *exact* dimensions listed above.

Instructions

Note: Seam allowances are ¼" and are included in fabric measurements.

1. Referring to Diagram 1, mark fold lines and X on 9½" x 31¼" flannel piece. Referring to Diagram 2, use vanishing fabric marker to mark fold lines and X on print fabric. Make ⅛" clips into seam allowances at fold lines to mark each location.

2. Referring to Diagram 3 and with right sides facing, align and stitch together X-marked edges of flannel and print pieces. Press seam open. This will be center bottom of bag lining.

3. Referring to Diagram 4 and leaving unit wrong side up, fold flannel along fold line 1, exposing right side. Fold flannel back along fold line 2, exposing wrong side and aligning fold line 2 with center bottom seam to create bag front and pocket area. Do not fold cuff area yet.

4. Leaving unit in same position and referring to Diagram 5, fold print fabric along fold line 3, overlapping flannel at center bottom seam and flannel pocket area and exposing right side. Align raw edge of print pocket area with flannel cuff fold line. Pin fabric layers together along raw side edges.

5. Referring to Diagram 6, fold flannel cuff over print pocket area. Fold raw edge of cuff under ¼" and baste. Slipstitch straight edge of lace to hemmed edge, if desired. Slipstitch cuff to print pocket layer. Baste layers together along raw side edges.

6. With all edges aligned, fold bag along center bottom seam and fold line 4 so that print bag back and print pocket area are facing each other inside bag. Pin and stitch raw side edges together ¼" from edge. Clip corners. Turn bag right side out and flatten edges. Reinforce seams and conceal seam allowances at each side with a few handstitches. Cut ribbon in half. With 1" of each end of 1 ribbon inside bag, pin handle along 1 top edge, 2¾" from each side. Repeat with remaining ribbon on other top edge of bag. Fold cut ends of ribbon under ¼". Machine-stitch.

7. To make pillow, with right sides facing and raw edges aligned, fold and pin ticking in half, short edges together, to measure 5½" x 3¾". Stitch together ¼" from raw edges, leaving small opening for turning. Turn right side out. Press flat. Stuff, maintaining flatness. Slipstitch opening closed.

8. To make pillowcase, with right sides facing and raw edges aligned, fold and pin 4½" x 13" flannel piece in half, short edges together, to measure 4½" x 6½". Stitch together along each long raw edge. Turn right side out and press flat. Fold raw edge under ¼" and press. Then fold under ¾" and hem. Slipstitch straight edge of lace to hemmed edge, if desired.

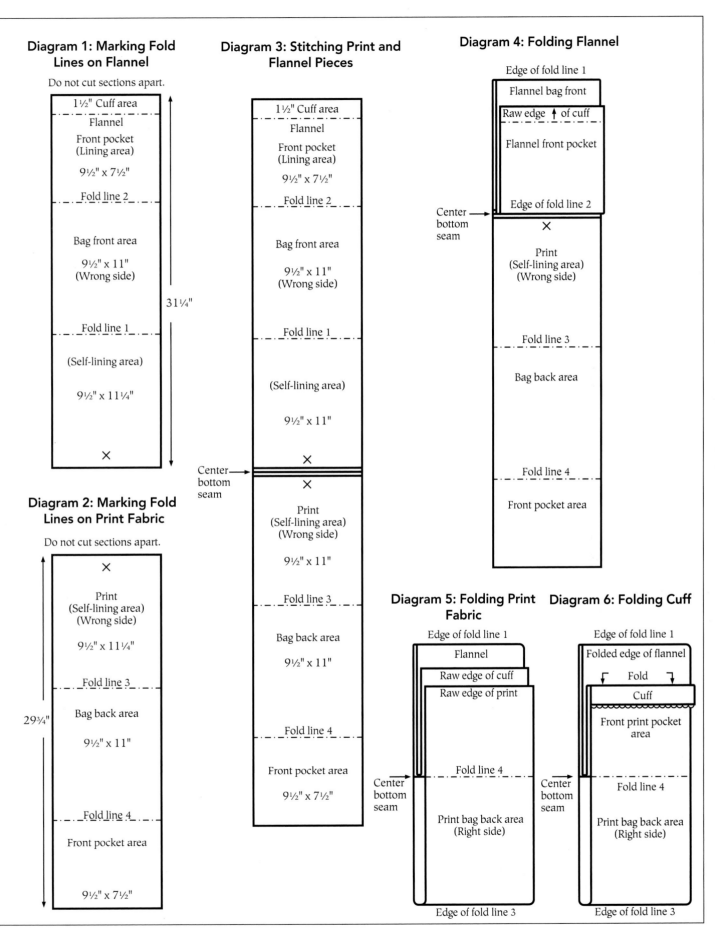

Diagram 1: Marking Fold Lines on Flannel

Do not cut sections apart.

1½" Cuff area

Flannel
Front pocket
(Lining area)

9½" x 7½"

Fold line 2

Bag front area

9½" x 11"
(Wrong side)

Fold line 1

(Self-lining area)

9½" x 11¼"

×

31¼"

Diagram 2: Marking Fold Lines on Print Fabric

Do not cut sections apart.

×

Print
(Self-lining area)
(Wrong side)

9½" x 11¼"

Fold line 3

Bag back area

9½" x 11"

Fold line 4

Front pocket area

9½" x 7½"

29¾"

Diagram 3: Stitching Print and Flannel Pieces

1½" Cuff area

Flannel
Front pocket
(Lining area)

9½" x 7½"

Fold line 2

Bag front area

9½" x 11"
(Wrong side)

Fold line 1

(Self-lining area)

9½" x 11"

×

Center bottom seam →

×

Print
(Self-lining area)
(Wrong side)

9½" x 11"

Fold line 3

Bag back area

9½" x 11"

Fold line 4

Front pocket area

9½" x 7½"

Diagram 4: Folding Flannel

Edge of fold line 1

Flannel bag front

Raw edge ↑ of cuff

Flannel front pocket

Edge of fold line 2

Center bottom seam →

×

Print
(Self-lining area)
(Wrong side)

Fold line 3

Bag back area

Fold line 4

Front pocket area

Diagram 5: Folding Print Fabric

Edge of fold line 1

Flannel

Raw edge of cuff

Raw edge of print

Fold line 4

Center bottom seam →

Print bag back area
(Right side)

Edge of fold line 3

Diagram 6: Folding Cuff

Edge of fold line 1

Folded edge of flannel

Fold

Cuff

Front print pocket area

Fold line 4

Center bottom seam →

Print bag back area
(Right side)

Edge of fold line 3

Hearth & Home Mercantile

As long as you're in the neighborhood, take time to explore the Hearth & Home Mercantile. Here are presents to enhance the cozy hours—nap times and snack times and all the leisure moments in between.

Dragon Hot Mitt

Materials

Patterns on pages 139–140
Tracing paper
13" x 18" piece green cotton fabric
3½" x 7" piece black fabric
9" square red bandanna (cut from corner)
⅜ yard quilted fabric
Quilt batting (optional)*
Thread to match
Pom-poms: 2 (½") black, 2 (1") white
Rickrack: 7" length narrow black, cut in half; 25" length jumbo white, cut in half
Small amount polyester stuffing
18" length ½"-wide black double-fold bias tape
*Note: If quilted fabric is thin, you will need to add a layer of batting between the 2 quilted layers to protect hands.

Instructions

Note: Seam allowances are ¼" and are included in patterns. Backstitch at beginning and end of each seam.

1. Trace patterns for eyelid and point, transferring markings. On folded paper, trace upper top, lower top, bottom, and mouth patterns, transferring markings. Cut out and unfold patterns. Tape upper and lower portions of top section together along dots.
2. On wrong side of green fabric, trace 1 top, 1 bottom, and 2 eyelids (do not transfer markings). On black fabric, trace 3 points. On bandanna square, trace 1 mouth. Cut out.
3. Pin and stitch fabric pieces (except eyelids and points) to double layer of quilted fabric. Cut out. Using pattern, transfer markings to back of each quilted shape. Baste dart stitching lines to keep fabric layers together. Stitch nose dart and center top dart. Using basting stitches, transfer eyelid placement lines to right side of head.
4. To make eyeballs, stitch 1 black pom-pom to center of each white pom-pom. Set aside.
5. Noting grain line direction on eyelid pattern, transfer rickrack placement line to right side of each fabric eyelid. Center, baste, and then stitch 1 piece of black rickrack on each placement line. Cut small slit for turning where indicated. With right sides facing and raw edges aligned, fold each circle in half along rickrack stitching line. Pin. Stitch each semicircular seam. Turn each right side out through slit. Finger-press flat. Whipstitch each opening closed. Slipstitch curved edge of each eyelid in place on head top. Insert reserved eyeballs and tack each securely to head. If eyeballs seem too small, first add a small amount of stuffing to back of each lid before inserting eyeballs.
6. Baste 1 piece of white rickrack to right side of lower portion of mouth and 1 piece to upper portion along seam line of each. Machine-stitch and set aside.
7. With right sides facing and raw edges aligned, stitch head top and bottom together along each side seam, from bottom edge to jaw dot. Leave wrong side out. Clip curves.

With right sides facing and raw edges aligned, pin reserved mouth in place, easing in fullness of dragon jaws. Baste and machine-stitch. Clip curves. Turn right side out. If teeth don't lie flat, slipstitch to mouth. Bind open end of dragon with bias tape, adding loop at center back for hanging, if desired.
8. To make 1 point, refer to Diagram and fold square diagonally. Fold back ¼" seam allowance along 2 edges as shown. Stitch seam along raw edges. Turn right side out. Finger-press. Slipstitch folded edges closed. Repeat to make remaining points. Arrange along center back dart, overlapping bottoms of points slightly. Slipstitch folded edge of each to dart seam so that points stand upright.

Diagram: Making Dragon Points

Slipstitch.
Fold under seam allowance.
Fold square in half diagonally.
Clip.

Heart Cluster Pot Holder

Materials

Pattern on page 140
8 (5¼") squares fabric (2 each of 4 different prints)
Thread to match
10" square batting
Vanishing fabric marker
Quilting thread to match
6" length ⅜"-wide ribbon for hanging loop (optional)
Tracing paper

Instructions

Note: Broken pattern line is stitching line. Add ¼" seam allowances when cutting fabrics.
1. Trace pattern on folded tracing paper, transferring markings. Cut out. Unfold pattern.

These gifts help make baking fun. The Cookie Cutter Couple is on page 45.

close to stitching. Clip curves and deeply into crevices.

7. Turn pot holder right side out. Use pencil with broken lead to push out curves, giving hearts an accurate shape. Pin pot holder so that seam is exactly on edge. Slipstitch opening closed. Stick pins through fabric layers to make sure seams are aligned on front and back of pot holder. Hand-quilt around each heart, approximately ½" from edge.

8. For hanging loop, fold each cut end of ribbon under ¼" and hem. Fold ribbon in half. Align ends and tack ribbon loop to back of pot holder at crevice of heart. Working from back, hand-stitch to reinforce crevices between hearts.

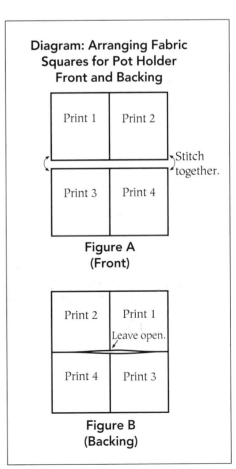

Diagram: Arranging Fabric Squares for Pot Holder Front and Backing

Print 1	Print 2
Print 3	Print 4

Stitch together.

Figure A (Front)

Print 2	Print 1 Leave open.
Print 4	Print 3

Figure B (Backing)

2. To make front piece, refer to Diagram, Figure A for print placement. With right sides facing and raw edges aligned, stitch Print 1 and Print 2 together to form rectangle. Repeat with Print 3 and Print 4. Join 2 units together along 1 long edge to make 10" square. Set front piece aside.

3. To make backing piece, refer to Diagram, Figure B for print placement. Repeat directions for front piece, leaving 2½" opening at center of final seam.

4. Place pattern on wrong side of backing piece, aligning dotted lines on pattern with seams on fabric unit. Trace along outside of pattern. Cut out backing, adding ¼" seam allowance.

5. With right sides facing and raw edges and seams aligned, center and pin backing on front piece. (Look inside opening to be sure centers also align.)

6. Pin batting square to back of pot holder unit, opening side up. Baste edges together securely but do not trim excess batting and backing yet. Machine-stitch around shape. Trim excess fabric and batting, leaving ¼" seam allowance. Then trim batting

Stitch this crescent moon and star place mat set for the midnight snacker in your home. It is just right for late-night treats.

Midnight Snack Mat Set

Materials for one set

Patterns on page 141
Tracing paper: 9" x 13¼" piece, 15" square
18" x 27" piece blue star print fabric
Thread: blue, gold
15" x 36" piece nonwoven fusible featherweight interfacing (to stabilize lamé fabric)
15" x 36" piece gold lamé fabric
Thin quilt batting: 15" square for mat, 6" square for coaster
Note: For a quicker version of this design, do not use metallic fabric and omit interfacing.

Instructions

Note: Broken pattern lines are stitching lines. Add ¼" seam allowance when cutting fabrics.
1. Fold 9" x 13¼" piece of tracing paper in quarters. Trace and cut out sky pattern. Fold 15" square of tracing paper in quarters. Trace and cut out moon pattern.
2. To make napkin, cut 18" square from star print fabric. Press under ¼" twice around edges and stitch. On remaining star fabric, trace and cut out 1 sky piece, adding ¼" seam allowance.
3. Working on *nonadhesive* side of interfacing and placing pattern pieces at least ½" apart, trace 1 star, 2 moons, and 2 (3¼" x 6") rectangles. Following manufacturer's instructions, fuse all interfacing pieces to 1 side of gold lamé fabric. Adding ¼" seam allowances, cut out.
4. Press under seam allowance along 1 edge of sky. Aligning raw edges, pin and baste sky to 1

moon circle. Slipstitch folded edge of sky to moon.

5. With right sides facing and raw edges aligned, stack moon circles. Pin 15" square of batting to back of fabric layers; place pins within seam allowance, as they may mar metallic fabric. Stitch around circle, leaving 3" opening for turning. At opening, handstitch batting to 1 fabric layer along seam line. On other single fabric layer, make line of basting stitches along seam line.

Trim batting close to stitching around circle. Trim stitched seam allowance with pinking shears. Turn unit right side out. Slipstitch opening closed. Quilt around moon and sky, ½" from edges of each.

6. To make coaster backing, pin interfaced lamé rectangles together along 1 long edge. Stitch seam, leaving 2" opening in center for turning. Press seam open. With right sides facing and seam running from top to

bottom, center and pin star on backing. Trim backing to match star. Pin this unit, with opening faceup, on top of batting square. Machine-stitch around star edges. Trim batting close to stitching. Trim fabric edges with pinking shears. Clip into crevices. Turn right side out. Slipstitch opening closed. Quilt around star, ½" from edges.

Just a Little Something

Cookie Cutter Couple

To make this charming couple, refer to photo and place a miniature heart cookie cutter between a miniature man and a miniature woman cookie cutter. Join the couple to the heart by tying with 18" lengths of ½"-wide ribbon. Then trim a wedding shower present with the decoration or, if you prefer, tuck a gift certificate or a check inside the heart for your newlywed friends.

Favorite Shirt Pillow

Materials

Pattern on page 142
Tracing paper
1 old shirt
Thread to match
1⅛ yards corded piping (size
  used for slipcovers)
Polyester stuffing

Instructions

Note: Broken pattern line is stitching line. Add ¼" seam allowance when cutting fabric.

1. Trace pattern on folded paper and cut out.

2. Rip out stitches around collar; remove collar from band and reserve. Remove pockets. Button shirt and then stitch down center placket near edge to keep shirt together.

3. To make pillow front, on wrong side of buttoned shirt front, trace pattern. Cut out pillow front, adding ¼" seam allowance. Rip out stitches around 1 cuff; remove cuff and set aside.

4. If collar is worn, use reverse side. Cut collar in half at center back. Referring to photo, pin and baste collar sections to center top of pillow front. Trim excess to match pillow shape. Button cuff and baste to 1 side of pillow front.

5. Trim piping seam allowance to ¼" if necessary. Aligning raw edges, baste and then machine-stitch piping to right side of heart, tapering into seam allowance at beginning and end. Set aside.

6. For pillow back, from shirt back or ripped out and flattened sleeves, cut 2 (6¾" x 13") pieces. With right sides facing and raw edges aligned, pin and stitch pieces together along 1 long edge, leaving 4" opening at center. Press seam open.

7. With right sides facing, center pillow front on back square. Machine-stitch completely around outside edge of heart. Trim back to match front. Clip curves and into crevice. Turn heart right side out and stuff, maintaining flatness. (This will take some time in order for edges to be even. Working from back, shift stuffing toward edges with darning needle. If piping puckers too much, gently pull on it to straighten.) Slipstitch opening closed. Tack collar and cuffs in place.

Blanket Statement

Materials

6¼ yards black cotton fabric
2¼ yards red cotton fabric
Rotary cutter (optional)
Rotary cutter mat (optional)
Quilter's acrylic ruler (optional)
Thread to match
61" x 78" piece polyester quilt
  batting
White pencil
Black embroidery floss (for
  tying quilt)
Tracing paper

Instructions

Note: Seam allowances are ¼" and are included in fabric measurements. Press seams open as you work.

Border pieces are cut an extra ½" long to allow for variations in size after joining blocks. Trim border to fit after stitching to patchwork area. Backing pieces and batting are cut a little large for the same reason.

Rotary cutting equipment allows you to quickly measure and cut in 1 step. But if you prefer, use a yardstick and marking tool to measure the pieces before cutting with scissors.

Diagrams 1, 2, and 3 are on pages 48–49.

1. Referring to Diagram 1, Figure A, cut 2 (39" x 60") backing pieces and 9 (1¼" x 40") strips from black fabric. Using ¼" seam, join 2 backing pieces together along 1 long edge to make 60" x 77½" unit. Set aside.

Referring to Figure B, cut 4 (9" x 60") border pieces, 6 (9"-square) blocks, and 27 (1¼" x 40") strips from remaining black fabric.

2. Referring to Diagram 2, cut 12 (9"-square) blocks and 36 (1¼" x 40") strips from red fabric.

3. Stitch strips together along long edges, alternating colors to make 40" x 72¼" striped piece. Draw 9" square on tracing paper. Fold square in half diagonally. Mark fold line with pencil. Draw parallel line ¾" away from center fold line. Use pattern to trace and cut out 17 striped blocks, always placing black diagonal stripe between parallel lines on pattern.

4. Referring to Diagram 3, lay out blocks and border strips on work surface. Be sure direction of stripes and placement of color is same on each pieced block. Starting at top, with right sides facing and raw edges aligned, stitch blocks together to make 7 horizontal rows of 5 blocks each. Press seams open as you work. (Continued on page 48)

A pillow made from a man's favorite old shirt and a patched blanket are cozy companions for lazy afternoons.

(*Continued from page 47*)

5. Referring to Diagram 3, lay out horizontal rows of blocks on work surface. Be sure direction of stripes is same with each striped block. With right sides facing and raw edges aligned, stitch rows together as shown. Stitch 1 border piece to each side edge of pieced unit. Stitch 1 border piece to top and bottom.

6. Trim backing to match size of quilt top if necessary. Stack batting, backing (right side up), and quilt top (right side down). Pin all layers together. Machine-stitch edges together, using ¼" seam and leaving 12" open for turning. Trim excess batting from seam allowance. Turn right side out so that batting is on inside. Slipstitch opening closed. Smooth out all wrinkles on quilt. Flatten and pin edges so that seam is exactly on edge. Also pin layers together at every point where block corners meet.

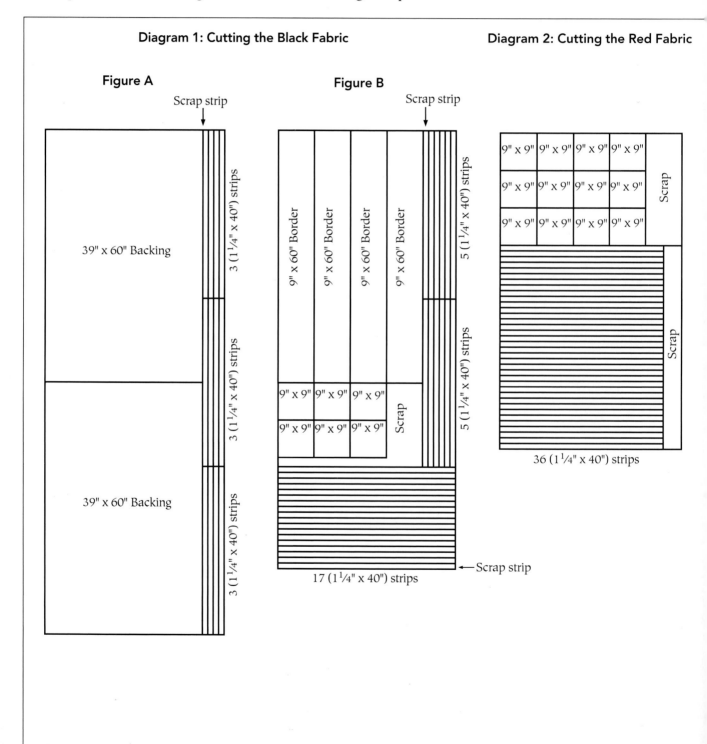

Diagram 1: Cutting the Black Fabric

Diagram 2: Cutting the Red Fabric

Figure A

Scrap strip

39" x 60" Backing

3 (1¼" x 40") strips

3 (1¼" x 40") strips

39" x 60" Backing

3 (1¼" x 40") strips

Figure B

Scrap strip

9" x 60" Border

9" x 60" Border

9" x 60" Border

9" x 60" Border

9" x 9" 9" x 9" 9" x 9"

9" x 9" 9" x 9" 9" x 9"

Scrap

5 (1¼" x 40") strips

5 (1¼" x 40") strips

5 (1¼" x 40") strips

17 (1¼" x 40") strips

9" x 9" 9" x 9" 9" x 9" 9" x 9"

9" x 9" 9" x 9" 9" x 9" 9" x 9"

9" x 9" 9" x 9" 9" x 9" 9" x 9"

Scrap

Scrap

36 (1¼" x 40") strips

Scrap strip

7. Thread needle with 6 strands of embroidery floss. At each corner of each block, take 1 stitch through all layers from back of quilt to front. Take another stitch from front to back, leaving 3"-long tails. Tie tails together with a double knot on back of blanket and trim tails as desired.

Diagram 3: Laying Out Blocks and Border Strips

Red	Stripe	Red	Stripe	Red
Stripe	Black	Stripe	Black	Stripe
Red	Stripe	Red	Stripe	Red
Stripe	Black	Stripe	Black	Stripe
Red	Stripe	Red	Stripe	Red
Stripe	Black	Stripe	Black	Stripe
Red	Stripe	Red	Stripe	Red

Just a Little Something

Corrugated Basket

Corrugated cardboard provides an inexpensive means for creating great-looking baskets. Begin by selecting an empty can or box to use as the base for your basket. To make the handle, cut a strip of corrugated cardboard (see Resources, page 173) at least 1" wide and whatever length you desire. Flatten the corrugations on the ends of the handle and, using white glue, glue the handle to the container.

Measure the perimeter and the height of the container. Cut a length of corrugated cardboard to match these dimensions. Glue the corrugated cardboard to the sides of the container.

Fill your basket with a variety of thoughtful items depending on the occasion for which you are giving it:
• A presentation of potpourri and a small wooden spoon for stirring makes a marvelous housewarming gift.
• Fill the basket with packing straw; then add cedar sachet blocks tied with narrow ribbon. The blocks resemble gift packages, making the presentation an ideal birthday remembrance for the man in your life.
• Unshelled nuts are also attractive and create a charming hostess gift.
• Summer flowering bulbs look sweet nestled in the packing straw. Just add planting instructions and you'll have a delightful May Day surprise.

Give this set for a tableful of love. Add the finishing touch by bundling the coasters with coordinating ribbon.

Heart Place Mat

Materials for one place mat

Patterns on pages 143–144
Tracing paper
2 (15" x 19") pieces heart print fabric
15" x 19" piece thin quilt batting (optional)
Thread to match
Heavy-duty or quilting thread for topstitching

Instructions

Note: Broken pattern line is stitching line. Add ¼" seam allowance when cutting fabric.

1. On folded paper, trace each heart pattern section. Cut out. Unfold patterns and match sections along dots. Tape together.

2. Trace complete heart pattern on wrong side of 1 fabric piece. With right sides facing and raw edges aligned, stack fabric pieces. (If desired, pin batting to back of fabric pieces.) Stitch along outline, leaving open between large dots on side. Cut out, adding ¼" seam allowance. Clip along curved edges and into crevice. (Trim batting close to stitching line.) Turn right side out. Slipstitch opening closed.

3. Machine-topstitch around place mat ¼" from edge.

Bow Napkin

Materials for one bow napkin

5½" to 6" length ⅜"-wide elastic
Thread to match
1 napkin *or* 22" square fabric with ¼" double-fold hem on each edge

Instructions

1. To make elastic napkin ring, refer to Diagram 1 to form elastic into ring and fold under cut ends. Whipstitch folds and finished edges to conceal cut ends.

2. Referring to Figures A through D of Diagram 2, fold napkin. Referring to Figure E, slide elastic ring over napkin at center to finish bow.

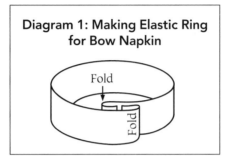

Diagram 1: Making Elastic Ring for Bow Napkin

Fold
Fold

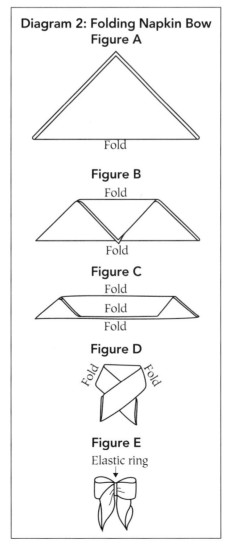

Diagram 2: Folding Napkin Bow

Figure A

Fold

Figure B

Fold
Fold

Figure C

Fold
Fold
Fold

Figure D

Fold
Fold

Figure E

Elastic ring

Heart Coasters

Materials for four coasters

Pattern on page 143
Tracing paper
8 (6") squares fabric (2 each of 4 different prints)
Thread to match
4 (6") squares thin batting
1 yard ⅜"-wide coordinating ribbon

Instructions

Note: Broken pattern line is stitching line. Add ¼" seam allowance when cutting fabrics.

1. Trace pattern onto folded tracing paper, transferring markings. Cut out. Unfold pattern.

2. For each, to make coaster backing, cut 1 square of fabric in half. With right sides facing and raw edges aligned, stitch together along 1 long side, leaving 2" opening in center. Press seam open. Place coaster pattern on wrong side of pieced coaster backing, aligning dots on pattern with seam on fabric. Trace pattern. Cut out, adding ¼" seam allowance.

3. With right sides facing, center coaster backing on matching fabric square. Pin this unit, with opening faceup, on top of 1 batting square. Do not trim yet. Machine-stitch around heart. Trim excess fabric and batting, leaving ¼" seam allowance. Then trim batting close to stitching. Clip seam allowance at crevice and around curves. Cut off seam allowance at tip. Turn right side out. Slipstitch opening closed.

4. Pin around edges to flatten. Hand-quilt around heart approximately ½" from edge. Repeat to complete remaining coasters. Stack coasters and tie together with ribbon.

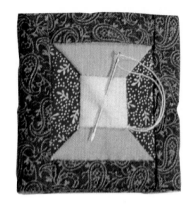

These pieced needle books that look like spools of thread make great little gifts for quilter friends or for a young person going off to college.

Pieced Needle Books

Materials

Patterns on page 144
Tracing paper
2" square fabric for thread area
3" square fabric for background
3" square fabric for spool ends
3" x 11" piece fabric for book
  (including border, back, and
  self-lining)
Thread to match
Small fine needle
Pinking shears
1¾" x 3¾" piece linen, flannel,
  or thin felt for book "pages"
Size 4/0 sew-on snap set
Assorted needles

Instructions

Note: Broken pattern lines are stitching lines. Add ¼" seam allowance when cutting fabrics.

1. Trace pattern pieces onto tracing paper, transferring markings. Cut out.

2. Place pattern pieces ½" apart on wrong side of fabrics. Trace and cut out pieces, adding ¼" seam allowances and transferring markings, including dots at corners of all seams. From thread fabric, cut 1 A. Using pattern B, cut 2 background pieces and 2 spool pieces. From border/lining fabric, cut 2 Cs, 1 D, and 1 E. Transfer fold lines to right side of fabric with basting stitches.

3. Referring to Diagram 1, place pieces on work surface. With right sides facing, raw edges aligned and using fine needle and tiny handstitches, stitch only from dot to dot to join 1 spool B to top of A. Join remaining spool B to bottom of A. Stitch 1 background B to each side of A. Stitch diagonal seams from dot to dot between B pieces. Finger-press.

4. With right sides facing and raw edges aligned, refer to Diagram 2 to stitch 1 C each to top and bottom of spool. Fold under and baste seam allowances on starred edges of D and E.

5. With right sides facing and raw edges aligned, refer to Diagram 3 to stitch D and E to joined spool piece. Referring to Diagram 4 and aligning starred edges with center fold line, fold and pin unit. Stitch along each long raw edge, leaving center folded edges open. Trim stitched seam allowances to ⅛"; turn book right side out. Slipstitch folded edges closed.

6. Use pinking shears to trim edges of fabric for pages. Fold in half, short edges together. Slipstitch center fold of pages to slipstitched center seam inside book. Center and stitch snap set inside book along side edges.

7. Thread needle with 8" length of thread that matches pieced thread area. Take small stitch in corner of pieced spool, inserting needle through thread loop to knot. Trim ends. Then run needle through spool as shown in photo. Fill pages of needle book with assorted needles.

Diagram 1: Placing Pattern Pieces

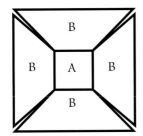

Diagram 2: Joining C Pieces to Spool

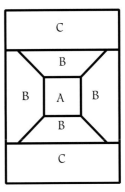

Diagram 3: Joining D and E Pieces to Spool

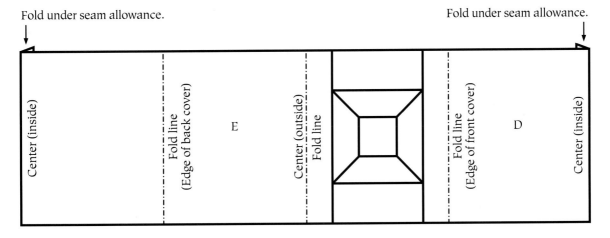

Fold under seam allowance.

Fold under seam allowance.

Center (inside)

Fold line (Edge of back cover)

E

Center (outside)
Fold line

Fold line (Edge of front cover)

D

Center (inside)

Diagram 4: Stitching Long Edges

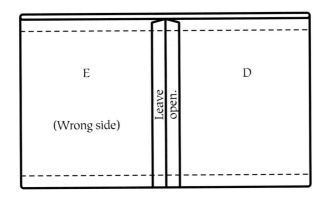

E

(Wrong side)

Leave open.

D

Celebration Station

Just ahead is Celebration Station, offering
year-round holiday fun! Catch the spirit
and celebrate the seasons. This is the
place to share an old tradition or start
one that's brand new.

*Make this Valentine Folder for the
one you love who loves to write.*

Valentine Folder

Materials for one folder
Pattern on page 145
Tracing paper
Acetate
11½" x 14" piece art paper
Craft knife
24" length ¼"-wide ribbon, cut
   in half
White glue
Transparent tape
Purchased package of formal
   note cards with envelopes
   (measuring no more than
   3⅝" x 5⅛")
Stickers

Instructions
1. Trace pattern onto tracing paper or photocopy; glue to acetate, if desired. Cut out, transferring markings.
2. Score and fold art paper in half, short ends together, to measure 11½" x 7".
3. Align pattern with folded edge of paper as indicated. Trace shape, transferring score and fold lines. Cut out. Score along all fold lines.
4. Without opening folder, flip to opposite side; also flip pattern.

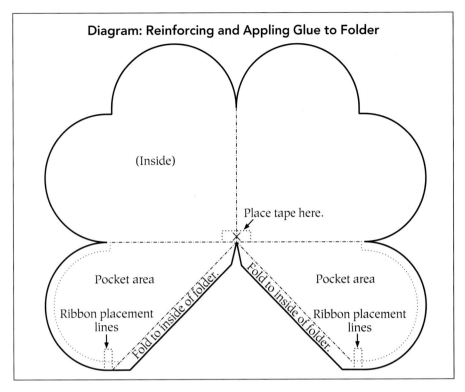

Diagram: Reinforcing and Appling Glue to Folder

(Inside)

Place tape here.

Pocket area

Pocket area

Fold to inside of folder.

Fold to inside of folder.

Ribbon placement lines

Ribbon placement lines

Transfer and score all fold lines.
5. Referring to Diagram, open folder so that inside faces you. To reinforce folder, place tape at base of hearts where indicated with X. Fold glue flaps on pocket areas to inside of folder. Open flaps and apply line of glue to each. Refold; hold flaps in place until dry.
6. Use pattern to transfer ribbon placement lines to each pocket.

Spread glue on 1 end of each ribbon piece. Place 1 ribbon on each pocket and let dry.
7. Add glue to curved edge of each pocket as indicated on pattern. Fold pockets to meet hearts as indicated. Press edges together until dry.
8. Fill folder with purchased note cards and stickers.

Just a Little Something

New Year's Fortune Cookie Jar

Give the hostess of a New Year's Eve party a bit of good fortune. Fill a glass canister with store-bought fortune cookies. Tie a bright bow around the neck of the jar. Add a "Good Luck" message by adhering inexpensive metallic paper letters to the ribbon.

Glove Bunnies

Materials for one bunny

1 child's or woman's stretch-
  knit glove (approximately
  4" x 6")
Thread to match
Polyester stuffing
Black embroidery floss
12" length ⅛"-wide
  coordinating satin ribbon

Instructions

1. To make seam guidelines,
handstitch through *single* layer of
glove to make line of basting
stitches, following straight knit
line from crevice of pinky to start
of cuff and from crevice between
index finger and middle finger to
start of cuff. (Stitches should go
through to wrong side of glove so
that line will be visible there.)
Repeat on opposite side of glove.
2. Turn glove inside out. Pull ring
finger until it matches length of
middle finger. Cut straight across
to remove cuff along hemline and
discard. Flatten glove on work
surface. Align basting stitches,
and pin layers together.
3. Referring to Diagram 1 (see
page 60) and using basting
stitches as guidelines, make
narrow machine-zigzag stitches
from finger crevices to cut edge.
Trim glove as indicated in
Diagram 1. Without stretching
cut edge of body area, make
small running stitches around
opening to prevent raveling. Turn
pieces right side out. Set aside
pieces for legs and tail.
4. To pleat ears, refer to Diagram
2 (see page 60) to fold 1 ear in
half, long edges together. Tack
layers together near head. Wrap
thread tightly around base of ear.
Secure thread and tie off. (This
will hold shape of head while it is
being stuffed; wrapped thread

can be removed after stuffing, if
desired.) Fold tip of ear forward
and slipstitch layers together.
Repeat with other ear.
5. With doubled thread, run
gathering stitches across bunny
approximately ¼" above midway
point on body, leaving tail of
thread. Stuff head. Pull thread to
slightly gather neckline. Continue
adding stuffing until head is 5"-
circumference ball. Pull thread as
tightly as possible to define head.
Secure thread and tie off. Run
gathering stitches ¼" from lower
cut edge, leaving tail of thread.
Stuff lower body area until it is
5¾"-circumference ball. Pull
thread tightly to gather, tucking
in seam allowance. Tie off.
6. To make tail, run gathering
stitches ⅛" from cut edge of
pinky tip, leaving tail of thread.
Stuff. Pull thread tightly to gather,
tucking in seam allowance.
Secure thread and tie off. Flatten
tail slightly and slipstitch to rear
of bunny, covering gathered
opening. (At this point, bunny
will look somewhat like snowman with small ball on the base.)
7. To make legs, stretch or trim
reserved glove fingers so that
both are same length (approximately 1½" long). Push small
amount of stuffing into paw
portion of 1 leg. Measure approximately 1" from cut edge and
make line of running stitches
through 1 layer of glove across
paw area, just above stuffing.
Fold stuffed area up along stitching line and slipstitch paw to leg
front to form a foot. (Leg and foot
will be at right angles.) Do not
stuff leg. Whipstitch leg opening
closed. Repeat for other leg.

(Continued on page 60)

*Bunnies made from little gloves
look sweet bouncing on boxes or
nestled in a fabric basket (page 61).*

(Continued from page 58)

8. Lifting bunny head, pin and tack legs to center front of body at neckline, easing in fullness of leg tops to fit between side seams on body. Whipstitch leg tops to neckline. To cover ragged edges of leg tops, slipstitch small area at top to neck edge of body (catching only top layer of leg).

9. Pin paws in place side by side at body center front. Underneath bunny, tack paws together and to body. Slipstitch outside edges of legs to bunny body.

10. Push head back so it is high up on body; securely slipstitch around neck. Compress bunny head and body so that bunny looks chubby and proportions resemble bunnies in photos.

11. To make face, satin-stitch eyes using 1 strand of black floss. Tie ribbon into bow around neck.

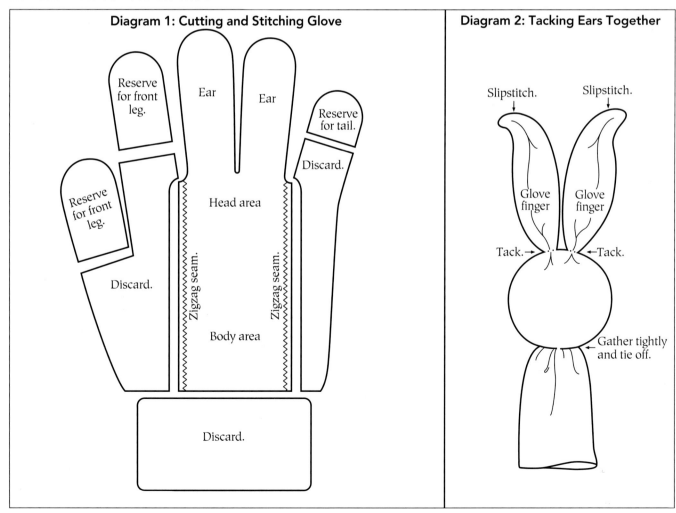

Diagram 1: Cutting and Stitching Glove

Reserve for front leg.

Ear

Ear

Reserve for tail.

Discard.

Reserve for front leg.

Head area

Zigzag seam.

Zigzag seam.

Discard.

Body area

Discard.

Diagram 2: Tacking Ears Together

Slipstitch.

Slipstitch.

Glove finger

Glove finger

Tack.→

←Tack.

Gather tightly and tie off.

Gathered Basket

Materials

9" x 44" piece fabric
Vanishing fabric marker
Fabric glue
1 empty, clean 6⅛-ounce tuna can
Plastic coffee can lid
Graph paper
Compass
Bodkin (optional)
Thread to match
10½" length 1⅜"- to 1½"-wide sturdy elastic
2 safety pins
Shredded paper grass

Instructions

1. Referring to Diagram, cut 6" x 35" piece of fabric for basket side and 1¾" x 30" strip for handle. Set aside. From remaining fabric, cut 1 (9") square.
2. With raw edges aligned, fold 9" fabric square in half diagonally and pin folded edge. Measure, mark, and cut 1¼" from folded edge to make 2½" x 12¾" bias strip. Square off 1 short end of strip. Fold under ¼" along trimmed end and glue. Let dry. Spread glue inside can on walls and base. Also make ½"-wide border of glue around rim on outside of can. Starting with pointed end of bias strip, press ½" of 1 long edge of strip around outside rim of can. Fold excess to inside of can. About ¼" of fabric should rest on base of can. Smooth wrinkles. Let dry.
3. Cut off rim of coffee can lid in continuous ¼"- to ⅜"-wide strip. Reserve for handle. Use graph paper and compass to draw circle pattern to fit inside tuna can (approximately 3¼"-diameter). Check for fit. Using pattern, cut 1 plastic circle from remaining portion of coffee can lid. Glue

circle to wrong side of corner scrap from 9" square of fabric. Trim fabric ¼" beyond plastic circle. Clip and fold raw edges to back of circle, gluing in place. When dry, glue circle inside tuna can onto base.
4. To make handle, fold under ¼" along each short edge of reserved 1¾" x 30" strip and press. With right sides facing and raw edges aligned, fold handle strip in half, long edges together. Machine-stitch long edges together ¼" from raw edge. Turn right side out with bodkin or safety pin. Rotate seam to center.
　Measure and cut 11"-long strip from lid rim. Slide strip inside fabric tube until plastic and fabric ends align at point of entry. Using sturdy needle, tack plastic and fabric together. Gather tube on handle until plastic and fabric align at other end; tack. Glue and tack handle to bias fabric outside can rim.
5. To make basket side, fold under ¼" along each short raw edge of reserved 6" x 35" piece and press. With right sides facing and raw edges aligned, fold side piece in half, long edges together. Machine-stitch long edges together ¼" from raw edge. Turn right side out and press so that seam is exactly on edge. Back-stitching at beginning and end, make casing on basket side piece by stitching 1" from folded edge along length of unit.
6. Using safety pins, pull elastic through casing until ¼" remains outside point of entry; pin elastic and fabric together there. Complete pulling elastic through tube, gathering fabric on it as you work. Let elastic extend ¼" beyond point of exit; pin elastic and fabric together there. Overlap elastic ends ¼" and securely stitch together. Pull fabric over

elastic ends, butting and slip-stitching folded edges together. Slip unit over can, concealing ends of handle. Fill with shredded paper grass.

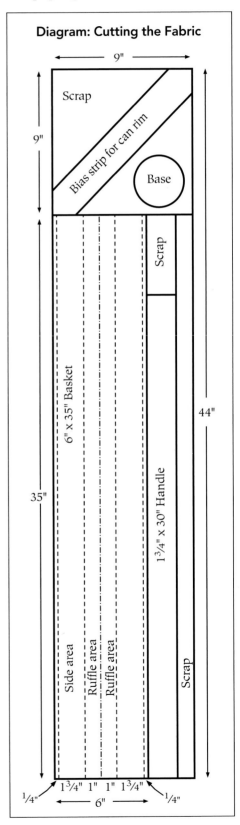

Diagram: Cutting the Fabric

Cedar Flag Bags

Materials for one bag

2 flag motifs from print fabric
(each approximately 4" x 6")
or 1 (4½" x 6¼") scrap star
fabric and 1 (4½" x 6¼")
scrap stripe fabric
Pinking shears
Thread to match
Cedar shavings*
15" length ⅛"-wide navy ribbon
or natural jute twine
4 (½") metallic paper stars
(optional)
Note: Inexpensive cedar shavings can be purchased from pet
shops.

Instructions

1. For flag print fabric, using
pinking shears, trim each motif
along short edge opposite navy.
With right sides facing and raw
edges aligned, stitch around 3
sides, ¼" from edge, leaving
pinked edge open. Clip corners
and turn.
2. For star and stripe scraps,
using pinking shears, trim 1 short
edge of each piece. With right
sides facing and raw edges
aligned, stitch side seams only,
¼" from edges. Referring to Diagram above, move side seams to
match at center front and back.
Press seams open. Stitch across
bottom of bag. Clip corners and
turn.
3. Fill bag halfway with cedar
shavings. Tie ribbon into bow
around bag. For each ribbon,
sandwich cut ends between stars,
if desired. Knot twine ½" above
ends and fray to make tassels.

*Protect your wardrobe with aro-
matic sachets filled with cedar, a
natural moth repellent. The all-
American heart can double as a
pincushion or an ornament.*

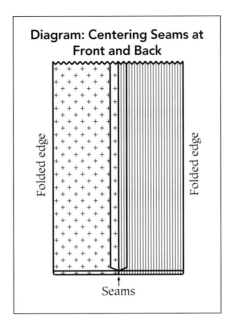

Diagram: Centering Seams at Front and Back

Folded edge
Folded edge
Seams

Patriotic Heart

Materials

Patterns on page 146
3" square navy-and-white star
fabric
4" square red-and-white stripe
fabric
4½" square fabric for back *or*
additional star and stripe
fabric*
Thread to match
13½" navy corded piping
(optional)*
8" length ⅛"-wide navy satin
ribbon
Tracing paper
Note: Heart can be backed with
plain fabric or front and back
can be made to match, requiring
extra star and stripe fabric.

Design can be made with or
without piping around edge.
Addition of piping requires using
zipper foot on sewing machine.

Instructions

Note: Broken pattern lines are
stitching lines. Add ¼" seam allowances when cutting fabrics.
1. Trace patterns onto tracing
paper and cut out.

2. On wrong side of star fabric,
trace 1 A. On wrong side of stripe
fabric, trace 2 Bs, 1 with stripes
parallel to straight edge and 1
with stripes perpendicular to
straight edge. Cut out, adding ¼"
seam allowance.
3. With right sides facing and
raw edges aligned, refer to
Diagram below to pin and stitch
Bs to A to form heart. Press
seams toward star fabric.
4. If adding piping, trim piping
seam allowance to ¼" if necessary. Open ½" of 1 end of piping;
trim ½" of cord inside and close.
Clip seam allowance of piping.
Starting at center top, pin piping
to right side of heart, folding
"empty" end of piping out of the
way and aligning cut edges of
piping and heart. Baste and
machine-stitch along ¼" from
raw edge. If edge of piping rolls
too much, baste it to heart.
5. With right sides facing and
raw edges aligned, pin heart front
to back. Stitch, leaving 1" open
along 1 straight edge. Using
pinking shears, trim edges
(except at opening) to ⅛". Clip
curves. Turn heart right side out.
Remove basting. Stuff and
flatten. Slipstitch opening closed.
For hanger, fold satin ribbon in
half to form loop; tack ends to
center of heart at crevice.

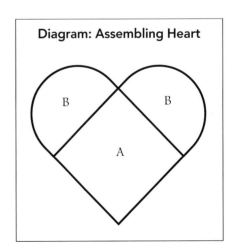

Diagram: Assembling Heart

B   B

A

Jack-o'-lantern Lampshade

Materials
Pattern on page 146
Tracing paper
Vanishing fabric marker
Purchased white fabric lampshade with bound rims
Orange fabric to cover shade
Orange thread
Fabric glue
Black ½"-wide double-fold bias tape (to equal total measurement around top and bottom shade rims plus 2")
5" square black paper
Craft knife
Purchased black lamp

Instructions
1. Trace face pattern onto tracing paper and cut out. Set aside.
2. To cover lampshade, leave shade intact and make pattern by taping pieces of paper around shade and trimming to fit. Trace this patched pattern onto single piece of paper, adding ¼" along each short straight edge for overlap. Cut out and tape final pattern onto shade; make fitting adjustments if necessary.

Using vanishing fabric marker, trace shade pattern onto orange fabric and cut out. Pin fabric onto shade along rims, pulling gently to tighten as you work. Fold 1 short straight edge under ¼" and overlap other short edge at center back. Whipstitch raw edges of fabric to rims, removing pins as you work and adjusting to make taut. Glue overlapped edge at center back. Open bias tape and align center fold with edge of rim. Fold excess tape over rim to inside of shade. Glue bias tape to rims, overlapping ends.

3. Transfer face pattern onto black paper and cut out. Referring to photo for placement or using cut out area of tracing paper as a template, center face on covered shade and glue cutouts in place.
4. Place shade on lamp.

Petite Pumpkin Trio

Materials for three pumpkins
Orange fabric: 5" x 12" strip for small 3"-diameter pumpkin; 6½" x 17½" strip for medium 4¼"-diameter pumpkin; 8" x 22" strip for large 5"-diameter pumpkin
Olive fabric: 1" x 4" scrap for small stem; 1⅛" x 5½" for medium stem; 1¼" x 6" scrap for large stem
Heavy-duty orange thread
Olive thread
Polyester stuffing
3 pipe cleaners

Instructions
1. To make small pumpkin, with right sides facing and raw edges aligned, fold 5" x 12" orange fabric strip in half, short ends together. Stitch short ends together, ½" from edge, to make a tube. Finger-press seam open.
2. Leaving tube wrong side out, use doubled thread to run gathering stitches ½" from edge along 1 long edge of tube, leaving tail of thread. Pull thread tightly to gather. Wrap loose thread around gathered edge. Secure and tie off. Turn right side out. Stuff pumpkin firmly. Set aside.
3. With right sides facing and raw edges aligned, fold 1" x 4" olive fabric scrap in half, short ends together. Leaving short end open, stitch along long edges ¼" from edge, rounding seam at top near fold as in Diagram. Trim stitched seam allowance to ⅛". Clip curves. Turn right side out. Cut 4" length from pipe cleaner and fold in half. Insert folded pipe cleaner and stuffing into stem. Set aside.
4. Run gathering stitches ½" from edge along open edge of pumpkin, leaving tail of thread. Pull slightly and fold ½" seam allowance to inside of pumpkin. Pull slightly again and insert stem so that 1¼" remains outside. Pull tightly to gather around stem. Secure and tie off. Tack pumpkin and stem together.
5. To make medium pumpkin, complete steps 1–4 using 6½" x 17½" strip of orange fabric, 5½" length of pipe cleaner, and 1⅛" x 5½" scrap of olive fabric for 1⅝" stem.
6. To make large pumpkin, complete steps 1–4 using 8" x 22" strip of orange fabric, 6" length of pipe cleaner, and 1¼" x 6" scrap of olive fabric for 2¼" stem.

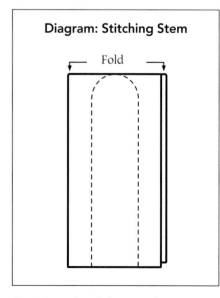

Diagram: Stitching Stem

Fold

Cast just the right mood over a Halloween party with these decorative accents. (Candy Corn Cup is on page 66.)

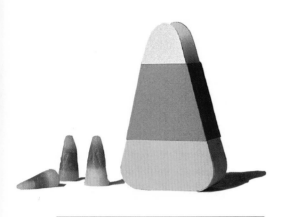

Candy Corn Cup

Materials

Patterns on page 147
Tracing paper
Scrap of acetate (optional)
Craft knife
White glue
8" x 8" square sturdy yellow
    paper
1¼" x 2" scrap white paper
2¾" x 5½" scrap orange paper

Instructions

1. Trace patterns onto tracing paper, transferring markings. Glue patterns to acetate, if desired. Cut out, making sure to clip to arrows on cup base.
2. Trace cup base pattern onto yellow paper, transferring markings. Cut out. Lightly score fold lines.
3. Fold cup base and tabs along score lines. Bring tabbed extensions up along sides of cup. Place small amount of glue on tabs and glue extensions to inside back and front of cup. Glue 1 tab at a time and hold in place until dry.
4. Trace 2 cup tips onto white paper and cut out. Glue tips in place on cup.
5. Trace cup side wrap pattern onto orange paper, transferring markings. Cut out. Score and fold along marked lines. Glue in place on cup.

Paper Witch

Materials

Patterns on pages 148–149
Tracing paper
Acetate (optional)
Craft knife
8" x 10" scrap sturdy black art
    paper
3" x 5" scrap light green art
    paper
4½" x 8" scrap purple art paper
Silver tinsel strands
Transparent tape
White glue
Paper punches: ⅛" for eyes, ¼"
    for cheeks
1" square pink art paper
Fine-line black felt-tip pen
12 (½"-wide) self-sticking silver
    stars (optional)
12" length ⅛"-wide black satin
    ribbon

Instructions

1. Trace patterns onto tracing paper or photocopy. Glue to acetate, if desired. Cut out. Make template on head pattern by cutting out nose, eyes, cheeks, and line for mouth.
2. Trace witch body, hat crown, and hat brim patterns onto black paper. Trace head and nose onto green paper. Trace cape and hat band onto purple paper. Transfer markings and cut out pieces. Do not punch out holes at cape closure yet. Also, do not clip slits on hat crown yet.
3. Gently pull head, cape, hatband, hat crown, and body across scissors blade or ruler to curl slightly. Turn body piece over so that wrong side faces you. Tape multiple strands of tinsel to top edge between dots as indicated on pattern. (Leave area at center top free of tinsel so that face will show.) Form piece into open-ended cone with taped

tinsel ends inside. Pushing tinsel aside, glue back tab edge. Let dry. Fold tinsel over top edge to right side.
4. Using paper punches and scraps of paper, make ⅛" black eyes and ¼" pink cheeks. Glue in place on head piece. Use pen to draw mouth.
    Score, fold, and glue nose in place. Lift tinsel "hair" and overlap body with head piece. Add glue to tab and hold in place until dry.
5. Reinforce hole areas at cape closure by putting pieces of tape on wrong side of paper and trimming excess tape. Punch out holes. Add stars to right side of cape, if desired. Place cape on witch. Overlap rounded tab with cape front edge and thread ribbon through holes. Tie ribbon into bow and trim ends.
6. To make hat, lightly score curved line at base of slits on crown. To make glue tabs, use craft knife, cut slits from scored line to edge. Form crown into cone, add glue to long center back tab, and hold in place until dry. Bend bottom glue tabs outward on crown to fan apart. Spread thin layer of glue on tabs. Insert hat crown through hole in hat brim; press glue tabs against brim. When hat is dry, add hatband. Glue hat in place on head.

Enhance the desk of your favorite school teacher with this whimsical witch.

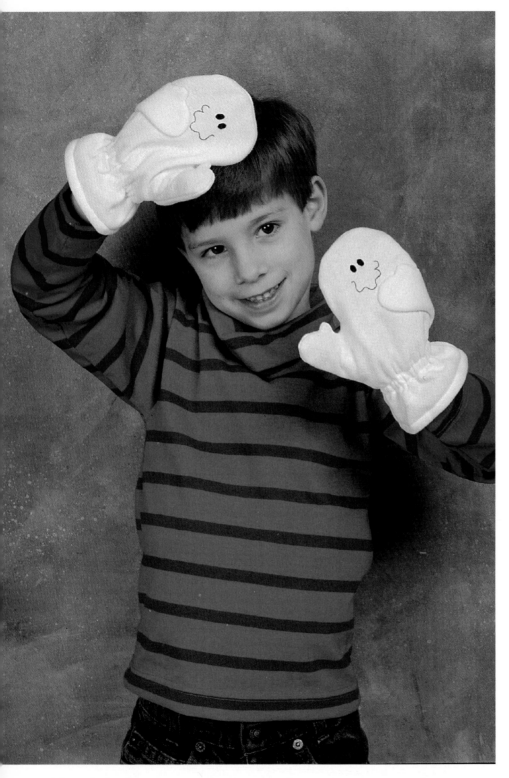

These little ghost mittens aren't meant for stormy winter weather, but they're great for chasing the chills away on a shivery October night.

Ghost Mittens

Materials for one pair of mittens

Pattern on page 150
Tracing paper
4 (8½" x 9") pieces white fleece sweatshirt fabric (9" dimension should run length of fabric from top to bottom)
Vanishing fabric marker
Black embroidery floss *or* black permanent marking pen
White thread
21" length ½"-wide single-fold white bias tape
¼"-wide soft elastic (loose wrist measurement plus 1½" or about 6½" for *each* mitten)
Small safety pin
Note: These mittens are intended for children ages 2 to 4.

Instructions

Note: Broken pattern line is stitching line. Add ¼" seam allowance when cutting fabric.

1. Trace pattern onto tracing paper, transferring markings. Cut out.

2. For 1 mitten, center and pin pattern on wrong side of 1 fabric piece. Trace mitten, transferring markings. Cut out, adding ¼" seam allowance.

3. Center pattern on right side of mitten piece; transfer face details. Using 1 strand of black floss, satin-stitch eyes and backstitch mouth. Or if you prefer, draw face using permanent marker.

4. With right sides facing, center and pin embroidered mitten piece to unmarked fabric piece. Trim excess fabric to match mitten shape. Using small machine stitches and starting at bottom edge below thumb, stitch side seam to dot on head.

5. Do not turn mitten right side out. Remove pins and open mitten so that wrist edge of wrong side faces you. Pin bias tape casing in place and stitch close to each long edge. Using safety pin, pull elastic through casing, letting each end extend ¼" beyond casing. Stitch across casing ends to secure elastic.

6. Fold mitten with right sides facing and raw edges aligned. Stitch remaining portion of seam, catching ends of elastic in stitching. Trim seam allowances above casing to ⅛". Clip curves and into thumb and arm crevices.

7. Turn right side out. Fold under hem along line indicated and machine-stitch. Fold arm to mitten front as indicated and slipstitch in place.
8. Repeat, reversing pattern, to make other mitten.

Just a Little Something

Thanksgiving Table Setting

This seasonal table setting costs very little to make and is quick to complete. Inexpensive corrugated cardboard can be purchased from paper product suppliers. The 12" width is a perfect size for these place mats and other corrugated projects (see Corrugated Basket, page 49).

To make the corrugated place mat, make a paper pattern by tracing a favorite oval or rectangular place mat. Cut it out. Trace the pattern on the back of the corrugated cardboard and cut out the shape using scissors or a craft knife with a new blade.

To make each napkin and napkin tie, cut an 18" square of cotton fabric. Press under a ¼" hem twice around each edge and stitch. Fold and roll the napkin. Cut 1 or 2 (28") lengths of jute twine and tie around the rolled napkin. Place a cinnamon stick and a small pressed leaf or dried flower on top of the twine. Tie

twine into a bow. Make a knot 1" from each cut end of the twine. Unravel the twine up to the knot to make tassels.

To make the autumn leaf place cards, collect a variety of colorful leaves. Dip them in warm, soapy water to wash away any hitchhiking critters. Rinse and spread them out on towels to air dry. Place leaves in a heavy book, sandwiching them between layers of smooth

paper towels to protect the pages of the book. (Textured towels will produce textured leaves.) Stack more books on top. Press at least a week before using. Remove the leaves from the book. Handle carefully as leaves will be brittle. Using a permanent marker or gold paint pen, gently write names on the leaves.

Decorations that will delight family members of all ages are nestled in this tissue paper-lined box. (Decorations shown here continue through page 75.)

Santa Beanbag Decoration

Materials

Patterns on pages 151–152
Tracing paper
6½" x 32" piece red print fabric
6" square peach fabric
Embroidery floss: black, pink, light pink, red
Extra-fine unwaxed dental floss
Polyester stuffing
2½" x 7½" scrap green print fabric
Thread to match fabrics
4½" x 6" scrap black minidot fabric
Plastic stuffing pellets*
1 woman's white stretch sport sock with terry cloth lining
1 (⅝") white pom-pom
*See Resources, page 173.
Note: Use tightly woven cotton fabrics and small machine stitches. Begin and end each seam with backstitches, ¼" below outline.

Instructions

Note: Broken pattern lines are stitching lines. Add ¼" seam allowances when cutting fabrics.
1. Trace patterns for body front/back, beard, foot, and mitten onto tracing paper. On folded tracing paper, trace patterns for head, sleeve, and hat. Transfer all markings and cut out. Unfold patterns.
2. Place patterns ½" apart on wrong side of fabrics. Trace and cut pieces from fabrics as indicated below, transferring markings and adding ¼" seam allowances, unless otherwise indicated.
3. From red print fabric, cut 2 body front/back pieces, 2 sleeves, and 1 hat. Set pieces aside.
On peach fabric, trace 1 head. Before cutting out, use 1 strand of floss to satin-stitch eyes with black and nose with light pink. Also backstitch mouth with red and straightstitch cheeks with pink. Cut out, adding ¼" seam allowance. Fold under seam allowance around head circle. Use dental floss to run small gathering stitches close to edge, leaving tail of thread. Pull thread slightly to gather edge. Stuff. Pull tightly, squeezing head. Secure thread and tie off. There will probably be a ½" opening. Add more stuffing through it so that head is firm. Set aside.
4. With right sides facing and raw edges aligned, fold green print fabric in half, short edges together, to measure 2½" x 3¾". Trace 2 mittens, but *do not cut out yet.* Machine-stitch mittens, leaving straight edge open on each. Cut out, adding ⅛" seam allowance around stitched seam and ¼" seam allowance at opening on each. Clip curves and into thumb crevices. Turn right side out. Stuff. Run small gathering stitches around each opening, ¼" from raw edge, leaving tail of thread. Pull thread to gather tightly. Secure thread and tie off. Seam allowance will form stem at bottom of each mitten. Set mittens aside.
With right sides facing and raw edges aligned, fold black minidot fabric in half, short ends together, to measure 4½" x 3". Trace 2 feet, but *do not cut out yet.* Machine-stitch, leaving ¾" open along straight edge on each. Cut out, adding ⅛" seam allowance around stitched seam and ¼" seam allowance at opening on each. Clip curves. Turn right side out. Stuff, maintaining flatness. Slipstitch openings closed. Set feet aside.
5. To make body, refer to Diagram 1 (see page 72). With right sides facing and raw edges and dots aligned, pin and stitch side edge of 1 sleeve to 1 front/back piece from neck edge to dot. Repeat to stitch remaining sleeve to remaining front/back piece. With right sides facing and raw edges aligned, place unit as shown in Diagram 2 (see page 72). Pin and stitch remaining side edge of 1 sleeve to remaining side edge of other front/back piece from neck edge to dot. Repeat to join pieces together to form front/back unit. Referring to Diagram 3 (see page 72), stitch each sleeve seam from wrist to underarm dot. Stitch each body side seam from lower edge to underarm dot. Check underarm seams at dot and reinforce if necessary.
Stitch inseam and cut through center of legs, leaving ⅛" seam allowance on each side. While unit is inside out, use doubled thread to run small gathering stitches along seam line around bottom of each leg, leaving tail of thread. Pull tightly to gather. Secure thread. Wrap thread around resulting seam allowance and tie off. Turn unit right side out. Mark body front. Tuck raw edge of neck under ¼". Use dental floss to run gathering stitches close to edge, leaving tail of floss. Pull to gather. Pour pellets inside body and legs. Santa will seem *very* full, but some pellets will later be distributed into arms. To gather neck edge, pull floss tightly. Because there is so much fabric, opening will remain. Pinch neck front and back layers together at opening and measure. Adjust gathers, if necessary, so that flattened neck edge measures 1½". Secure floss and tie off. To close opening, whipstitch neck edges together.

(Continued on page 72)

(Continued from page 71)

6. Tuck 1 sleeve opening under ¼". Run gathering stitches along folded edge, leaving tail of thread. Pull thread to gather. Insert stem of 1 mitten so that palm faces body side and thumb faces forward. Pull thread to gather sleeve tightly around mitten wrist. Secure thread and tie off. Slipstitch mitten and sleeve together. Repeat with other sleeve and mitten. Work pellets from body into sleeves. Tack feet to leg bottoms where indicated on foot pattern by X.

7. Securely stitch head to neck edge along line indicated. To make beard, trace pattern on cuff area of sock, aligning with folded edges of sock as indicated. Cut out, adding ¼" seam allowance. *Do not cut folds.* Stitch lower curved edge by hand. Clip seam allowance. Trim upper unstitched seam allowance exactly on outline. Carefully turn beard right side out and add very small amount of stuffing. Whipstitch cut edges of beard together. Pin and slipstitch whipstitched edge of beard along placement line on face. Tack underside of beard to face.

8. To make hat, with right sides facing and raw edges aligned, stitch center back seam. Turn right side out. Make line of machine basting stitches along curved edge, leaving tail of thread. Pull to gather slightly. Place hat on head, aligning raw edge of hat with placement line on face. Slipstitch hat in place. Tack pom-pom to tip of hat. To make hatband, cut 1" x 7" scrap across width of sock. Fold long cut edges to center; butt and whipstitch ends together. Wrap hatband around head, covering hat seam allowance. Slipstitch in place. To make cuffs, use 1"-wide strips of sock, prepared as above and trimmed to fit wrists and legs.

Diagram 1: Stitching Sleeves

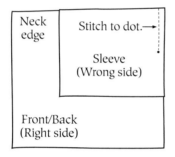

Diagram 2: Joining Front/Back Units with Sleeves

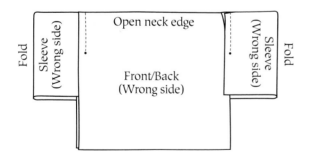

Diagram 3: Stitching Side Seams and Inseam

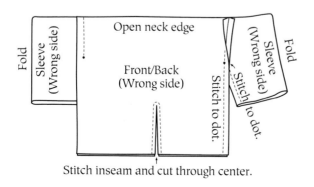

Stitch inseam and cut through center.

Little Stocking Ornaments

Materials for one stocking
Patterns on page 152
Tracing paper
2 (4" x 6") scraps fabric
4" square fabric for stockings with patches (optional)
Vanishing fabric marker
Thread to match
4" length string or yarn *or* ⅛"-wide ribbon

Instructions
Note: Broken pattern lines are stitching lines. Add ¼" seam allowances when cutting fabrics.
1. Trace patterns onto tracing paper, transferring markings. Cut out.
2. For bandanna stocking, turn 1 short edge of each fabric scrap under ¼" twice. Press and machine-stitch.

3. Align top edge of stocking pattern with hemmed edge of 1 scrap. Lightly trace stocking shape on right side of fabric. Transfer stitching line to wrong side with basting stitches.

4. With right sides facing and hemmed edges aligned, pin marked scrap to remaining unmarked scrap. Stitch along outline, leaving top open. Cut out, adding ¼" seam allowance. Trim seams and clip curves. Turn right side out and lightly press edges. At opening, tack all seam allowances to stocking front.

5. For hanger, fold string in half. Tack ends of loop to side seam allowance at top right of stocking.

6. For fabric scrap stocking, complete steps 2 and 3 above. Trace heel, toe, and cuff patterns onto wrong side of patch fabric square. Cut out, adding ¼" seam allowance. Fold long edges on cuff piece and straight edges on heel and toe under ¼". Pin pieces in place on right side of stocking front. Slipstitch folded edges to stocking. Baste raw edges together. Complete steps 4 and 5.

7. For dish towel stocking, if towel edge is unfinished, or border is very far from towel edge, complete Step 2. Otherwise, start with Step 3. For patched toe, trace toe pattern onto wrong side of border scrap. Cut out, adding ¼" seam allowance. Fold straight edge under ¼". Pin in place on right side of stocking front. Slipstitch folded edge to stocking. To make patched heel, cut 2 (2") squares from border. With right sides facing and raw edges aligned, stitch diagonally across squares to make bias seam. Trim seam allowance to ¼" on 1 side of seam. Press seam open. Trace 1 heel, aligning dotted line of pattern with seam. Cut out,

adding ¼" seam allowance. Fold and slipstitch patched heel to stocking in same manner as fabric scrap stocking. Complete steps 4 and 5.

8. For mitten or sweater stocking, complete steps 3–5 above, aligning top edge of stocking pattern with finished edge of knitwear.

Button Wheel Wagon

Materials
Graph paper
Small box
Vanishing fabric marker
Fabric scraps
Thread to match
Craft glue
Cardboard scrap (same size as box base)
4 big flat buttons for wheels
Twine *or* ribbon for handle
Ball or toggle button for handle

Instructions
1. Refer to Diagram 1 for guidance in making pattern. In center of graph paper, draw rectangle equal to base of box. Measure depth of box. Extend *each* edge of box base pattern by drawing lines to equal twice depth of box. Draw larger rectangle to enclose these lines. Draw diagonal lines from corners of box base to corners of outside rectangle.

2. Trace pattern onto wrong side of fabric scrap, transferring markings. Cut out fabric, adding ⅛" around edges.

3. Referring to Diagram 2, with right side up, fold fabric diagonally at each corner and stitch. Trim to ⅛" from stitching. Turn fabric right side out. Insert box.

Fold excess fabric around edges to inside of box and glue in place.

4. Trim cardboard scrap so that it will fit inside box. Cut fabric scrap ½" larger all around than cardboard. Wrap fabric around cardboard, gluing or taping excess to back. Push base, fabric side up, inside box.

5. Glue button wheels in place. To make wagon handle, center and glue twine under box. Stitch or glue button to free end of twine.

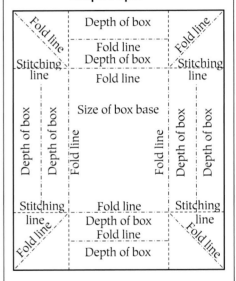

Diagram 1: Making Pattern on Graph Paper

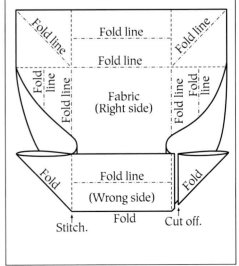

Diagram 2: Folding and Stitching Corners

Folded Ribbon Stars

Materials for one 4" star
Pattern Guide on page 153
Tracing paper
Tacky glue
Cardboard scraps (optional)
20¼" length ⅝"-wide stripe grosgrain ribbon
Transparent tape
6" length fine gold cord for hanging loop
Thread to match

Instructions
1. Trace pattern guide onto tracing paper or photocopy. Glue to cardboard for added support, if desired.

2. Referring to Figures A–D, leave ribbon tail and tape ribbon in place directly on pattern as you fold and weave to form star. At each folded star tip, use 1 piece of tape to hold ribbon on pattern and 1 piece to attach ribbon to itself (see Figure A). Add tape to each overlapped woven area. Fold down and tape end as shown in Figure D.

3. After completing star, remove tape from extended ribbon tail at beginning. Fold down tail and tuck into star to conceal cut ends. Tape closed.

4. Remove tape at star tips only. Lift star and flip it over to reverse side. Place spot of glue between ribbon layers where indicated by dots in Figure E. Press under heavy books until dry.

5. Flip star to taped side. Remove all tape. To make hanger, thread gold cord onto needle, leaving ends unknotted. Slip needle between ribbon layers at 1 star tip. Take 1 small stitch and then push needle back between layers, leaving loop of thread at top. Knot loose ends; bury knot in fold. Referring to Figure F, use small overcasting stitches to join edges where ribbon ends overlap. Cover star with cloth and gently press.

Crocheted Stars

Materials for one star
Pattern on page 154
Tracing paper
2 (5") squares ecru satin
Thread to match
Polyester stuffing
Pinking shears
Size 30 mercerized crochet cotton: 67 yards ecru, 6 yards red
Size 10 steel crochet hook

Instructions
Note: Broken pattern line is stitching line. Add ¼" seam allowance when cutting fabric.
1. Trace star pattern onto tracing paper.
2. Trace star onto wrong side of 1 satin square. With right sides facing and raw edges aligned, pin marked square to unmarked square.
3. Stitch along outline, leaving ½" opening along 1 straight edge. Using pinking shears, trim seam allowance to ⅛" around stitched seam and ¼" at opening. Clip into crevices. Turn right side out. Stuff, maintaining flatness. Slip-stitch opening closed. Set aside.
4. Make first crocheted star: Using ecru crochet thread, ch 8, join with sl st to form ring. **Rnd 1:** Ch 3 for first dc, 3 dc in ring, (ch 2, 4 dc in ring) 4 times, ch 2, sl st in top of beginning ch-3. **Rnd 2:** Ch 3 for first dc, * dc in each of next 3 dc, 4 dc in ch-2 space, dc in next dc, rep from * around, end with sl st in top of

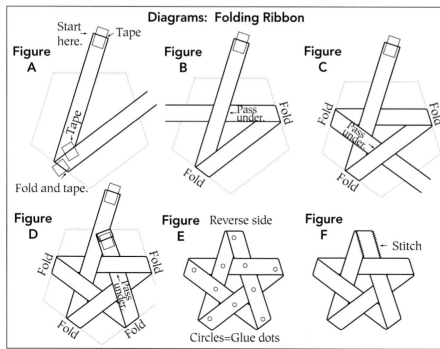

Diagrams: Folding Ribbon

Figure A — Start here. Tape. Tape. Fold and tape.

Figure B — Pass under. Fold. Fold.

Figure C — Fold. Pass under. Fold. Fold.

Figure D — Fold. Fold. Pass under. Fold. Fold.

Figure E — Reverse side. Circles=Glue dots

Figure F — Stitch

beginning ch-3 = 40 dc around. **Rnd 3:** Ch 3 for first dc, * dc in each of next 3 dc, ch 2, skip 1 dc, dc in next dc, ch 2, dc in next dc, ch 2, skip next dc **, dc in next dc, rep from * around, ending last rep at **, sl st in top of beginning ch-3. **Rnd 4:** Ch 6 for first dc and ch 3, * skip 2 dc, dc in next dc, 2 dc in ch-2 space, dc in next dc, 4 dc in next ch-2 space, dc in next dc, 2 dc in next ch-2 space **, dc in next dc, ch 3, rep from * around, ending last rep at **, sl st in top of beginning ch-3. **Rnd 5:** Sc in next ch-3 space, * ch 5, skip 1 dc, sc in next dc, (ch 5, skip next 2 dc, sc in next dc) 3 times, ch 5 **, sc in ch-3 space, rep from * around, ending last rep at **, sl st in top of first sc = 25 loops around.
5. Make first point of star: Sc in next loop, (ch 5, sc in next loop) 4 times, turn, sc in next loop, (ch 5, sc in next loop) 3 times, turn, sc in next loop, (ch 5, sc in next loop) twice, turn, sc in next loop, ch 5, sc in next loop. Fasten off = 1 point of star completed. Second point: With right side facing, join thread with sc in next ch-5 loop after first point of star, rep directions for first point to complete second point. Complete 3 more points as established. Edging: Join thread with sl st in top loop

of first point, 2 sc in same loop, * 3 sc in each loop down side of point, sc in sc between points, 3 sc in each loop up side of next point **, (4 sc, ch 2, 4 sc) in loop at top of point, rep from * around, ending last rep at **, 2 sc in same loop as beg, ch 2, sl st in top of first sc. Fasten off.
6. Repeat to make second star.
7. Joining 2 stars: Holding 2 stars with wrong sides facing and working through both pieces at same time, join red crochet thread with sc in ch-2 space at tip of any point, (sc in each sc to next ch-2 space, 2 sc in ch-2 space) 3 times, insert satin star into crocheted star, and continue joining crocheted stars as established, ending with sl st in top of first sc. Do not fasten off. Hanging loop: Ch 25, sl st in 20th ch from hook to form ring, work 25 sc in ring, sl st in top of first sc. Fasten off.

Abbreviations

beg—beginning
ch—chain
dc—double crochet
rep—repeat
sc—single crochet
sl st—slip stitch

Miniature Mittens Ornaments

Materials for each pair

Pattern on page 154
4 (3½" x 5½") scraps matching fabric
Thread to match
3" length ⅛"-wide soft-stretch elastic
20" length cotton yarn *or* pearl cotton *or* ¹⁄₁₆"-wide ribbon
Spool (1⅜" in diameter)
Tracing paper

Instructions

Note: Broken pattern line is stitching line. Add ¼" seam allowance when cutting fabric.
1. Trace pattern onto tracing paper, transferring markings. Cut out.
2. Center and trace mitten shape onto wrong side of 1 fabric scrap, transferring markings. With right sides facing, pin marked scrap to unmarked scrap but do not cut out. Starting at straight bottom edge of mitten below thumb, backstitch ¼" below outline and then stitch side seam to dot at mitten top.
3. Cut out shape, adding ¼" seam allowance. Trim stitched seam allowance to ⅛". Clip curves and into thumb crevice. Do not turn mitten right side out, but remove pins and open it so that wrist edge and wrong side face you. Fold elastic in half and mark center point. Tack center to seam on elastic placement lines. Also tack ends to mitten sides. Zigzag elastic in place while stretching it, using stitches same width as elastic. Fold mittens with right sides facing and raw edges aligned. Stitch remaining portion of seam and clip curve.
4. Before turning right side out, fold along hemline. To assist with hemming, pull mitten over spool to stretch elastic. Tuck under ¼" of cut edge and slipstitch folded edge to elastic. Turn right side out. Repeat steps 1–4 to make other mitten. Knot and tack yarn ends inside mittens at side seams.

Angel with Baby Jesus

Materials for Angel
Patterns on page 137
Tracing paper
4½" x 31" piece cotton fabric for body
Thread to match fabrics
Polyester stuffing
White or silver fabric marking pencil
Embroidery floss: blue, red
3" x 4¾" piece cotton fabric to match hair color
10 yards 3-ply crewel yarn for hair
Large-eyed needle
Powdered blusher for cheeks (optional)
2 (4" x 2¾") scraps knit T-shirt fabric for pantie
11" length ⅛"-wide elastic for pantie
7" x 21" piece star fabric for robe
5½" length ⅛"-wide elastic for robe
18" length gold cord for belt (optional)
5½"- to 6"-diameter purchased heart-shaped or round doily for wings (starch if too soft)
9" length ¼"-wide gold braid for halo
Gold thread (optional)
Note: Use tightly woven cotton fabric and small stitches for Angel and Baby Jesus.

Instructions
1. Complete angel using Dress-up Doll instructions on pages 34–35 and patterns on page 137. Add powdered blusher to cheeks, if desired.

These soft figures are ideal toys to help teach your child the true meaning of Christmas.

2. Complete pantie using instructions for Dress-up Doll Pantie on pages 35–36. To make robe, refer to Dress-up Doll Nightgown instructions on pages 35–37 (omitting lace) and patterns on page 138. Tie gold cord around waist, if desired. Trim and knot ends of cord. Fray ends to make tassels.
3. To make wings, pleat or scrunch doily at center and tack to center back of angel. To add halo, overlap ends of gold braid and securely stitch to prevent raveling. Tack to center back of head above neck.

Materials for Baby Jesus
Patterns on page 155
Tracing paper
2" x 9" piece cotton fabric for face, head side, and hands
Embroidery floss: blue, red, light brown
Thread to match fabrics
Polyester stuffing
Powdered blusher for cheeks (optional)
4½" x 9" piece fabric for bunting body, arms, and cap
4½" length ¼"-wide gold braid for halo
13" length ⅛"-wide ribbon
2 (6") squares fabric for blanket
Gold thread (optional)

Instructions
Note: Broken pattern lines are stitching lines. Add ¼" seam allowances when cutting fabrics.
1. Trace patterns onto tracing paper, transferring markings. Cut out.
2. Placing patterns at least ½" apart on wrong side of 2" x 9" fabric piece, trace 1 face, 1 head side, and 2 hands. Transfer markings. Before cutting fabric, using 1 strand of floss, satin-stitch eyes with blue and backstitch mouth with red. Cut out, adding ¼" seam allowances.

3. To make head side, with right sides facing and raw edges aligned, fold piece in half, short ends together. Stitch short ends together, ¼" from edges to form ring. Clip seam allowance at ¼" intervals along 1 long edge of head side. With right sides facing and raw edges aligned, match center top and center bottom dots on head side ring and head. Pin and securely baste using tiny stitches. Machine-stitch. Trim and clip seam allowance. Turn right side out. Tuck under ¼" around opening. Using doubled thread, run gathering stitches close to open edge, leaving tail of thread. Pull to gather slightly. Stuff firmly. Pull thread tightly. Secure thread and tie off. There will probably be a circular opening remaining. If so, push in a little more stuffing and whipstitch opening closed. Dust cheeks with powdered blusher, if desired. Set head aside.
4. To make hands, use doubled thread to gather fabric circles. For each, insert small amount of stuffing. Pull thread to gather tightly, making hand a ball. Secure thread and tie off. Set aside. Hands will have a "stem" on them, formed by gathered seam allowance; do not trim.
5. On wrong side of 4½" x 9" fabric piece, trace 1 bunting body, 1 arm unit, and 1 cap. Cut out, adding ¼" seam allowances.
6. To make bunting body, with right sides facing and raw edges aligned, fold piece in half, short ends together. Stitch center back seam. Flatten unit and rotate seam to center back. Stitch seam across bottom. Turn right side out. Using doubled thread, run gathering stitches close to edge of opening, leaving tail of thread. Pull to gather slightly. Stuff

(Continued on page 78)

(Continued from page 77)

firmly. Pull thread tightly to gather. Secure thread and tie off. If desired, square off bottom of bunting by tucking in corners and slipstitching fabric layers together.

7. To make arms, with right sides facing and raw edges aligned, fold piece in half, long edges together. Stitch long edges together to make tube. Turn right side out. Tuck each open edge under ¼". Run tiny gathering stitches close to edge around openings, leaving tail of thread. Do not stuff sleeves. Insert stem of 1 hand into 1 opening in arm unit. Pull thread to gather sleeve tightly around stem. Secure thread and tie off. Securely slipstitch hand to sleeve. Repeat for other hand. Run 2 parallel rows of gathering stitches where indicated on arm pattern. Pull to gather to ½". Secure thread and tie off. Set unit aside.

8. To make cap, with right sides facing and raw edges aligned, fold piece in half, short edges together. Stitch short seam to form ring. Leaving unit wrong side out, run tiny gathering stitches around 1 raw edge of ring, ¼" from edge. Pull tightly to form center back of cap. Knot thread, wrap it around seam allowance stem, and tie off. Trim stem to ⅛". Turn cap right side out. Tuck under ½" and baste remaining long edge. Try cap on head, adjusting fit with deeper or shallower fold if necessary. Tack cap to head at center bottom seam. Securely stitch head to body. Place arms across center top of body back and slipstitch in place.

9. To make hair, push cap away from face and, using 1 strand of light brown floss, knot floss and take a stitch on head. Pull floss forward over face and trim to make hair. Continue until bangs are desired thickness. To add halo, overlap ends of gold braid and securely stitch to prevent raveling. Tack to center back of head above arms.

10. Center ribbon on front of baby, ⅝" from lower edge of bunting. Wrap ribbon to back, crossing it there. Bring ribbon to front again and cross it over body. Tie ribbon at neck back. Tack ribbon if necessary.

11. To make blanket, with right sides facing and raw edges aligned, stitch fabric squares together, ¼" from edge, leaving opening for turning. Clip corners. Turn right side out. Slipstitch opening closed. Topstitch close to edges.

This candy cane heart makes a great ornament or package topper.

Candy Cane Heart Ornament

Materials for one 4¼" ornament

Patterns on page 155
Tracing paper
Vanishing fabric marker
5½" x 8" scrap red fabric
5½" x 8" scrap white fabric
Thread: red, white, green
Polyester stuffing
16" length ⅛"-wide white satin ribbon
16" length ⅛"-wide red satin ribbon
6" length ⅟₁₆"-wide green satin ribbon for hanging loop
12" length ¼"-wide green satin ribbon for bow

Instructions

Note: Broken pattern lines are stitching lines. Add ¼" seam allowances when cutting fabrics.

1. Trace ornament pattern onto tracing paper, transferring markings. Cut out.

2. Fold white fabric and red fabric each in half, with short ends together and right sides facing. On each folded piece, trace 1 candy cane. *Do not cut out yet.*

3. Using matching thread and small machine stitches, stitch along outline of each candy cane, leaving open between dots. Cut out, adding ¼" seam allowances. Trim stitched seams to ⅛", leaving ¼" along openings. Clip curves and turn each candy cane right side out.

4. Firmly stuff each cane. Mold and shape in hands so that canes are rounded. Slipstitch openings closed.

5. Referring to photo, place white cane on left (facing right) and red cane on right (facing left) on work surface. To form temporary heart, red hook overlaps white cane at top and white end overlaps red cane at bottom.

6. Pin 1 end of white ribbon to center back of red hook, extending length of ribbon strip up and to left of hook. Bring ribbon to front and proceed to wrap it in spiral fashion around cane, making 6 evenly spaced diagonal stripes. Pin remaining end of ribbon to center front of red cane end. Set aside.

7. Pin 1 end of red ribbon to center front of white hook, extending length of ribbon strip down and to left of hook. Bring ribbon to back and proceed to wrap it in spiral fashion around cane, making 6 evenly spaced diagonal stripes. Pin remaining end of ribbon to center back of white cane end. Place canes in heart shape, as described in Step 5. Check position of stripes and adjust if necessary. (Canes should be mirror images of each other.) Place pins in ribbons where they cross seams. Tack ribbons at seams.

8. For hanging loop, fold ⅟₁₆"-wide green ribbon in half. Lift top of red cane and tack cut ends of ribbon to center front of white cane hook. Check placement of canes again and adjust if necessary. Flatten hooks and ends slightly. Pin and tack canes together. Tie ¼"-wide green ribbon into bow and tack to heart base.

When attending a holiday open house, give this mitt as a hostess gift. Fill it with kitchen utensils, baking supplies, and small treats. The snowman can be used to top a small tree. For mittens, see page 75.

Santa's Baking Mitt

Materials

Pattern on page 156
Tracing paper
10" x 15" piece thick reversible quilted fabric *or* 2 (10" x 15") pieces matching or contrasting traditional quilted fabric
Thread to match
6" length ⅜"-wide white grosgrain ribbon for hanging loop
5" x 11¼" piece white terry cloth
Note: If quilted fabric is thin, you will need to add a layer of batting between the 2 quilted layers to protect hands. To make a cuffless hot mitt, encase lower edge in 12" of extra-wide bias tape before stitching side seam.

Instructions

Note: Seam allowance is ¼" and is included in pattern.
1. Trace pattern onto folded paper, transferring markings. Cut out. Unfold pattern.
2. Trace pattern onto wrong side of fabric and cut out. If using 2 layers of fabric, baste 2 mitt pieces together, with wrong sides of mitt fabric and lining fabric facing.
3. With right sides of *outside* mitt fabric facing and raw edges aligned, fold mitt in half. Pin and stitch mitt, leaving lower cuff edge open and taking stitch across crevice at dot in thumb area instead of pivoting and stitching a V. Trim 1 layer of seam allowance to ⅛". Clip curves and into crevice. Turn mitt right side out and flatten. Fold ribbon in half and whipstitch ends together. Aligning raw edges of ribbon with raw edge of mitt opening, tuck ribbon loop inside mitt at fold and tack.
4. To make cuff, with raw edges aligned, fold terry cloth piece in half, short edges together. Stitch short ends together ¼" from edge to form ring. Turn right side out. Insert cuff inside mitt. With cuff side seam at mitt fold, align raw edges of cuff and mitt. Pin layers of lower edge together. Stitch around mitt opening. Pull cuff fabric outside mitt. Fold up raw edge of cuff to meet raw edge of mitt. Fold again so that cuff overlaps mitt. Align cuff fold with placement line on mitt and slipstitch in place.

Tree Topper Snowman

Materials

1¾"-diameter empty paper towel tube *or* 6" x 7½" scrap sturdy paper (rolled and glued to make 7½"-high tube with 1¾" diameter)
11½" x 16" piece quilt batting (traditional weight)*
Sturdy black art paper for hat: 4"-diameter circle, 6" x 7½" rectangle
Compass
Craft glue
Craft knife
Felt-tip black marker
⅞"-wide ribbon: 6" length for hatband, 22" length for bow
4 (¼") black ball buttons
White thread
Note: Quilt batting used on model was ⅜" thick, making snowman approximately 11¼" in circumference.

Instructions

1. Measure and cut paper towel tube so that it is 7½" high. Use cut edge as bottom of snowman. Dab pen along opposite end to darken edge. Wrap 6" x 7½" black paper scrap around tube; glue.
2. Using compass, draw circle with same diameter as tube on center of black paper circle. Cut out, using craft knife. Glue this smaller circle to darkened top end of tube. Reserve remaining doughnut shape for hat brim. Measure and mark line around tube, 2" from top.
3. Fold batting in half, long edges together, to measure 5 ¾" x 16". Whipstitch long edges together. Rotate seam to center. Whipstitch short ends of batting. Wrap batting around tube, aligning 1 short whipstitched edge of batting with glued edge of paper wrapped around tube. As you wrap, align folded edges of batting with marked line and bottom edge of tube. When finished, whipstitch end to batting. Along folded edge of final layer of batting at each end of tube, use doubled thread to run gathering stitches right along each fold, leaving tails of thread. Pull threads tightly to make batting hug each end of tube. Secure thread and tie off.
4. To define head and body, wrap doubled thread around batting, just above midpoint. Pull thread tightly. Secure thread and tie off.
5. To make face, stitch 2 buttons to center front of head, approximately ⅝" apart. Also stitch 2 buttons to center front of body, approximately ⅝" apart.
6. Slide hat brim over hat portion of tube. Add dab of glue under brim at center front and back. Push brim onto batting and hold in place until dry.
7. Glue hatband around hat. Tie ribbon into bow around neck.

Linen & Lace Boutique

Welcome to the Linen and Lace Boutique, where yesterday's keepsakes become tomorrow's treasures. If you collect little pieces of the past, such as antique buttons, snippets of lace, dried flowers, and vintage linens, this shop is for you.

Add a romantic touch to any wicker rocker or porch swing with these lacy pillows.

Quick Bolster Pillow

Materials

Pastel floral fabric: 12½" x 20" piece for pillow center, 2 (4" x 20") pieces for pillow ends
Thread to match
1⅛ yard 3"-wide pregathered lace, cut in half
26" x 45" piece thick batting
1¼ yard ⅜"-wide satin ribbon
Small safety pin

Note: Inexpensive (45"-wide) thick batting, sold by the yard, is a good choice for this project. To use up odd scraps of batting, cut them into 13"-wide pieces and whipstitch 13" ends together. Keep adding batting pieces, rolling tightly into tube until it is 6" in diameter.

Sometimes pregathered lace looks skimpy. If you prefer, purchase 3 yards of 3"-wide flat lace, cut in half, and gather each piece to 54" length.

Instructions

Note: Seam allowances are ¼" and are included in fabric measurements.

1. To make pillow center, with right sides facing and raw edges aligned, fold 12½" x 20" fabric piece in half, short edges together. Stitch 12½" edges together to form tube. Press seam open. Turn right side out.

2. With gathered edge of lace aligned with raw edge of fabric, pin and stitch 1 piece of pregathered lace to right side of

84

fabric at each end. To minimize appearance of seam on lace, overlap motifs and slipstitch together if possible.

3. To prepare pillow ends, with right sides facing and raw edges aligned, fold 1 (4" x 20") fabric piece in half, short edges together. Stitch 4" edges together to form tube. Press seam open. To make casing, fold under ¼" along 1 long edge; press. Then fold under ½" and press; stitch. With right sides facing and raw edges aligned, stitch tube to 1 end of pillow cover. Fold and baste all seam allowances toward open end of pillow cover. Repeat for opposite end of pillow cover.

4. Cut batting into 2 (13" x 45") pieces. Whipstitch 1 (13") end of each batting piece together to make 1 long piece. Roll piece tightly to make 6"-diameter cylinder. Whipstitch loose end of batting to roll. Insert into pillow cover, aligning ends of batting cylinder with pillow cover end seams. Smooth batting at pillow ends if it has wrinkled or folded.

5. Clip a few stitches of each casing seam on wrong side. Cut ribbon in half. Fold under 1" on 1 end of each length. Attach safety pin to folded end and pull 1 ribbon length through small opening in each casing. Remove safety pin. Pull ribbons tightly to gather ends and tie each into bow. Remove basting threads along seams.

Lace Fan Pillow

Materials
Patterns on page 157
Tracing paper
Darning needle
10" square pastel print fabric
Vanishing fabric marker
8"-diameter round doily (with enough scallops to be equally divided into 4 sections)
4 (4⅜") squares solid pastel fabric
Thread to match doily and fabric
11⅜" square thin quilt batting
42" length corded piping (jumbo piping as used for upholstery projects)
Zipper foot for sewing machine
11⅜" square fabric for back
Polyester stuffing

Instructions
Note: Seam allowances are ¼" and are included in patterns.

1. Trace patterns onto tracing paper, transferring markings. Cut out. Using darning needle, pierce placement lines for quarter section of doily fan shape on square pattern.

2. On wrong side of 10" fabric square, trace 4 pillow corner pieces, transferring dots. Cut out.

3. Stretch doily into perfect circle shape if necessary. Cut doily into quarter sections and set pieces aside.

Using vanishing fabric marker, transfer doily section placement lines to right side of 1 (4⅜") fabric square. Pin 1 doily section on right side of square. (Place cut edges of doily section approximately ⅛" from raw edges of fabric.) Securely baste cut edges of doily section to fabric. Tack scalloped edge of doily section to fabric. Repeat with remaining fabric squares and

doily sections. Be sure cut edges of doily sections are secured to fabric; whipstitch if necessary.

4. Referring to Diagram, with right sides facing and raw edges aligned, pin and stitch 2 squares together to make unit. Repeat with remaining squares to make another unit. Join units together to make center square. Press seams open.

5. Referring to Diagram, with right sides facing and raw edges aligned, pin 1 corner piece to 1 side of center square. Stitch between dots. Press seam allowance toward corner piece. Repeat to join remaining corners.

Baste edges of pillow front to batting. Trim excess batting to match size of pillow front.

6. Trim piping seam allowance to ¼" if necessary. With raw edges aligned, pin and baste piping to right side of pillow front, clipping piping seam allowance at corners; taper piping into seam allowance at beginning and end. Using zipper foot, machine-stitch piping to pillow front. Clip curves.

7. With right sides facing, center pillow front on pillow back; pin and baste. Stitch together along stitching line of piping, leaving 3" opening. Trim back to match front. Clip curves; turn right side out. Stuff firmly. Slipstitch opening closed.

Diagram: Assembling Lace Fan Pillow Top

Antique Hankie Nosegay

Materials
Dried flowers
Antique hankie
Thread to match
24" length each ⅛"-wide
    ribbon in 2 colors

Instructions
1. Referring to Diagram below, fold box pleat along center of each hankie edge. Pin pleats in place.
2. Arrange small bouquet of dried flowers, 5" to 6" tall. Tie stems together with thread.
3. Place base of bouquet stems in center of hankie. Pull up hankie sides to cover stems. Tie ribbons into bow around stem. Remove pins.

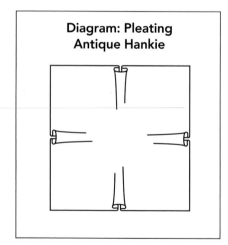

Diagram: Pleating Antique Hankie

Lace Carnation Pin

Materials
1 yard 1⅞"-wide flat lace
    with 1 scalloped edge
Thread to match
Craft glue
3 velvet leaves
1 (1") bar pin

Instructions
1. Referring to Diagram below, fold each cut end of lace to align with straight edge. Run small gathering stitches close to straight edge of lace, leaving tail of thread. Pull thread tightly to gather lace. Secure thread and tie off. Coil gathered lace to form carnation. Whipstitch gathered edges together.
2. Glue leaves to back of carnation. When dry, glue bar pin to back.

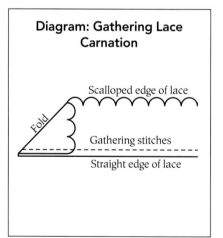

Diagram: Gathering Lace Carnation

Scalloped edge of lace

Fold

Gathering stitches

Straight edge of lace

Antique Button Pins

Materials for one pin
Scrap of felt
Antique button
Thread to match
Scrap of lace
Water-based craft glue
    (optional)
Bar pin *or* small safety pin

Instructions
1. Cut 2 circles from felt to match size of button. Run small gathering stitches close to straight edge of lace, leaving tail of thread. Pull thread tightly to gather lace. Secure thread and tie off. Whipstitch gathered edge of lace to 1 felt circle approximately ⅛" from edge.
2. Stitch button to gathered lace side of circle. If desired, glue lace to edges of button to secure.
3. Blanket-stitch remaining felt circle to back of lace-edged circle. Stitch bar pin or small safety pin to back.

Brighten a grandmother's day with one of these sentimental accessories. Clockwise from top; Antique Hankie Nosegay, Antique Button Pins, and Lace Carnation Pin

Dainty Doily Basket

Materials
Pattern on page 158
Tracing paper
Darning needle
3 (10"- to 12"-diameter) round lace doilies, all of same size and design
Vanishing fabric marker
Thread to match
24" length ¹⁄₁₆"- to ⅛"-wide coordinating ribbon
Note: For best results, select doilies with scallops that can be divided equally into 6 sections. Dense designs work better for this project than light, open ones.

Instructions
Note: Pattern guide may be slightly larger or smaller than doilies used. However, stitching lines should touch edges of doilies. It's best to hand-wash doilies and starch them while wet. If doilies are irregular, spray with heavy starch; stack, aligning motifs, and stretch into shape. Let dry.

1. On folded paper, trace pattern guide, transferring markings. Using darning needle, pierce stitching lines with needle. Place pattern on Doily 1, positioning so that stitching segments will divide scallops equally. Trace a few doily design motifs onto pattern guide so that guide can be placed in same position on each doily.

2. Referring to Figure A, transfer dots and lines to right side of Doily 1. Referring to Figure B, transfer all lines to right side of Doily 2. Referring to Figure C, transfer incomplete lines to right side of Doily 3.

Tuck fruit or muffins into this basket and dress up homemade jelly.

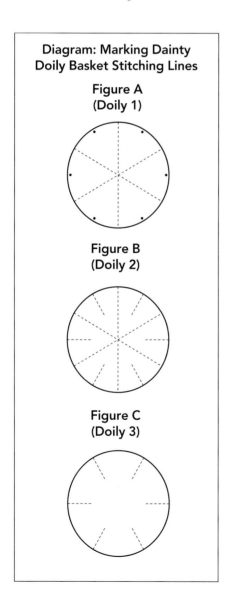

Diagram: Marking Dainty Doily Basket Stitching Lines

Figure A (Doily 1)

Figure B (Doily 2)

Figure C (Doily 3)

3. Aligning stitching lines and design motifs, stack and pin Doily 1 (marked side up) on top of Doily 2 (marked side up). Stitch only complete stitching lines as in Figure A. For best results, stitch by hand using small back stitches.

4. Stack and pin this stitched doily unit on top of Doily 3 (marked side up), aligning stitching lines. Working between layers of doilies 1 and 2, stitch only incomplete diagonal lines. This joins only doilies 2 and 3.

5. Referring to Figure A, weave ribbon through scallops at dots only on edge of Doily 1. Pull ribbon tightly to gather doily, bringing scallops together at center top to form a star. Tie ribbon into bow. Support basket on dinner plate or in shallow straw basket for serving. Remove ribbon before washing. Dry doily basket flat.

Lacy Jelly Jars

Materials

Jam jar with gold metallic lid
1 large and 1 small gold notary seal (optional)
22" length elastic gold cord
5"-diameter round doily
4 (½"-wide) self-sticking gold stars (optional)

Instructions

Note: If jam jar has motif on lid, cover with large notary seal.

Run gold cord through openings around edge of doily, allowing enough margin to make ruffle. Place doily over jar lid. Pull cord and tie into bow. Knot ends of cord or sandwich between stars. Attach small notary seal to jar for label, if desired.

Just a Little Something

Lace Napkin Ring Set

A lace bow adorning each cloth napkin is the perfect finishing touch for your luncheon table setting. To make a napkin, cut a 20" square of fabric. Hem the napkin by folding the edges under ¼" twice. Press and stitch. To finish, with wrong sides facing, fold the napkin in half and roll. Using 24" of 1"- to 1¼"-wide lace, tie a bow around the napkin. Trim around motifs on cut ends of lace.

Bunny Bunch

Materials for both bunnies
Patterns on pages 159–161
Tracing paper
Vanishing fabric marker
Thread to match fabrics
Polyester stuffing

For Mama Bunny
9" x 44" piece pastel print
  cotton fabric
7" square contrasting cotton
  fabric for inner ears
  (optional)
2 (¼") black short-shank ball
  buttons
24" length 1½"-wide lace,
  scalloped on 1 edge, for tail
18" length ¼"- to ⅜"-wide satin
  ribbon

For Baby Bunny
9" x 22" piece pastel print
  cotton fabric
4" square contrasting cotton
  fabric for inner ears
  (optional)
2 (⅛") black short-shank ball
  buttons
18" length 1"-wide lace,
  scalloped on 1 edge, for tail
18" length ⅛"-wide satin ribbon
Note: Because of button eyes
and tacked-on tail, bunny is not
intended for children under 3
years of age.

Instructions for Mama Bunny
Note: Seam allowances are ¼"
and are included in patterns.
Choose closely woven cotton
fabrics that do not fray easily.
For constructing bunny, use
small machine stitches and
backstitch at beginning and
end of all seams. Clip all
curved seams as you work.
1. Trace pattern pieces onto
tracing paper, transferring
markings. Cut out.

2. With right sides facing and
raw edges aligned, fold print
fabric in half, short ends together.
Trace patterns, except head top
and head center back, on wrong
side of doubled fabric. Cut out.

For inner ears, trace and cut 2
additional ears on single layer of
same or contrasting fabric.

Trace 1 head top and 1 head
center back on remaining single
layer print scraps. Cut out.
3. On wrong side of fabric,
transfer all pattern markings and
seam lines. On right side of each
head side, use basting stitches to
mark placement lines for eyes.
4. With right sides facing and
raw edges aligned, pin 2 body
side pieces together along top
edge from neck to rear. Machine-
stitch from neck edge to rear dot.

With right sides facing and
raw edges aligned, pin 2 underbody pieces together from neck
to rear along center tummy
seam. Machine-stitch from neck
edge to rear dot.

Carefully clip unstitched
curved seam allowances around
leg areas of body side units and
underbody unit. With right sides
facing and raw edges aligned,
pin units together from rear dot,
around legs, and up to leg bottom. While pinning, ease in fullness. Baste and stitch seams.
Clip curves. Use doubled thread
to hand-staystitch along placement line at neck line. Turn.

Stuff body firmly. For each
front leg, pinch front and back
seams together to make leg more
rounded. Working from the
outside, use a sturdy needle to
pull stuffing into puckered areas.
5. With right sides facing and
raw edges aligned, pin pairs of
ear pieces together. For each ear,
machine-stitch around long
curved edge only. Trim stitched
seam allowance and clip curves.

Turn right side out. Run gathering
stitches, by hand, along seam
line of open raw edge. Pull to
gather to ¾".

To place ears at top of bunny
head, with raw edges aligned,
pin and baste each ear (inner
ear side down) to right side of
head top along straight edge.
Place ears close together, touching dot at center top. Clip
stitched seam allowance. With
right sides facing and raw edges
aligned, spread clipped seam allowance and pin head top to
head center back. Baste and
then machine-stitch.
6. With right sides facing and
raw edges aligned, pin head side
pieces together along chin seam;
machine-stitch. Trim stitched
seam allowance, clipping curves.
Working on 1 side at a time, pin,
baste, and stitch head side unit
to head top/head center back
from neck to nose, easing in
fullness. Use doubled thread to
hand-staystitch along neck on
line indicated. Turn right side
out. Stuff head firmly. Turn
neckline seam allowance under
along fold line and baste.
7. Pin head to body, matching
center front and center back
seams. Use doubled thread to
hand-slipstitch head to body.
Using long needle, stitch back
and forth between eye placement
lines to shape head. Pull thread
tightly and secure. Tie off. Stitch
buttons in place.
8. To make tail, referring to
Diagram, fold each cut end of
lace to align with straight edge.
Run small gathering stitches
close to straight edge, leaving tail
of thread. Pull tightly to gather
lace. Secure thread and tie off.
Coil gathered lace to form ruffled
tail. Whipstitch gathered edges
together. Slipstitch tail to body.
Tie ribbon into bow around neck.

Instructions for Baby Bunny

Follow instructions for Mama Bunny, pulling gathered ears to ½" in Step 5.

If you wish to place ears at side of bunny head, with right sides facing and raw edges aligned, stitch head top to head center back. Baste ears (inner ear side up) to side edges of head top, just in front of seam.

Use coordinating prints and little puffs of gathered lace to create this pastel family portrait.

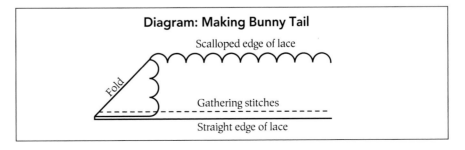

Diagram: Making Bunny Tail

Scalloped edge of lace

Fold

Gathering stitches

Straight edge of lace

Just a Little Something

Mini Motifs

Place individual motifs of special laces in miniature frames to accent a little nook or cranny. Back the motifs with neutral-colored paper or, if you prefer, select a color that complements your room. Mounting several framed lace motifs on a length of ribbon creates an attractive vertical grouping.

Lace Sachets

Materials for four sachets
Lace scraps for rectangular and heart sachets
2 miniature round doilies for circular sachet
Scrap 3"-wide lace trim, finished on both edges, for bow sachet
Scraps fine tulle
Vanishing fabric marker
Thread to match
Potpourri*
Gathered lace trim for rectangular and heart sachets
1"-wide moiré ribbon for bow sachet
*See Resources, page 173.

Instructions
1. For rectangular sachet, cut 2 matching lace scraps in desired size. Place 1 piece of tulle, cut to fit, on wrong side of each lace scrap; baste along edges. With right sides facing and raw edges aligned, stitch lace scraps together along long edges and 1 short end, ¼" from edge. Turn right side out. Fill with potpourri and whipstitch opening closed. Whipstitch gathered lace trim along seam lines.

2. For circular sachet, back doilies by placing tulle, cut to fit, on wrong side of each doily and basting along edges. With tulle sides facing, whipstitch edges together, leaving small opening. Fill sachet with potpourri. Whipstitch opening closed.

3. For heart sachet, draw heart pattern onto paper that accommodates size of lace scraps. Back lace by placing tulle, cut to

Salvage tattered scraps of antique lace and transform them into little sachet pillows.

fit, on wrong side of each lace scrap and basting around edges. With right sides facing, pin lace scraps together. Using vanishing fabric marker, transfer heart pattern to 1 scrap. Do *not* cut out. Stitch along heart shape. Cut out, adding ¼" seam allowance. Open approximately 1" of seam. Clip curves and into crevice. Turn right side out. Fill with potpourri and slipstitch opening closed. Whipstitch gathered lace trim along seam line.

4. For bow sachet, cut length of lace trim. Back trim by placing tulle, cut to fit, on wrong side of lace trim and basting along edges. With lace on outside, fold short edges to center to create 2 pouches. Whipstitch long outer edges of lace together, leaving shorter inner edges open. Fill pouches with potpourri and whipstitch openings closed. Wrap ribbon around center, overlapping ends at back. Tuck under cut edge of ribbon and whipstitch in place.

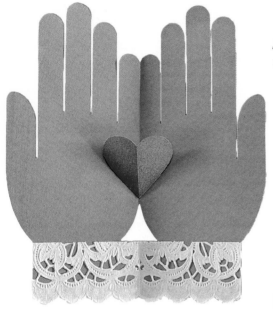

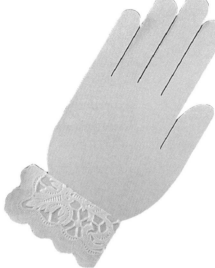

Send a handful of love with this unique note card.

Heart Doily Pincushion

Materials
Tracing paper
5"-wide heart-shaped doily*
7" x 16" piece pastel fabric
Vanishing fabric marker
Thread to match
Polyester stuffing
See Resources, page 173.

Instructions
1. Create heart pattern by tracing heart-shaped doily along base of scallops onto tracing paper. Add $\frac{1}{16}$" outside traced outline. Cut out.
2. With right sides facing and raw edges aligned, fold fabric in half, short ends together. Trace pattern onto folded fabric. *Do not cut out.* Stitch along outline, leaving 1" opening for turning.

Find a pretty doily and stitch this pincushion in no time at all.

Heart in Hand Valentine

Materials
Patterns on page 161
Tracing paper
7" square sturdy pink or brown paper
Craft knife
1$\frac{3}{8}$" x 9$\frac{3}{4}$" scalloped end of paper lace place mat
White glue
2" square red paper

Instructions
1. Trace patterns onto tracing paper, transferring markings. Cut out.
2. Score and fold 7" square in half. Place hand pattern along folded edge of paper as indicated. Hold in place with paper clips. Trace around shape. Remove pattern, keeping paper clips in place to prevent shifting of layers. Cut out as indicated. Open hands so that card is flat and inside is facing up. Transfer markings.
3. With right sides facing and raw edges aligned, fold paper lace strip in half, short edges together. Align center fold of lace with bottom center of opened card. Glue lace to inside of card on cuff. Wrap each end of lace to outside of card, matching scallops, and glue in place. Glue layers of scallops together along side of cuff. (If desired, in place of paper lace, trace cuff onto contrasting paper. Cut out and glue in place.)
4. On red square, trace heart pattern, transferring markings. Cut out. On right side of paper, score and fold as indicated on pattern. Align heart with placement lines and glue tabs to inside of card at center fold. (One cut edge of each tab behind heart will almost rest on center fold of card.) Before glue dries, close card with center fold of heart forward.

3. Trim around shape, adding ⅛" around stitched seam and ¼" at opening. Clip curves and into crevice. Turn right side out. Stuff. Flatten to 1¼" thickness. Slipstitch opening closed.

4. Pin doily on stuffed heart, stretching to extend scallops beyond seam line. Tack doily in place along seam line.

Fill these little boxes with candy, potpourri, or special buttons.

Lacy Boxes

Materials for one small box
6"-diameter round lace doily with 8, 12, or 16 scallops around edge
Thread to match
Graph paper
Transparent tape
5" square acetate
Craft knife
⅛"-wide white satin ribbon (optional)

Diagram 1: Folding Doily Scallops

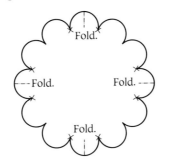

Fold.
Fold. Fold.
Fold.

Diagram 2: Marking Small Liner Pattern

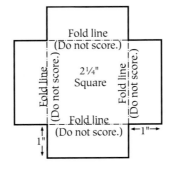

Fold line (Do not score.)
Fold line (Do not score.)
Fold line (Do not score.)
2¼" Square
Fold line (Do not score.)
1"
1"

Diagram 3: Tacking Doily

Stitch, if desired.

Diagram 4: Marking Large Liner Pattern

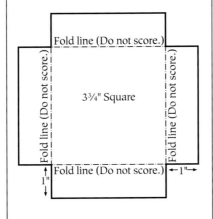

Fold line (Do not score.)
Fold line (Do not score.)
Fold line (Do not score.)
3¾" Square
Fold line (Do not score.)
1"
1"

Instructions

1. Referring to Diagram 1, fold and pin lace doily at designated scallops. Tack layers together at Xs to form sides. Be sure to have same number of scallops in each section.

2. Referring to Diagram 2 and using indicated measurements as guide, make graph paper pattern for small acetate liner. Fold and lightly tape corners. Insert paper liner pattern into lace doily form to check fit. Make adjustments, if necessary, so that paper pattern fits snugly inside lace form.

3. Remove tape from paper liner. Tape flattened pattern to work surface. Tape acetate over pattern. Using straight edge and craft knife, score pattern outline and trace fold lines onto acetate. Fold along scored lines to break away excess acetate. Crease liner along fold lines. Tape corners. Insert acetate box into lace form.

4. Referring to Diagram 3, if desired, baste doily along corners so that it hugs liner. At each corner, thread 9" length of ribbon through openings in doily at Xs and tie into bow, if desired.

5. For large box, follow instructions for small box, substituting 8"-diameter round doily and 6½" square of acetate and referring to Diagram 1, Diagram 4, and Diagram 3.

Lace Hanger

Materials

1 purchased padded satin
 hanger
Vanishing fabric marker
1 yard 3¾"- to 4"-wide lace*
½ yard ½"-wide picot-edged
 taffeta ribbon
See Resources, page 173.

Instructions

1. If hanger has bow at top, untie
it, knot ribbon, and cut off ends.
2. Straighten covering on hanger.
Using vanishing fabric marker,
draw guideline along center top
of padded hanger arms.
3. Extending 1 end of lace
approximately 2" beyond 1 arm
of hanger, center lace design
motif just below hook. Pin
straight edge of lace to guideline
along length of hanger. At end of
opposite arm, refer to Diagram to
make box pleat. This will round
lace around end of arm. Butting
straight edges of lace together
along guideline, pin remaining
portion of lace to other side of
hanger.
4. Whipstitch straight edges of
lace together along guideline,
catching hanger fabric in process.

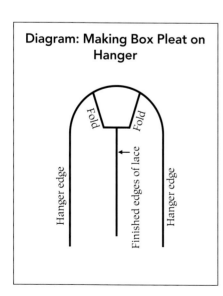

**Diagram: Making Box Pleat on
Hanger**

Fold   Fold

Hanger edge   Finished edges of lace   Hanger edge

*This dainty gift selection is made up of a Lace Hanger, Lace
Carnation Pin (page 86), and Pillow Cover Purses.*

For loose lace at end of hanger
arm (starting point), trim
around lace motifs and overlap
to minimize appearance of
seam. Stitch motif edges
together. Tack lace along hanger
sides, easing in any extra
fullness. Make additional
slipstitches at ends of arms, if
necessary, to flatten lace against
hanger. Tie taffeta ribbon into
bow at top of hanger.

Pillow Cover Purses

Materials for one purse

Vanishing fabric marker
2 purchased 12"-square
   identical lace or crochet
   cushion covers (fabric lining
   and back attached)
12" strip poly boning*
Thread to match
46" length ⅝"-wide ribbon *or*
   46" length ¼"-wide cording
   for purse strap
2 (2½") lengths ⅞"-wide ribbon
   for covering ends of cording
   strap (optional)
1 (1⅛") button (optional)
3 sets small white Velcro dots
See Resources, page 173.

Instructions

1. Referring to Diagram 1, use vanishing fabric marker to draw horizontal line across back of 1 cushion cover, 4" from top edge. Aligning top edge of boning strip with line, machine-stitch fabric edges of strip to cushion cover.

2. Referring to Diagram 2, measure and mark shoulder strap positions 1¼" below lower edge of boning on lace side of same cushion cover.

For ribbon purse strap, pin ribbon in place 1" from scalloped side edge, tucking cut ends under ¼". Machine-stitch ribbon in place as shown in Figure A.

For cording purse strap, refer to Figure B and wrap thread tightly around cut ends to prevent raveling. Pin cording in place 1" from scalloped side edges and whipstitch in place. Fold under cut ends of 2½" lengths of ribbon. Pin in place, covering ends of cording. Slip-stitch to pillow cover as shown in Figure B.

3. With backs of covers facing and edges aligned, pin side and bottom edges, folding 1 layer of scallops to inside and leaving top open. Stitch by hand, using strong thread and whipstitches.

If greater stability is needed, slide piece of lightweight cardboard, cut to fit purse area, between layers.

4. Fold open end of purse to form flap. (Straps are at back of purse.) Tack scallops on lower inside flap to inside of purse. If desired, stitch button to center of flap through 1 layer of fabric. Stitch half of 1 Velcro dot set inside bag, under button on upper portion of flap. Stitch dot mate inside bag on lower portion of flap. Stitch remaining Velcro dot sets to each end of flap and purse sides to close.

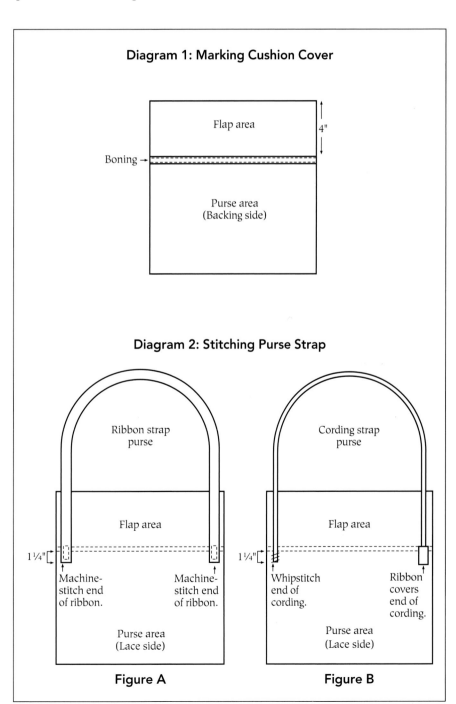

Diagram 1: Marking Cushion Cover

Flap area

4"

Boning →

Purse area
(Backing side)

Diagram 2: Stitching Purse Strap

Ribbon strap purse

Flap area

1¼"

Machine-stitch end of ribbon.

Machine-stitch end of ribbon.

Purse area
(Lace side)

Figure A

Cording strap purse

Flap area

1¼"

Whipstitch end of cording.

Ribbon covers end of cording.

Purse area
(Lace side)

Figure B

Pillow Cover Envelope

Materials

Purchased 12"-square
    Battenberg lace cushion
    cover (fabric lining and
    back attached)
Thread to match
1 (¾") button

Instructions

With lace side of pillow cover
down, refer to Diagram at right
to fold, pin, and slipstitch edges
to make envelope. (A graph
paper-covered work surface will
help align edges.) Stitch button
to envelope at dot. Use opening
in lace as buttonhole.

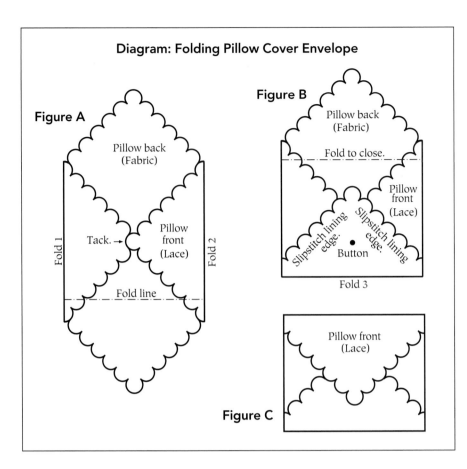

Diagram: Folding Pillow Cover Envelope

Figure A — Pillow back (Fabric), Tack., Pillow front (Lace), Fold 1, Fold 2, Fold line

Figure B — Pillow back (Fabric), Fold to close., Pillow front (Lace), Slipstitch lining edge., Slipstitch lining edge., Button, Fold 3

Figure C — Pillow front (Lace)

Embroidered Napkin Envelope

Materials

9"- to 10"-square tea napkin
9" to 10" square fabric for
    lining (optional)
Thread to match
Snap set *or* small Velcro dot set
    (optional)

Instructions

1. If lining envelope, turn raw
edges of lining fabric under ¼".
With wrong sides facing, slipstitch lining to napkin.
2. With right side of napkin
down, refer to Diagram at right
to make envelope. If desired,
attach snap set or Velcro dot set
to secure flap.

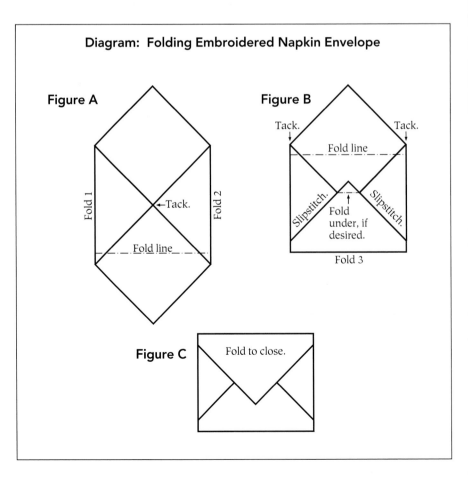

Diagram: Folding Embroidered Napkin Envelope

Figure A — Fold 1, Tack., Fold 2, Fold line

Figure B — Tack., Tack., Fold line, Slipstitch., Slipstitch., Fold under, if desired., Fold 3

Figure C — Fold to close.

These envelopes are two gifts in one. After holding mementoes, the stitches can be removed, and the material can be used as originally intended. Clockwise from top left: Embroidered Napkin Envelope, Pillow Cover Envelope, and Doily Envelope

Doily Envelope

Materials
9"- to 10"-diameter round doily
Thread to match
15" length ⅛"-wide ribbon

Instructions
1. With right side of doily down, refer to Diagram at right to fold.
2. Tack center of ribbon to center of lower flap behind holes in upper flap. Thread ribbon ends through holes. Tie into bow.

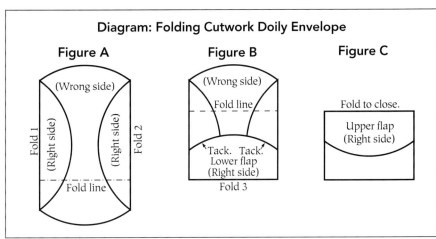

Diagram: Folding Cutwork Doily Envelope

Figure A

(Wrong side)
Fold 1
(Right side)
(Right side)
Fold 2
Fold line

Figure B

(Wrong side)
Fold line
Tack. Tack.
Lower flap
(Right side)
Fold 3

Figure C

Fold to close.
Upper flap
(Right side)

Lace Coverlet

Materials

Soft lace curtain fabric or panel
Vanishing fabric marker
Twin-size cotton flannel flat
    sheet (Must be at least 8"
    longer and 8" wider than lace
    after prewashing.)
Thread to match

Instructions

Note: Curtain and sheet sizes vary greatly, so these are general instructions. For example, a 60" x 72" curtain will require a prewashed flat piece of flannel trimmed to 68" x 90". Rip out hems on sheet, if necessary, to increase dimensions.

1. Trim lace, if necessary, so that edges are even. Referring to Diagram 1, center and place lace, right side up, on flannel sheet, leaving at least 4" border around lace edges. Pin layers together approximately 3" inside lace edges. Measure and trim flannel border to exactly 4" wide. Using vanishing fabric marker, draw placement lines 2" inside raw edges of lace. Folded edge of flannel border will eventually align with this line.

2. Referring to Diagram 2, from each corner of flannel, measure and mark 5" and 8" along each side. Draw line connecting 5" marks; trim 5" (*not* 8") corner triangles. Then mark fold line by connecting 8" marks, touching corner of lace with line.

3. Referring to Diagram 3, fold flannel over corner of lace along marked line.

4. Referring to Diagram 4, fold raw side edges of flannel to align with raw edge of lace.

5. Referring to Diagram 5, fold sides again to miter corner; align

Back an inexpensive lace curtain with flannel to create this elegant throw.

edges with placement lines.
6. Pin folds and borders securely in place.
7. Tack lace and flannel layers together at close intervals, using lace design to determine placement of tacks. Machine-stitch border close to folded edge of flannel near lace.

Diagram 1: Placing Lace

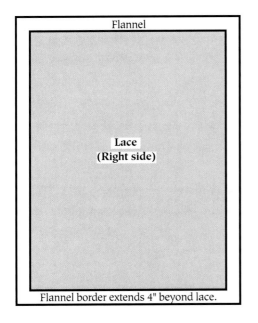

Flannel

Lace
(Right side)

Flannel border extends 4" beyond lace.

Diagram 2: Marking Corners

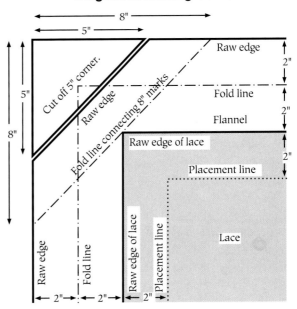

8"

5"

Cut off 5" corner.

5"

8"

Raw edge

Fold line connecting 8" marks

Raw edge

Raw edge

Fold line

Flannel

Raw edge of lace

Placement line

Lace

Raw edge of lace

Placement line

2"

2"

2"

2"

2"

2"

Raw edge

Fold line

Diagram 3: Folding Corners

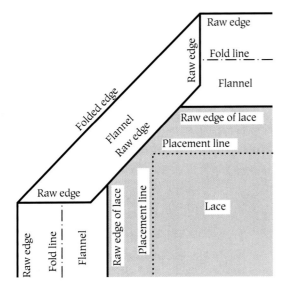

Raw edge

Fold line

Flannel

Folded edge

Flannel

Raw edge

Raw edge of lace

Placement line

Lace

Raw edge

Raw edge

Fold line

Flannel

Raw edge of lace

Placement line

Diagram 4: Folding Sides

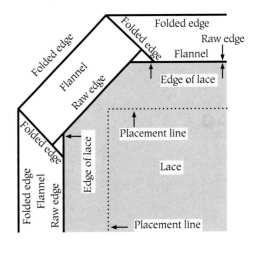

Folded edge

Folded edge

Folded edge

Flannel

Raw edge

Folded edge

Flannel

Raw edge

Folded edge

Folded edge

Flannel

Raw edge

Edge of lace

Flannel

Raw edge

Edge of lace

Placement line

Placement line

Lace

Placement line

Diagram 5: Making Mitered Corners

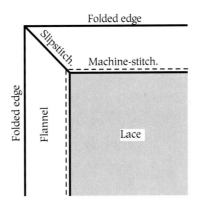

Folded edge

Slipstitch.

Machine-stitch.

Folded edge

Flannel

Lace

Village Emporium

Make a quick stop by the
Village Emporium, where you are sure to
find a little bit of what you fancy. Search
for real bargains here and make use
of materials you might otherwise
throw away.

In this cupboard full of gifts you'll find, from the top, Heart Needle Case (page 106),
Balsam Label Pillow (page 106), and Shaggy Denim Pony.

Shaggy Denim Pony

Materials
Patterns on pages 162–163

For Pony
Tracing paper
14" x 18" piece lightweight denim
Thread to match fabric and mane
Polyester stuffing
Black embroidery floss *or* 2 (⅛") black "doll" buttons for eyes
Twine *or* string *or* embroidery floss for mane
Large-eyed needle (optional)

For Stable Blanket
6" x 13" piece plaid fabric
Thread to match
20" length corded piping
20" length ¼"-wide double-fold bias tape

Instructions
Note: Broken pattern lines are stitching lines. Add ¼" seam allowances when cutting fabric. Tightly woven fabric is best to use for pony. Use small machine stitches. Because mane and tail pieces may pull out, this toy is not intended for children under 3 years of age.

1. Trace patterns onto tracing paper, transferring markings. Cut out.

2. For pony, placing pattern pieces ½" apart on wrong side of denim, trace 1 side body, 1 lower body, and 1 upper body strip. Reverse pattern and trace 1 side body and 1 lower body. Transfer markings. Cut out, adding ¼" seam allowances.

3. With right sides facing and raw edges aligned, pin 2 lower body pieces together along tummy seam. Stitch, leaving open between dots. Clip stitched seam allowance. Turn under ¼" and baste seam allowance along each side of opening. Set aside.

4. To make dart in upper body strip, with right sides facing, fold along center line as indicated. Pin and stitch dart. Trim dart seam allowance to ⅛" and clip. With right sides facing and raw edges aligned at chest and rear, stitch upper body and lower body together, making ring with legs. Clip each long edge of upper body piece at ¼" intervals.

5. Staystitch chin area as indicated on body side pattern. Make 1 clip up to staystitching under chin. With right sides facing and raw edges aligned, pin 1 body side to 1 edge of upper/lower body unit, matching numbered dots. Clip swayback of pony if necessary. Carefully hand-baste pieces together using thread to match. Basting is essential for best results. If necessary, clip upper body strip again to make it fit around pony shape. Machine-stitch around shape. Clip curves and into crevices. Attach remaining body side in same manner. Area under chin is a bit tricky. If not stitched correctly, hand-stitch. Spreading the head and neck far apart while stitching may be helpful.

6. Turn pony right side out. Stuff firmly, filling legs and head before body. Slipstitch opening closed. Mold and shape horse by hand. Pinch head and neck sides to make them narrow and more realistically shaped, if desired. Using 1 strand of floss, satin-stitch each eye. Or stitch on button eyes. Stitch through head from eye to eye to shape head.

7. To make ears, cut 4 (2") squares from denim. Fold ¼" hem along 1 edge of each square and baste. On wrong side of 1 square, trace 1 ear as indicated. With right sides facing and hemmed edges aligned, pin marked square to unmarked square. Stitch around ear, leaving folded edge open. Trim stitched seam allowance to ⅛" and clip curves. Turn right side out. Slipstitch opening closed. Repeat with remaining pieces to make other ear. Fold sides of each ear toward center. Whipstitch overlapping edges together along base of each ear. Securely slipstitch ears between dots on head top.

8. To make tail and mane, cut twine into 10" lengths and fold each in half. For tail, securely stitch lengths to rear. If using floss, stitch at least 8 (6-strand) lengths directly into fabric. Tie floss in knot. Trim unevenly until tail clears tabletop. For mane, stitch lengths in place, starting between ears and continuing along dart. Referring to photo, bring lengths forward at head top and trim. Cut irregular lengths along neck.

9. For stable blanket, cut 2 blanket pieces from plaid fabric, adding ¼" seam allowance except to neck edge. Trim seam allowance on corded piping to ¼" if necessary. With raw edges aligned, baste and machine-stitch corded piping to right side of 1 blanket piece except along neck edge. Clip and spread piping seam allowance at curves. With right sides facing and raw edges aligned, pin blanket pieces together. Stitch along stitching line of piping. Turn right side out through neck opening. Align and baste raw neck edges. Center and stitch bias binding along neck edge. Slipstitch open edges of ties together. Knot ends of ties. Tie blanket around pony's neck.

Heart Needle Case

Materials

Patterns on page 163
Tracing paper
3" x 5½" scrap lightweight cardboard
1 old silk necktie
Vanishing fabric marker
Thread to match
Masking tape
16" length ¼"-wide coordinating satin ribbon
3" x 8" scrap dark felt
Liquid ravel preventer
Small needles

Instructions

1. Trace patterns onto tracing paper and cut out.
2. Trace 2 large hearts on cardboard. Cut out.
3. Open tie by clipping stitches along center back. Remove and reserve interfacing.
4. Place tie (lining side up) on work surface. Align tip of 1 cardboard heart with tip of tie. Referring to Diagram, Figure A, trace heart on tie. Cut out, adding ¼" seam allowance to top curved edges as shown in Figure B. Cut away seam allowance of lining *only* as shown in Figure C. Clip

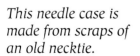

This needle case is made from scraps of an old necktie.

into crevice at center top, approximately ⅛" from top of lining fabric.
5. Insert cardboard heart between layers of lining and silk, aligning edges. Fold seam allowance toward lining side and use overcast stitches to tightly "slipcover" cardboard heart. Make sure silk side fits smoothly. Make adjustments if necessary. Repeat steps 4 and 5 for other heart.
6. Tape hearts (lining side up) to Placement Guide (see page 163) with ⅛" between them. Cut 2 (1") pieces from ribbon. Pin each in place on curves of hearts. Cut remaining ribbon in half. Pin each piece in place on pointed tip of hearts. Remove hearts from page and stitch ribbons securely in place.
7. From felt, cut 2 small hearts. Center and pin felt hearts on lining side of needle case hearts,

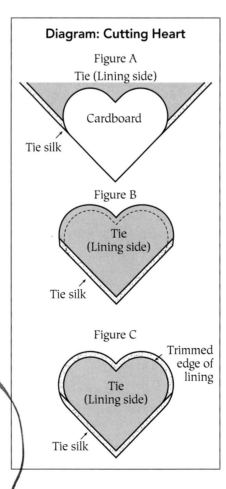

Diagram: Cutting Heart

Figure A
Tie (Lining side)

Cardboard

Tie silk

Figure B

Tie (Lining side)

Tie silk

Figure C

Trimmed edge of lining

Tie (Lining side)

Tie silk

covering overcast stitches and ends of ribbons. Whipstitch edge of felt to silk.
8. From tie interfacing, cut 2 small hearts for "pages." Apply liquid ravel preventer to cut edges. When dry, trim edges evenly if necessary. Stack heart pages; center on felt. Whipstitch top curved edges to felt. (A single felt heart may be used in place of 2 interfacing pages.)
9. Insert needles as shown in photos. Close case and tie ribbons into bow.

Balsam Label Pillow

Materials

Labels clipped from clothing
Velvet scrap
Thread to match
Drapery cording
Balsam tips*
See Resources, page 173.

Instructions

1. Arrange labels in square or rectangle on velvet, overlapping edges. Pin and slipstitch labels in place. Trim fabric ½" beyond outside of label arrangement. From remaining velvet, cut back piece to match label piece.
2. Baste cording to right side of label piece ½" from raw edge. Fold all seam allowances to wrong side of pillow front and baste in place. Also fold seam allowances to wrong side of back piece and baste in place.
3. With wrong sides facing, pin front and back pieces together. Slipstitch edges together, leaving opening for filling. Fill pillow with balsam tips. (Do not pack balsam too tightly.) Slipstitch opening closed. Remove basting.

Sachet Purses

Materials for one sachet
4" x 5⅝" scrap fabric
Thread to match
Balsam tips *or dried lavender**
9" metallic cord *or beading for handle*
4¼" length ¼"-wide metallic trim
Metallic thread to match
1 (¼") button
Liquid ravel preventer
*See Resources, page 173.
Note: Before trimming metallic braid to proper length, saturate areas to be cut with liquid ravel preventer. When dry, cut proper length and dab ends again with liquid ravel preventer.

Instructions
Note: Seam allowances are ¼" and are included in fabric measurements.

1. Referring to Diagram, with right sides facing and raw edges aligned, fold fabric in half, short edges together. Finger-press. Fold back ¼" along each edge opposite fold and press. Mark ¼" side seams; use large spool or other curved object to mark curves at lower corners as shown. Stitch side seams along marked lines. Trim extra fabric at each lower corner as shown, leaving ¼" seam allowance. Clip curves. Turn right side out.

These purses are ideal for tucking in gifts or giving as tea party favors.

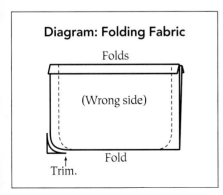

Diagram: Folding Fabric

Folds

(Wrong side)

Fold

Trim.

2. Run small gathering stitches along open edge, ¹⁄₁₆" from fold, leaving needle on thread when finished. Partially fill purse with balsam tips or dried lavender. Pull thread to gather top edge to measure 1¾" and tie off. For handle, insert 1 end of cord or beading into each end of opening and tack in place. Whipstitch opening closed. Referring to photo, use metallic thread to handstitch metallic trim around top edge. Stitch button to center top of sachet.

Cozy Cottage Box

Materials

Patterns on page 164
Graph paper with ⅛" grid
Metal file box (approximately
   5¼" wide x 3½" high x 3¼"
   deep)
Masking tape
Oak tag *or* lightweight
   posterboard
Craft knife
Darning needle
Craft glue
7" x 18" piece fabric for house
Vanishing fabric marker
4" x 3¾" scrap light-colored
   heavy art paper for windows
4" x 5¼" scrap dark-colored
   heavy art paper for door
   frame and window frames
⅛" hole punch
1" x 1¾" scrap bright-colored
   heavy art paper for door
2" x 5¼" scrap heavy art paper
   to line chimney
5½" square fabric for chimney

Instructions

1. Trace patterns for door frame, windows, and chimney onto graph paper, transferring markings. Cut out.
2. Use graph paper to draw custom patterns for file box. Measure and draw lower box area (below hinged lid), including box front, back, and both sides, but not bottom. (Height of front and back of box may not be same.) To make complete pattern for lower box area, join pieces together as shown in Diagram 1, adding ¼"-wide glue tab to 1 side edge. Cut out.
3. Measure and draw lid front, back, and both sides on graph paper. Cut out. To make complete pattern for lid, join pieces together as in Diagram 2, adding ¼"-wide glue tab to side edge of

Welcome new neighbors by giving them this decorative box filled with the names and phone numbers of favorite local shops.

lid back. Draw 90° peak on top edge of each lid side section. Add ¼"-wide glue tab to each side of peak and to top edge of lid front and back sections.
4. To make roof pattern, measure peak and width of lid front or back. Referring to Diagram 3, trace roof, adding ⅝" to each edge for overhang.
5. Referring to photo: Place door frame and large window patterns

on graph paper pattern of front and sides. Trace. (There are no windows on back of box.) Place small window pattern on graph paper pattern of lid sides. Trace.
6. Tape graph paper patterns to box to check for accuracy. Make adjustments if necessary. Remove patterns. Glue graph paper patterns, except door frame and windows, to oak tag. Cut out. Score all fold lines. Pierce

corners of traced windows and door frame using darning needle. Fold and tape oak tag pieces to box to check fit again. Trim oak tag until box can be opened easily without oak tag catching at back.

7. Glue graph paper side of oak tag lower box piece to house fabric. Cut out. Push darning needle through previously pierced holes to transfer placement of windows and door frame to fabric side of unit. Mark placement holes with vanishing fabric marker. Glue unit to lower area of box. Hold in place with rubber bands until dry.

8. Repeat Step 7 with box lid.

9. From light-colored art paper, cut 2 small windows and 4 large windows (do not cut out window panes). From dark-colored paper, cut 2 small windows and 4 large windows. Cut out panes to make window frames. Glue frames on windows. Glue windows on house. From remaining dark-colored paper, cut 1 door frame; use paper punch to make door knob. Center and glue bright door on frame. Glue door knob in place. Glue door unit on house.

10. Use darning needle to pierce a few dots along each placement line of roof. Cut out and score fold line. Center graph paper side of oak tag roof on roof fabric and glue. Wrap fabric around edges, mitering folds at corners. Apply glue to tabs on lid front, back, and peaks. Place roof on tabs, center-ing roof on house. Let dry.

11. To make chimney, glue chimney pattern to art paper. Cut out and score fold lines. Glue paper chimney to chimney fabric. Cut out. Fold and glue together along tab. Glue in place on roof.

12. To open box, grasp front and back of lid and lift.

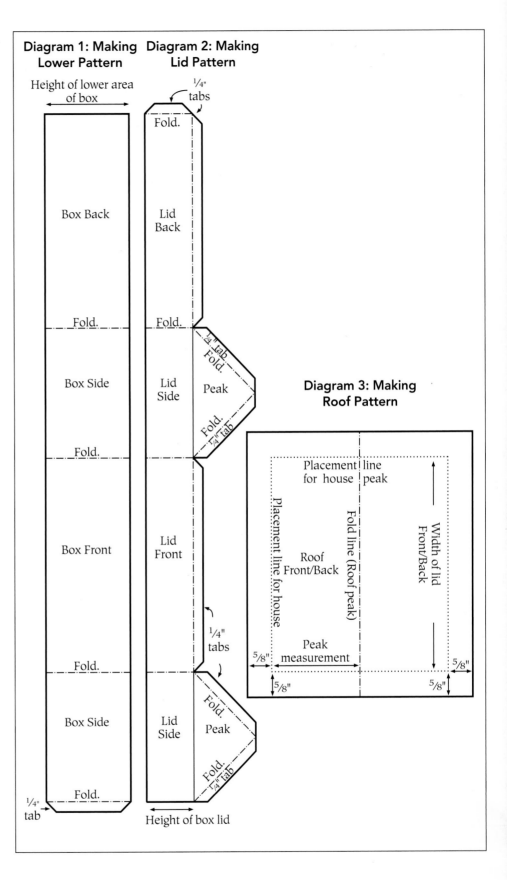

Diagram 1: Making Lower Pattern

Height of lower area of box

Box Back

Fold.

Box Side

Fold.

Box Front

Fold.

Box Side

Fold.

¼" tab

Diagram 2: Making Lid Pattern

¼" tabs

Fold.

Lid Back

Fold.

Lid Side   Peak

¼" Tab Fold.

Fold. ¼" Tab

Lid Front

¼" tabs

Lid Side   Peak

Fold.

Fold. ¼" Tab

Height of box lid

Diagram 3: Making Roof Pattern

Placement line for house peak

Placement line for house

Fold line (Roof peak)

Roof Front/Back

Width of lid Front/Back

Peak measurement

⅝"

⅝"

⅝"

⅝"

Miniature Sailboat Quilt

Materials

Patterns on pages 164–165
Tracing paper
3" x 5" scrap opaque white fabric
7" x 16" piece star or dot fabric with navy background
3" x 7" scrap dark red fabric
1 navy blue bandanna (preferably with wide border at least 3⅛" deep)
White pencil
Thread to match fabrics
9½" square thin quilt batting
Note: Narrow strips of bandanna border were used to bind edges. If desired, substitute 40" length of extra wide double-fold bias tape.

Instructions

Note: Seam allowances are ¼" and are included in patterns.
1. Trace patterns A–E onto tracing paper. Trace pattern F onto folded tracing paper. Transfer markings. Cut out. Unfold pattern F.
2. From white fabric, cut 4 As. From star or dot fabric, cut 6 As, 2 Bs, 1 D, and 2 Es. From red fabric, cut 1 C. From bandanna border, cut 1 F (can be pieced to attain desired depth). Transfer markings on each piece.
3. With right sides facing and raw edges aligned, refer to photo and Diagram to pin together and join pieces as follows, pressing seam allowances toward darker fabric as you work. For sails, make 4 squares by joining 4 white As and 4 star or dot As. Join 2 squares along 1 side edge. Repeat with remaining 2 squares. Then join pairs together along 1 long edge. Join 1 B to each side of

sail unit. For boat, join 1 star or dot A to each short side of red C. Join sail and boat units along 1 long edge. Join star or dot D along top of sails. Join star or dot E to each side edge of boat unit. Join bandanna print F to bottom.
4. Center, pin, and baste 9" patchwork square on 9½" batting square, stitching ¼ from edge. Do not trim edges. Cut 9½" square for backing from center of bandana. With right side up, pin pieced unit to wrong side of backing. Baste edges of unit together.
5. For border/binding, cut 2"-wide strips from bandanna border scraps: cut 2 (9½"-long) strips for sides, and 2 (10½"-long) strips for top and bottom. With long edges together and wrong sides facing, fold and press each strip in half. Fold and press each long raw edge ½" to wrong side. Beginning with 1 side strip, with right sides facing and raw edges aligned, place 1 long edge of unfolded binding on quilt block top. Stitch binding to quilt block along fold, ½" from edge. Fold binding over quilt block edge and slipstitch to backing. Repeat for opposite side. Attach top and bottom bindings in same manner.

Diagram: Joining Pieces

Pentagon Star Ball

Materials

Pattern on page 165
4" square sandpaper
Darning needle
11" x 14" piece crisp fusible interfacing
12 (4½") squares variety of solid cotton fabrics
Metallic thread
Thread to match
Polyester stuffing

Instructions

1. For best results, photocopy pattern. Glue pattern to smooth side of sandpaper. Cut out. Pierce star topstitching lines with darning needle.
2. Place rough side of pattern on interfacing and, using sharp pencil, trace pattern to draw 12 accurate pentagons (edges can be adjacent). Also trace star topstitching lines, connecting dots with ruler to make continuous line. Cut out pentagons. Following manufacturer's instructions, center and fuse 1 pentagon to wrong side of each fabric square. Cut out fabric pentagons, adding ¼" hem allowance beyond interfacing. Using metallic thread, machine-stitch star shape on interfacing.
3. Fold, finger-press, and baste seam allowance to interfacing side of each pentagon. In order for all pentagons to fit together perfectly, fabric must be folded *exactly* along edges of interfacing. As you work, hold unit to light to check edges.
4. Referring to Diagram at right, place 6 pentagons right side down on work surface. Label center pentagon. With right sides facing and folded edges aligned, join side pentagons 1 at a time to center pentagon by whipstitching

Teddy's two favorite belongings are his Miniature Sailboat Quilt and his Pentagon Star Ball.

adjoining edges together. Knot securely at beginning and end of each line of stitches. Keep closely placed, tight stitches right on edge of fabric where it folds over interfacing. Finished unit will resemble a flower with 5 "petals" around center.

5. Noting arrows on Diagram, use whipstitches to join adjacent edges of 5 pentagon petals. The resulting bowl-like unit is half of ball. Repeat with remaining 6 pentagons to make other half of ball.

6. Turn both "bowl" units inside out. Bring 2 units together to form ball, fitting "peaks" of 1 into "valleys" of other. Whip-stitch edges together, knotting thread securely at beginning and end of each line of stitches and leaving 2 edges of 1 pentagon open for turning.

7. Turn ball right side out and stuff. Slipstitch opening closed.

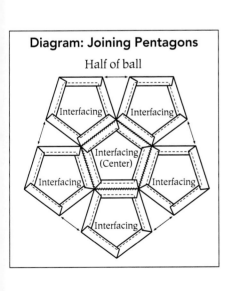

Diagram: Joining Pentagons

Half of ball

Interfacing | Interfacing

Interfacing (Center)

Interfacing | Interfacing

Interfacing

Bear Hugs

Materials for one bear

Patterns on pages 133–134
Tracing paper
8" x 29" piece tightly woven fabric for bear
4" x 5" piece contrasting fabric for muzzle and inner ears
Thread to match
2 (¼") buttons with low shanks *or* dark embroidery thread for eyes*
Polyester stuffing
24" length ½"-wide coordinating ribbon

Note: If teddy bear is intended for child younger than 3 years of age, use embroidery floss for eyes.

Instructions

Note: Seam allowances are ¼" and are included in patterns.

To make this bear, follow instructions for making Quilt Scrap Teddy Bear on pages 28–29 and patterns on pages 133–134. Substitute tightly woven fabric for lightweight quilt scraps.

Address Book Cover

Materials

9" length 3½"-wide burlap
  upholstery webbing tape
Thread to match
Miniature address book with
  flexible cover (2¼" wide x
  3¼" high and less than ⅛"
  thick)

Instructions

Fold each cut end of tape under
½". Whipstitch ends to tape
without going through to right
side. Fold edges under 1¼"; test
to see if unit comfortably wraps
address book without warping
cover. Make adjustments if necessary. Whipstitch finished
edges of overlapped upholstery
tape at top and bottom to form
pockets. Insert cover of address
book into pockets.

Zippered Bag

Materials

2 (8¼") lengths 3½"-wide
  burlap upholstery webbing
  tape
Thread to match
7½" square fabric for lining
7" all-purpose zipper

Instructions

Note: If you don't have a zipper
foot attachment for your sewing
machine, stitch zipper in place
by hand.
1. Place closed zipper, right side
up, on work surface. Baste 1 long
edge of 1 length of upholstery
tape, right side up, on each side
of zipper. (Be sure tape lengths
are far enough apart to allow
zipper to run on track.) Stitch
along each side of zipper, ¹⁄₁₆"
from edge of tape.
2. With right sides of upholstery
tape facing and zipper closed,
fold unit in half down length of
zipper. Machine-stitch side edges
of unit together ½" from each
edge. Do not stitch bottom. Flatten seam allowances and whipstitch to bag. Open zipper. Leave
bag wrong side out. Set aside.
3. To prepare lining, press 2
opposite edges under ¼" so that
piece measures 7" x 7½". With
right sides facing and raw edges
aligned, fold lining in half, long
edges together, to measure 3½" x
7½". Stitch short raw ends, ¼"
from edge. Turn right side out.
4. With wrong sides facing and
aligning side seams of lining and
upholstery tape unit, place upholstery tape unit inside lining.
Slipstitch lining to zipper tape
approximately 1" on each side of
each seam (keep lining away
from zipper track). Turn bag right
side out. Push lining inside bag.
Slipstitch lining to zipper tape.
Whipstitch finished edges of
upholstery tape at bottom of bag,
making sure not to catch lining in
stitches.

Eyeglass Case

Materials

3⅞" x 12½" piece fabric for
  lining
14½" length 3½"-wide burlap
  upholstery webbing tape
Thread to match
3⅜" x 12¾" piece thin batting
  or felt

Instructions

1. On both long ends of lining
fabric, press under ¼".
2. With right sides facing and
long folded ends of lining approximately ¹⁄₁₆" inside finished
edges of upholstery tape, align 1
short raw end of lining with 1
short raw end of upholstery tape.
Machine-stitch short ends
together, ¼" from edge. Repeat
with other short ends. Turn
resulting uneven ring unit right
side out.
3. With lining side up, flatten
unit so that there is ½" border of
upholstery tape on each end.
Slide layer of batting between
lining and upholstery tape. Align
edges and baste batting to lining
close to edge (stitches will remain
once complete). Pull lining unit
away from upholstery tape. Fold
lining, batting sides together, and
whipstitch side edges of lining
together.
4. Tuck lining inside upholstery
tape. Align top folded ends and
finished side edges of upholstery
tape. Whipstitch finished edges
together, leaving top open.

*These purse accessories are made from small pieces of burlap upholstery
webbing, usually sold in fabric shops and sometimes in hardware
stores. Color choice is limited—it is almost always jute color with red or
black bands, but it wears like iron and the price is right! The geometric
basket (page 115) is an ideal jewelry keeper.*

Coin Purse

Materials

10½" length 3½"-wide burlap upholstery webbing tape
Thread to match
4" x 7⅜" scrap fabric for lining
3 (½"-wide) Velcro dots

Instructions

1. With right sides facing, center and align 1 short raw end of upholstery tape on 1 short raw end of lining piece. (On each long side edge, lining will extend ¼" beyond finished edge of tape.) Machine-stitch short ends together ¼" from edge. Repeat with other short ends. Turn resulting uneven ring unit right side out.
2. Referring to Diagram, Figure A, flatten and fold unit; on lining side, center and stitch looped Velcro dot halves across top flap. Turn unit over to upholstery tape side. Referring to Figure B, center and stitch remaining Velcro dot halves in place on opposite edge.
3. Turn unit over to lining side again. Fold under each long edge of lining ¼" and baste to upholstery tape. Starting at top of flap on 1 side, stitch open edges together, first whipstitching upholstery tape to upholstery tape along flap and then slip-stitching lining to upholstery tape, allowing edge of tape to extend slightly beyond lining. Repeat on other side.
4. Fold lower portion of purse up 3¼" along fold line so that lining is on inside. Securely whipstitch finished edges of upholstery tape together to form pocket. Fold flap down 1¾" along folding line. Align Velcro dots and close.

This little Coin Purse has a Velcro closure to keep you from having to fumble with a snap.

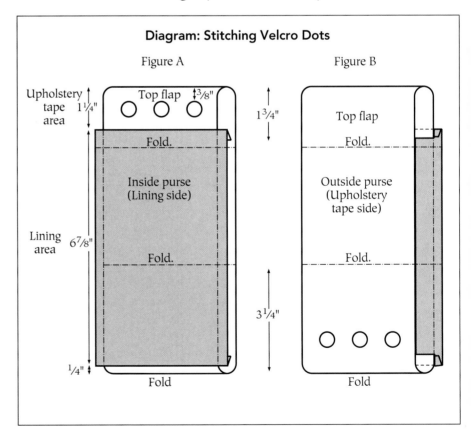

Pentagon Basket

Materials for one 5½"-diameter basket

Pattern on page 165
Tracing paper
4" square sandpaper
11" x 14" piece crisp fusible interfacing
12 (4½") squares cotton fabric (2 each of 6 different prints)
Thread to match

Instructions

1. For best results, photocopy pattern. Glue pattern to smooth smooth side of sandpaper. Cut out.

2. Place rough side of pattern on interfacing and, using a sharp pencil, trace pattern to draw 12 accurate pentagons (edges can be adjacent). Cut out. Following manufacturer's instructions, center and fuse 1 pentagon to wrong side of each fabric square. Cut out, adding ¼" seam allowance beyond interfacing.

3. Fold, finger-press, and baste seam allowances to interfacing side of each pentagon. In order for all pentagons to fit together perfectly, fabric must be folded *exactly* along edges of interfacing. As you work, hold unit up to light to check edges.

4. Referring to Diagram, place 6 pentagons right side down on work surface. Label center pentagon. With right sides facing and folded edges aligned, join side pentagons 1 at a time to center pentagon, whipstitching adjoining edges together. Knot securely at beginning and end of each line of stitches. Keep closely placed, tight stitches right on edge of fabric where it folds over interfacing. Finished unit will resemble a flower with 5 "petals" around center.

5. Noting arrows on Diagram, use whipstitches to join adjacent edges of 5 pentagon petals. This will form a bowl-like unit. Repeat with remaining 6 pentagons to make another bowl-like unit.

6. With wrong sides facing, fit and pin 1 bowl inside other, matching points and crevices. Slipstitch edges together. Curl points downward.

Just a Little Something

Simply Framed Stamps

These framed stamps are great small remembrances. Simply purchase a miniature frame, select an interesting stamp, and choose a coordinating scrap of paper for the background. Cut the paper to fit in the opening of the frame. Center the stamp on the background paper and insert the unit into the frame to check for placement. Lightly mark placement lines with a pencil. Apply a stamp hinge, available where stamp collecting supplies are sold, to the back of the stamp and then stick the hinged stamp to the background paper. Assemble the frame according to the manufacturer's instructions.

Diagram: Placing Pentagons

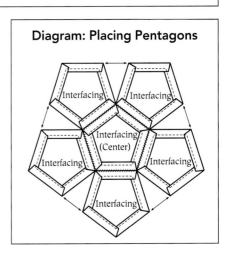

Ribbon Sunflower

Materials for each sunflower
Liquid ravel preventer
Thread to match ribbons
Small amount polyester stuffing
Extra-fine unwaxed dental floss
Craft glue

Materials for small sunflower
1½ yards ⅞"-wide yellow
  grosgrain ribbon for flower
26" length 1½"-wide green
  grosgrain ribbon, cut into 4
  (6½") pieces, for 2 leaves
2 (3¼") lengths fine wire
9" length ⅞"-wide green
  grosgrain ribbon for flower
  backing
4"-diameter circle black fabric
4"-diameter circle thin batting
1¾"-diameter circle cardboard
3"-long and ⅜"-wide metal
  barrette base

*Add a sunny accent to a barrette
base or a straw hat with this
ribbon flower.*

Materials for large sunflower
2⅓ yards 1½"-wide yellow
  grosgrain ribbon for flower
40" length 2¼"-wide green
  grosgrain ribbon, cut into 4
  (10") pieces, for 2 leaves
2 (4½") lengths fine wire
12" length 1½"-wide green
  grosgrain ribbon for backing
5¼"-diameter circle black fabric
4⅝"-diameter circle thin batting
2⅜"-diameter circle cardboard
Purchased hat

Instructions
Note: Sunflower is made by folding and tacking 1 continuous length of ribbon. To keep folds perpendicular, align finished ribbon edges with textured grosgrain stripes as you fold. Finger-press folds as you work.

Coat all raw edges of ribbons with liquid ravel preventer.

1. Thread needle with yellow thread and set aside. Referring to Diagram 1, fold 1 end of yellow grosgrain ribbon, allowing remaining length of ribbon to extend to right.

2. Fold extended length of ribbon to form peak as shown in Diagram 2.

3. Fold peak in half as shown in Diagram 3. Tack layers together securely at X, knotting thread and leaving it in place so that it will be ready to make next tack. Tacked area will form center back of sunflower.

4. Referring to Diagram 4, fold extended length of ribbon to form peak.

5. Referring to Diagram 5, fold ribbon peak in half and tack.

6. Fold extended ribbon as shown in Diagram 6. Refer back to Diagram 3 to fold ribbon in half and tack. Continue repeating steps 3–6 until you have 24 petals. Trim end of ribbon so that it extends ½" beyond last petal. At beginning and end of ribbon, fold extended ½" ends on diagonal as shown in Diagram 7 and tack. Tuck extensions inside folds of adjacent petals. (The final loose end tucks into folds of first petal. The first loose end tucks into folds of last petal.) Stitch securely in place.

7. Some petals may curl. If this happens, place finger inside each petal and move ribbon edges so that they butt together. Without going through front of petal, whipstitch butted ribbon edges together ¼" at petal tip.

8. To make padded flower center, run gathering stitches along edge of batting circle and gather slightly. Place small amount of stuffing on cardboard circle. Insert cardboard circle into

gathered batting, stuffing side toward batting. Pull to gather batting tightly around cardboard and tie off to make domed flower center. Use dental floss to slightly gather edge of black circle. Insert flower center into gathered black circle. Pull to gather tightly around flower center and tie off. Glue flower center in place on unstitched side of flower, pressing it gently into inner curve of flower and leaving border of weaving around it.

9. To make leaves, fold 1 piece of wide green grosgrain ribbon in half as shown in Diagram 9,

Figure A. Draw diagonal seam line, starting ⅛" from 1 finished edge at top fold and ending in opposite corner at bottom raw edge. Stitch along line. Trim seam allowance to ¼" as shown in Figure B. Stretch length of wire along line. Fold back each end of wire to make small hook, eliminating sharp end. Whipstitch wire to seam allowance. Repeat to make second layer of leaf. Referring to Figure C, flatten each leaf layer and, with wrong sides facing, whipstitch finished edges of ribbon together. Using dental floss, gather raw edge. Referring

to photo, tack or glue in place at back of sunflower. Repeat entire step to make another leaf.

10. To make flower backing, stitch cut ends of narrow green grosgrain ribbon together to form a ring. Run gathering stitches along 1 finished edge of ribbon. Pull to gather tightly to make a ruffled disc. Slipstitch in place on back of sunflower, covering raw ends of leaves. Glue and stitch flower on barrette or slipstitch flower on hat.

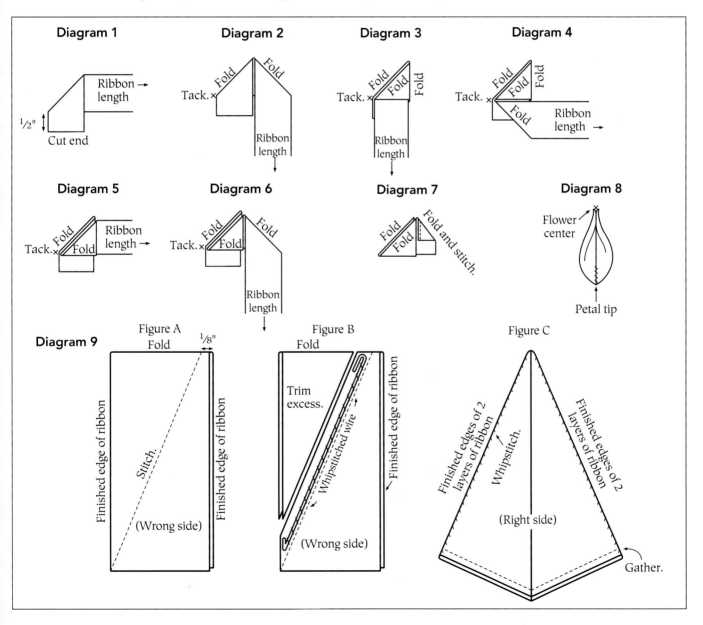

117

Use a pair of cotton bargain socks to make one of these cuddly kittens.

Sock Kittens

Materials for one kitten

Patterns on pages 166–167
Tracing paper
1 pair men's socks size 10–13
  (*not* crew socks)*
Thread to match
Polyester stuffing
Vanishing fabric marker
2 (½" to 9/16" diameter) flat
  black, low-shank buttons
  for eyes *or* black embroidery
  floss
Ribbon

*Note: Knit in foot and calf areas
should be same even texture,
not ribbed. Calf area should be
at least 10" high, including cuff
and heel. Cuff portions should
be 2½" or less. Socks do not
have to be exact width of patterns, but if they seem *much* too
wide, wash them in warm water
and then machine dry or enlarge
patterns with photocopier.

Instructions

Note: Seam allowances are ⅛"
wide and are included in patterns. Hem allowances at openings are ¼" wide.

  Substitute ½"-wide satin-
stitched eyes for buttons on toys
for children younger than 3
years of age.

1. Trace patterns A–E onto tracing paper, transferring markings.
Cut out. Turn socks inside out.

2. Refer to Diagram 1 for placing
patterns and cutting socks. Lay-
out can be varied somewhat, but
note that pieces A, B, and E *must*
be placed on folded edges of
socks. Pin all patterns in place
and be sure that everything,
including 2 ears, will fit. Transfer
markings and cut out.

3. On body piece A, carefully cut
to dot on each folded edge of
hind leg area as indicated. Referring to Diagram 2, with right
sides facing and raw edges aligned, refold piece A along lines
indicated on legs and match dots
at crotch. Machine-stitch legs
with 1 continuous seam, ⅛" from
edge. Turn right side out; stuff
legs until they measure 2½" to

2¾" long and approximately 5¾" around. Stuff body until it measures 6½" to 7" long and approximately 11" around middle. Using doubled thread and starting at top, run gathering stitches ¼" from cut edge around open neck area. Pull very tightly and tie off high on body.

4. For head, referring to Diagram 3, with right sides facing and raw edges aligned, refold piece B and match dots at head top. Machine-stitch between dots, ⅛" from edges, leaving opening at each end of seam. By hand, run gathering stitches ⅛" from cut edge around each small opening. Pull stitches very tightly and tie off. Turn right side out. Fold under ¼" hem allowance around neck opening and baste, leaving thread end free so that stitches can be gathered after stuffing. Stuff head; pull thread so that opening is approximately 1¼" wide. Tie off. Head should be approximately 11" in circumference. Pin in place on body and slipstitch units together with doubled thread.

5. For each ear, stitch curved seam, ⅛" from edge, leaving open along straight edge. Turn right side out. Do not stuff. Fold under ¼" hem allowance and baste; slipstitch opening closed. Pin ears 1" apart along head top seam. Slipstitch each front and back of ear in place.

6. With right sides facing and cut edges aligned, fold each front leg as indicated. Stitch side and foot seam, ⅛" from edge, leaving top open. Turn right side out. Fold under ¼" hem allowance at top and baste, leaving thread free. Stuff each leg to measure 2½" to 2¾" long at seam side and 5¼" to 5½" around. Pin legs approximately ¾" apart, 1¼" to 1½" below neck. Securely slipstitch.

7. Stitch folded tail as indicated, ⅛" from edge. Turn. Fold under ¼" hem allowance around opening and baste, leaving thread free. Stuff. Referring to photo, pin tail to top of rear. Slipstitch in place using remaining thread.

8. Referring to photo for placement, stitch button eyes to center of head. If cat is intended for a young child, using vanishing fabric marker, draw 2 (½"-wide) eyes approximately ¾" apart at center of head. Using 2 strands of floss, satin-stitch eyes. Use straight stitches to add nose and mouth. Tie ribbon into bow around neck.

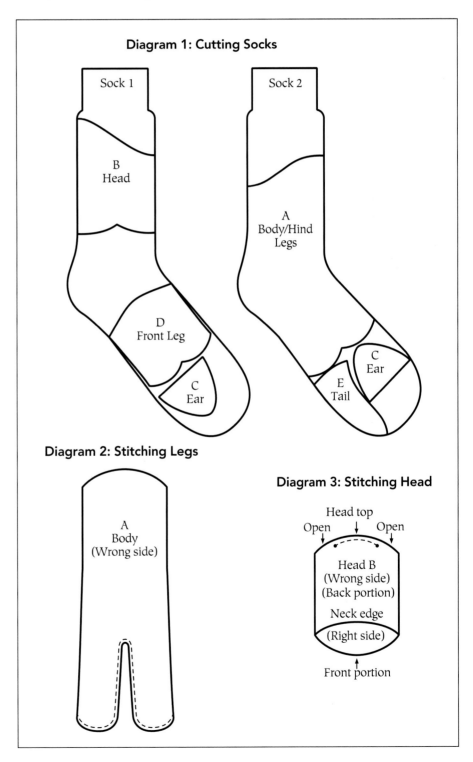

Diagram 1: Cutting Socks

Sock 1

Sock 2

B
Head

A
Body/Hind
Legs

D
Front Leg

C
Ear

C
Ear

E
Tail

Diagram 2: Stitching Legs

A
Body
(Wrong side)

Diagram 3: Stitching Head

Head top
Open ↓ Open

Head B
(Wrong side)
(Back portion)

Neck edge

(Right side)

Front portion

Stacked Pincushion

Materials

2 (3") squares black-red-and-white print fabric
2 (3¾") squares red-and-black print fabric
2 (4½") squares black-and-white print fabric
Thread to match fabrics
Polyester stuffing
40" length ⅛"-wide coordinating ribbon
Assorted pins: dressmaker pins, quilting pins, T-pins

Instructions

Note: Use small machine stitches and fabric that does not fray easily. Seam allowances are ¼" and are included in fabric measurements.

1. With right sides facing and raw edges aligned, pin matching squares together.

2. Stitch each pair of squares together, leaving 1" opening on 1 side of each for stuffing. Clip off corners of fabric close to stitching.

3. Turn each right side out and stuff firmly. Slipstitch openings closed.

4. Stack cushions with largest at bottom and smallest at top. Wrap ribbon around sides of cushions and tie into bow at top. Insert pins.

Here are two gifts that help make life simpler. Make the pocketed Sewing Basket Pincushion to leave in a car or a desk for on-the-spot mending. Avid sewers can stay organized by grouping similar-weight pins on different layers of the Stacked Pincushion.

Sewing Basket Pincushion

Materials

Patterns on page 167
Tracing paper
5" x 13" piece star print fabric for basket
6" square floral print fabric for background
2" x 4" piece checked fabric for tabletop
Thread to match fabrics
18" length corded piping
18" ribbon, cord, *or* braided embroidery floss for hanging loop
Zipper foot for sewing machine
Contents of purchased miniature sewing kit

Instructions

Note: Broken pattern lines are stitching lines. Add ¼" seam allowances when cutting fabrics unless indicated otherwise. Pincushion front is made in 2 layers to form a functional basket pocket.

1. Trace patterns onto tracing paper, transferring markings. Cut out.

2. From star print fabric, cut 5" square for pincushion back. Set aside. Place pattern pieces, except handle B, ½" apart on wrong side of fabrics indicated. Trace patterns, transferring markings. Cut out, adding ¼" seam allowances. Trace handle B on right side of star print fabric. Cut out, adding ⅛" seam allowance.

3. To make Layer 1, refer to Diagram 1. Use basting stitches to transfer handle placement lines onto right side of floral piece A. Fold under handle B seam allowance. Pin and slip-stitch handle in place on right side of floral piece A. With right sides facing and raw edges aligned, pin and stitch floral piece A to matching edge of 1 star print A. Press seam allowance toward floral piece. Set aside.

4. To make Layer 2, refer to Diagram 2. Press seams open as you work. With right sides facing and raw edges aligned, join 1 star print base D to 1 floral print background E. In same manner, join remaining D to reverse E. Join 1 unit to each side of basket C. Join tabletop F to base of basket C; press this seam allowance away from basket. Stitch remaining star print A to top edge of basket unit. Press seam allowance toward star print A.

Fold unit along basket top seam. With wrong sides facing and raw edges aligned, press star print A to back of basket as facing. Baste raw edges together. Pin; baste folded Layer 2 in place on Layer 1. Slipstitch Layer 2 to Layer 1 along top seam line of each floral print E piece only. Stitch in-the-ditch around basket C shape; do not stitch top of basket.

5. Trim seam allowance of piping to ¼" if necessary. With raw edges aligned, baste piping to right side of pincushion front. Clip seam allowance of piping at curves. Using zipper foot, machine-stitch piping to pincushion front along basting line.

6. With right sides facing, center pincushion front on reserved back fabric. Pin and stitch along stitching line of piping, leaving 2" opening for turning. Clip curves. Turn right side out. Stuff firmly. Slipstitch opening closed.

7. Fold ribbon, cord, or braided floss in half. Tack fold in place at center top of pincushion. Leaving 2" loop, tie ends of ribbon into bow. Insert pins into pincushion and fill basket pocket with sewing supplies.

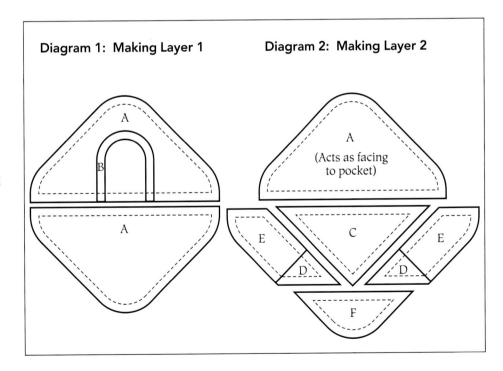

Diagram 1: Making Layer 1

Diagram 2: Making Layer 2

Twine Vases

Materials for one vase

Spool of twine
Scrap lightweight cardboard
Craft glue
Small empty plastic container to fit inside spool opening (candy tube, film canister, medicine container)

Instructions

Measure and cut circle of cardboard a little larger than opening on 1 end of spool of twine. Glue cardboard to 1 end of twine. Slide plastic container into spool opening. Fill container with water and flowers.

Button-Top Peanut Butter Jar

Materials

Pattern on page 166
Tracing paper
1 clean 18-ounce peanut butter jar with colored lid
3" square paper, fabric, or plastic to match lid color
3" square oak tag *or* lightweight posterboard for paper, fabric, or plastic backing
Craft glue
Craft knife
27" length white pearl cotton
Transparent tape
Wide variety of buttons

Instructions

1. Trace small button insert pattern for peanut butter jar onto

Ladybug Garden Gloves

Materials for gloves with one appliquéd ladybug

Patterns on page 167
Tracing paper
Darning needle
1 pair purchased garden gloves
Vanishing fabric marker
White pencil (for drawing on black fabric)
2½" square red polka-dot fabric
1½" square black fabric
Thread (for basting)
Black embroidery floss
Note: To appliqué *both* gloves, double amount of fabric.

Instructions

Note: Broken pattern lines are stitching lines. Add ¼" hem allowances when cutting fabrics.
1. Trace patterns for bug back and head onto tracing paper, transferring markings. Cut out. Use darning needle to pierce wing lines on back. On square of tracing paper, trace Placement Guide. Do not cut out. Pierce all lines and pin Placement Guide on 1 glove. Using vanishing fabric marker, transfer outline onto back of glove.
2. Using vanishing fabric marker or white pencil, trace patterns and markings on right side of fabrics. Cut out pieces.
3. Clip curves of hem allowances. Fold under; baste in place. Pin and baste head on glove. Pin and baste bug back in place, overlapping head. Using 1 strand of floss, appliqué bug in place with blanket stitches. Remove basting stitches. Using 1 strand of floss, chainstitch antennae and vertical wing line on bug. To make wings, using 2 strands of floss, make running stitches along traced outline.

tracing paper. Cut out pattern and holes.

2. Glue paper, fabric, or plastic to oak tag. Trace pattern and cut out insert and holes.

3. Cut 12 (2¼") lengths of pearl cotton. Working from back to front, pass ends of 6 strands through 2 diagonally opposite holes. Flatten strands if necessary. Tape ends to back of insert. Repeat with remaining strands and holes.

4. Glue insert on lid. Fill jar with buttons.

Button-Top Mason Jar

Materials
Pattern on page 166
Tracing paper
1 (8-ounce) mason jar with 2-piece gold-tone lid
3" square gold foil card stock (or foil glued to oak tag)
Craft knife
27" length pearl cotton
Transparent tape

Instructions
1. Trace small button insert pattern for mason jar onto tracing paper. Cut out pattern and holes.
2. On foil, trace pattern and cut out insert and holes.
3. Cut 12 (2¼") lengths of pearl cotton. Working from front to back, pass ends of 6 strands through 2 diagonally opposite holes. Flatten strands if necessary. Tape ends to back of insert. Repeat with remaining strands and holes.
4. Place foil insert inside lid ring. Place metal disc portion of lid behind foil to secure. Fill jar with buttons.

Button-Top Coffee Can

Materials
Pattern on page 167
Tracing paper
1 clean 1-pound coffee can with unprinted, opaque, colored lid
Craft knife
22½" length ⅛" cable cord
Transparent tape
3¾"-diameter circle white felt
Craft glue
6" x 14" scrap oak tag
6" x 14" scrap paper or fabric to cover can
Wide variety of buttons

Instructions
1. Trace large button pattern for coffee can onto tracing paper. Cut out pattern and holes.

2. Place pattern on lid. Trace holes and cut out.
3. Cut 6 (3¾") lengths of cable cord. Working from back to front, pass 3 strands through 2 diagonally opposite holes. Flatten lengths if necessary. Tape ends to back of lid. Repeat with remaining strands and holes.
4. Trim felt circle to fit inside lid if necessary. Glue in place, covering taped ends of cord.
5. Measure height and circumference of can. Measure and mark oak tag to fit can, adding ½" overlap to 1 side. Center oak tag on paper or fabric and glue. If using paper, trim to fit oak tag. If using fabric, wrap it around oak tag edges and tape or glue to wrong side. Wrap oak tag around can and glue in place. Hold in place with rubber bands until dry. Fill container with buttons.

These playful jars are topped with great big button-like lids. They will hold bunches of smaller buttons inside.

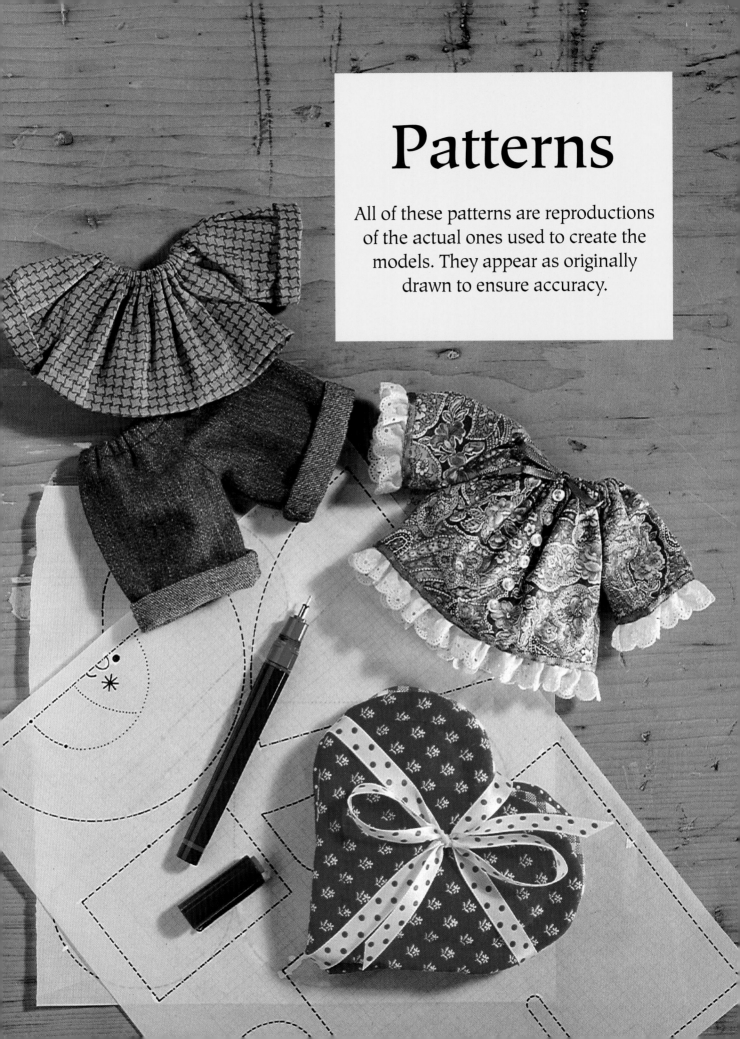

Patterns

All of these patterns are reproductions of the actual ones used to create the models. They appear as originally drawn to ensure accuracy.

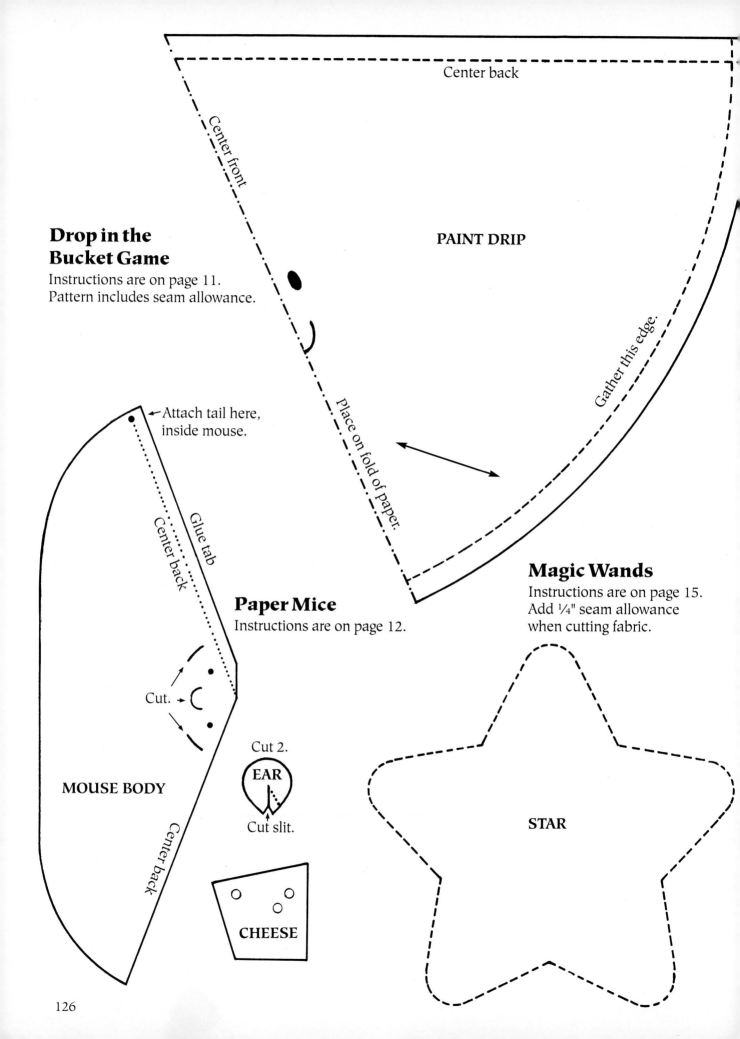

Drop in the Bucket Game

Instructions are on page 11.
Pattern includes seam allowance.

PAINT DRIP

Center back

Center front

Place on fold of paper.

Gather this edge.

Attach tail here,
inside mouse.

Glue tab

Center back

Paper Mice

Instructions are on page 12.

Cut.

MOUSE BODY

Center back

Cut 2.

EAR

Cut slit.

CHEESE

Magic Wands

Instructions are on page 15.
Add ¼" seam allowance
when cutting fabric.

STAR

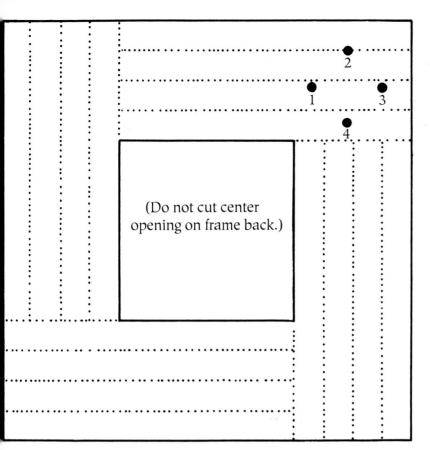

Crayon Frame

Instructions are on page 13.

2

1   3

4

(Do not cut center
opening on frame back.)

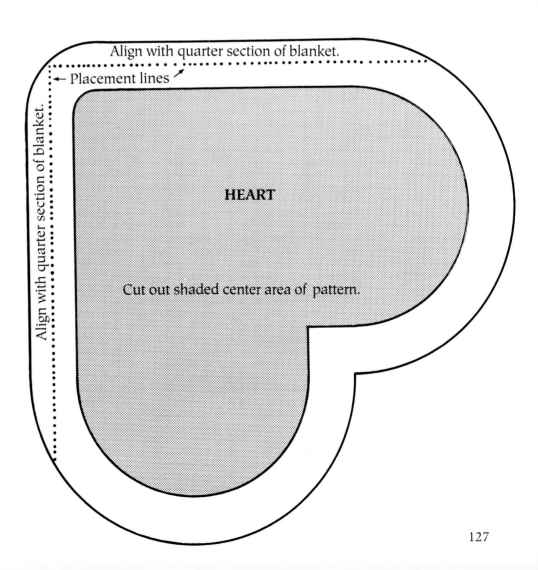

Align with quarter section of blanket.

← Placement lines ↗

Align with quarter section of blanket.

HEART

Cut out shaded center area of pattern.

Little Sweetheart
Receiving Blanket

Instructions are on page 16.

Pentagon Play Shirt

Instructions are on page 17.
Add ¼" hem allowance when cutting fabrics.

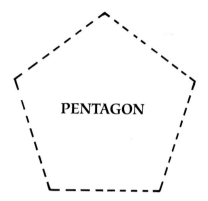

PENTAGON

Playful Pentagon Ball

Instructions are on page 17.

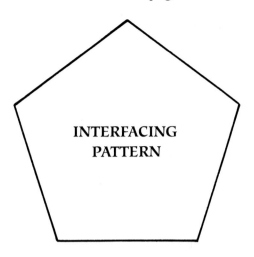

INTERFACING
PATTERN

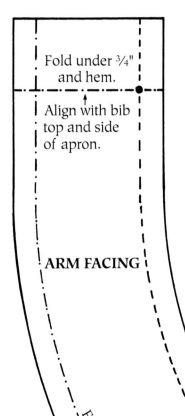

Fold under ¾"
and hem.

Align with bib
top and side
of apron.

ARM FACING

Fold under ¼" and hem.

Place on fold of paper.

Child's Aprons

Instructions are on pages 18–21.
Pattern includes seam allowance.

Front edge   Place piping here.

Baste ribbon here.

Long end of ribbon goes this way.

Place piping here.

Newborn Cap

Instructions are on page 23.
Add ¼" seam allowances when cutting fabrics.

CAP SIDE

Place on fold of paper.

Center top

Neck edge

Center back seam

Gather back edge to fit circle.

Newborn Booties

Instructions are on page 22.
Add ¼" seam allowance when cutting fabrics.

Place on fold of paper.

CAP BACK

Topstitch for casing.

Leave open.

Center front seam

BOOTIE

Center back seam

B

A

A

Sole Area

B

Place on fold of paper.

Center bottom

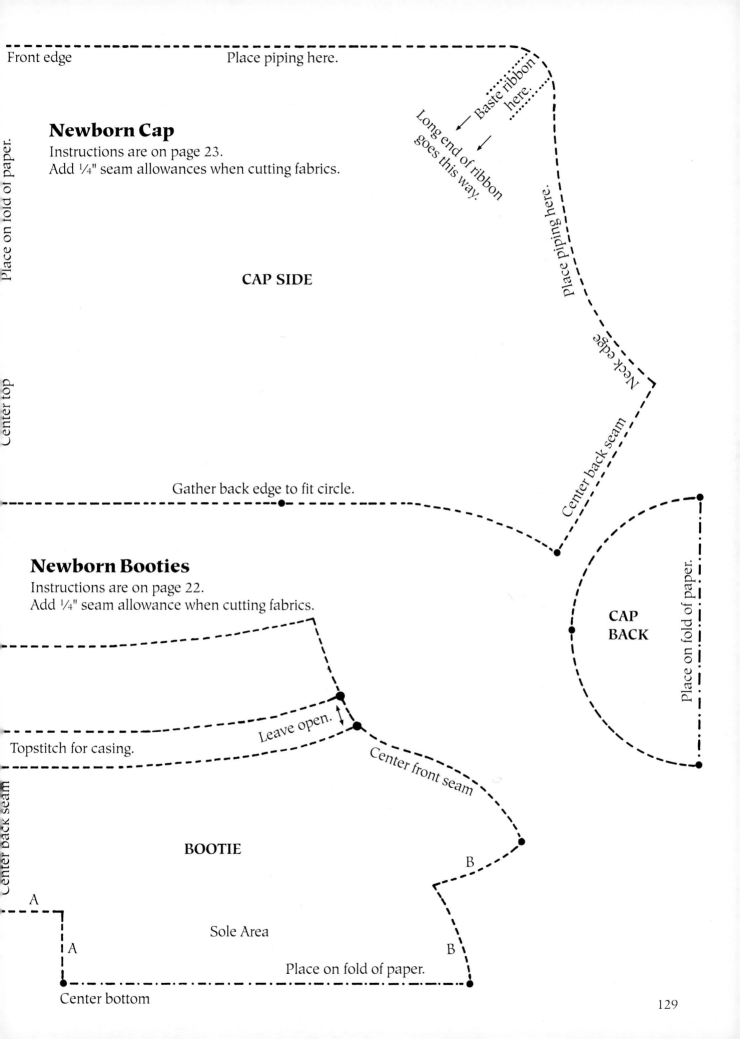

Scalloped Heart Bib

Instructions are on page 23.
Add ¼" seam allowance when cutting fabric.

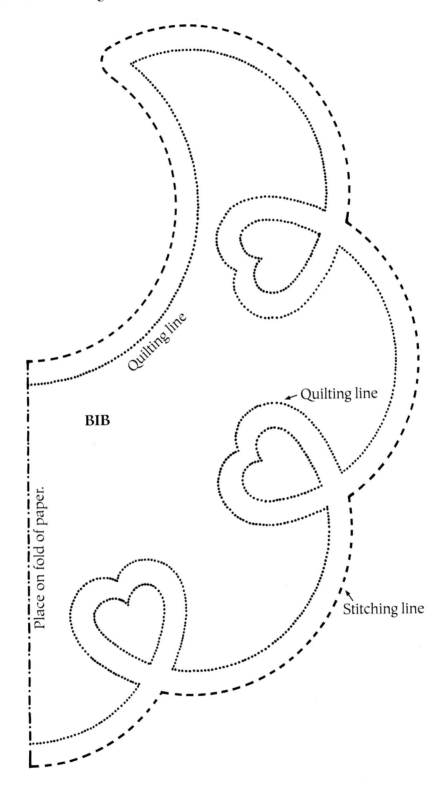

Quilting line

Quilting line

BIB

Place on fold of paper.

Stitching line

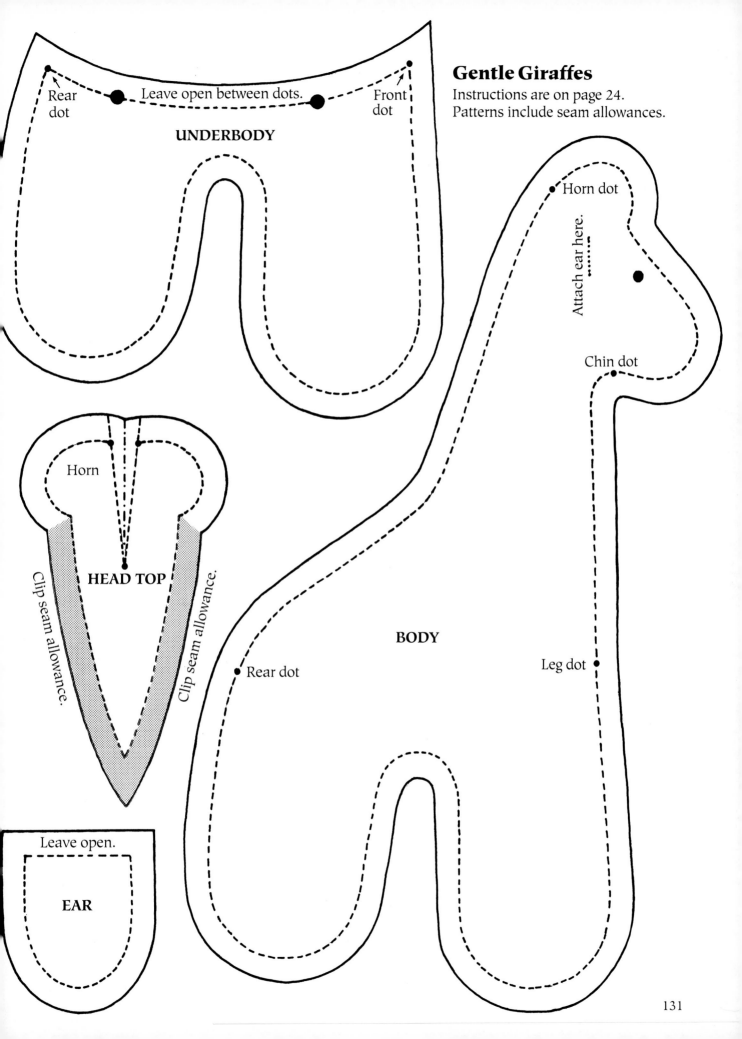

Gentle Giraffes
Instructions are on page 24.
Patterns include seam allowances.

Rear dot

Leave open between dots.

Front dot

UNDERBODY

Horn dot

Attach ear here.

Chin dot

Horn

Clip seam allowance.

HEAD TOP

Clip seam allowance.

Rear dot

BODY

Leg dot

Leave open.

EAR

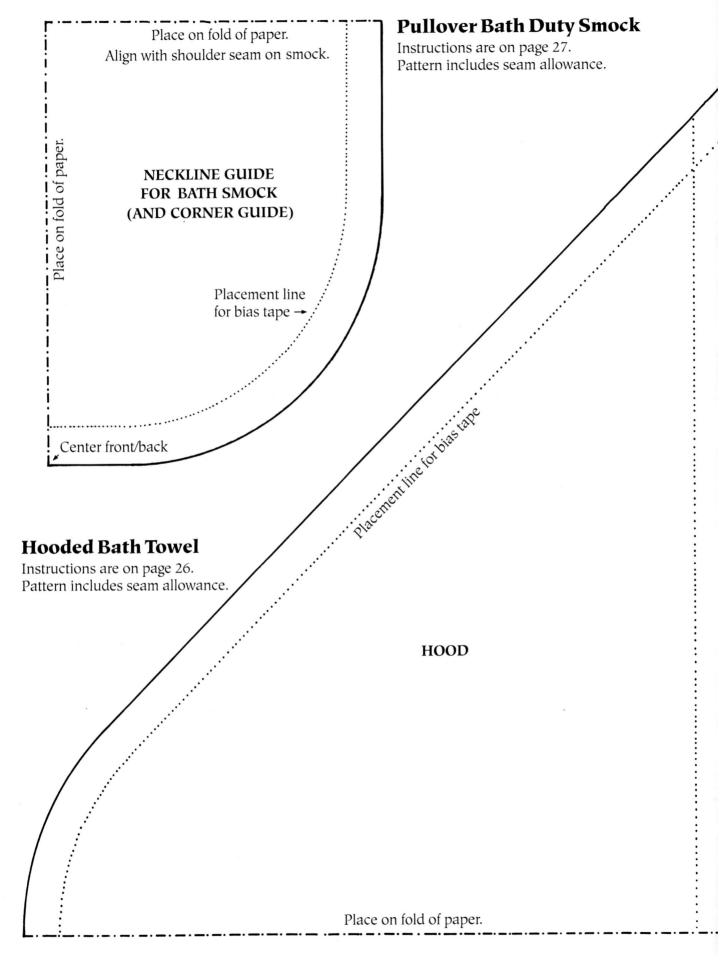

Place on fold of paper.
Align with shoulder seam on smock.

Pullover Bath Duty Smock

Instructions are on page 27.
Pattern includes seam allowance.

Place on fold of paper.

NECKLINE GUIDE
FOR BATH SMOCK
(AND CORNER GUIDE)

Placement line
for bias tape →

Center front/back

Placement line for bias tape

Hooded Bath Towel

Instructions are on page 26.
Pattern includes seam allowance.

HOOD

Place on fold of paper.

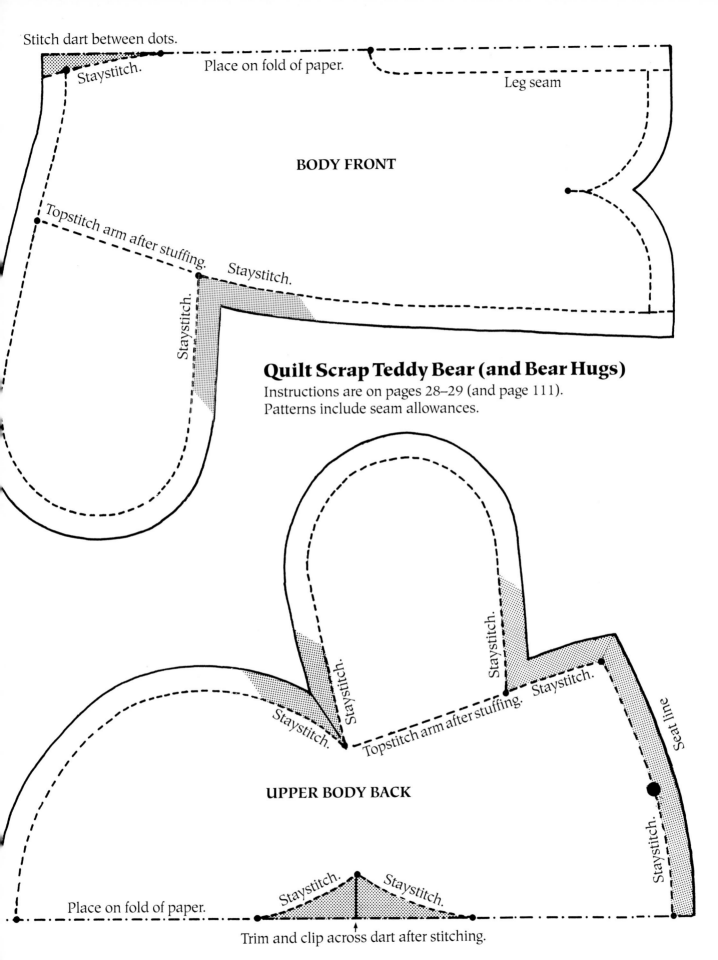

Stitch dart between dots.

Staystitch.

Place on fold of paper.

Leg seam

BODY FRONT

Topstitch arm after stuffing.

Staystitch.

Staystitch.

Quilt Scrap Teddy Bear (and Bear Hugs)

Instructions are on pages 28–29 (and page 111).
Patterns include seam allowances.

Staystitch.

Staystitch.

Staystitch.

Staystitch.

Seat line

Staystitch.

UPPER BODY BACK

Place on fold of paper.

Staystitch.

Staystitch.

Trim and clip across dart after stitching.

**QUILT SCRAP TEDDY BEAR
(AND BEAR HUGS)**
(*Continued on page 134*)

133

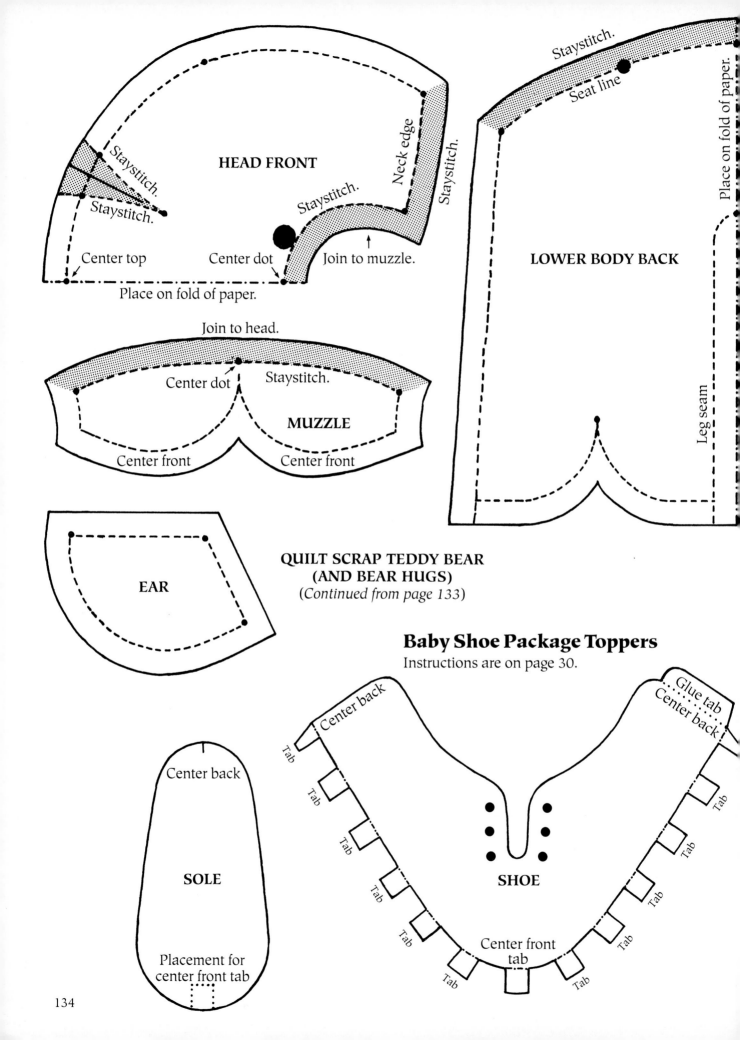

HEAD FRONT

Staystitch.

Staystitch.

Neck edge

Staystitch.

Staystitch.

Center top

Center dot

Join to muzzle.

Place on fold of paper.

LOWER BODY BACK

Staystitch.

Seat line

Place on fold of paper.

Leg seam

Join to head.

Center dot

Staystitch.

MUZZLE

Center front

Center front

EAR

QUILT SCRAP TEDDY BEAR
(AND BEAR HUGS)
(Continued from page 133)

Baby Shoe Package Toppers

Instructions are on page 30.

Center back

Glue tab

Center back

Tab

Tab

Tab

Tab

Tab

Center back

SOLE

Tab

Tab

Tab

Tab

Tab

Tab

SHOE

Placement for
center front tab

Center front
tab

Tab

Tab

Tab

Tab

134

Scrubby Monkey Mitts

Instructions are on pages 30–31.
Add ¼" seam allowances when cutting fabrics.

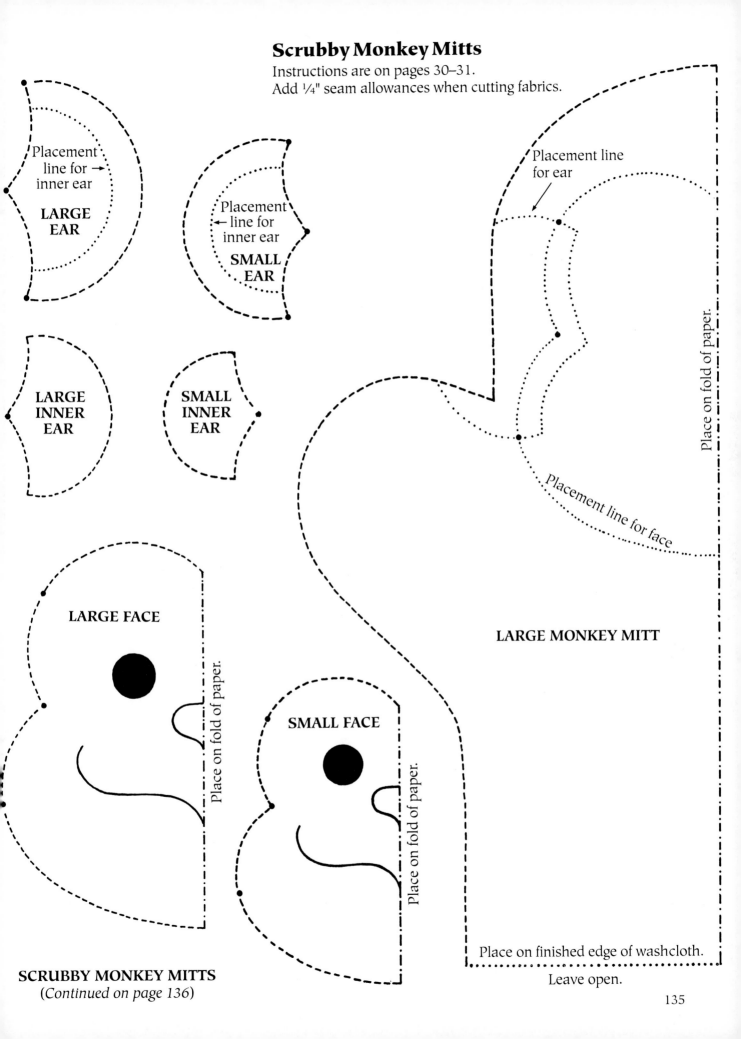

Placement line for inner ear

LARGE EAR

Placement line for inner ear

SMALL EAR

Placement line for ear

Placement line for face

Place on fold of paper.

LARGE INNER EAR

SMALL INNER EAR

LARGE FACE

SMALL FACE

Place on fold of paper.

Place on fold of paper.

LARGE MONKEY MITT

Place on finished edge of washcloth.

Leave open.

SCRUBBY MONKEY MITTS

(Continued on page 136)

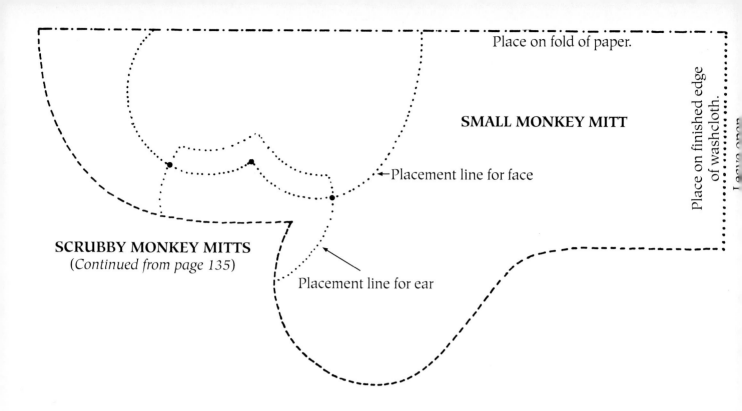

Place on fold of paper.

SMALL MONKEY MITT

Place on finished edge of washcloth.

←Placement line for face

SCRUBBY MONKEY MITTS
(*Continued from page 135*)

Placement line for ear

Lazy Lion Toy and Lion Hanger

Instructions are on pages 32–33.
Add ¼" seam allowances when cutting fabric.

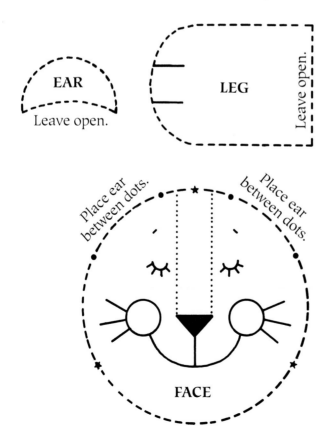

EAR
Leave open.

LEG
Leave open.

Place ear between dots.

Place ear between dots.

FACE

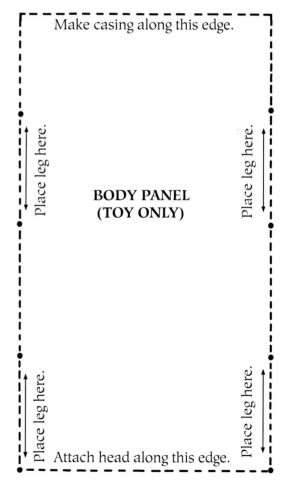

Make casing along this edge.

Place leg here.

Place leg here.

**BODY PANEL
(TOY ONLY)**

Place leg here.

Place leg here.

Attach head along this edge.

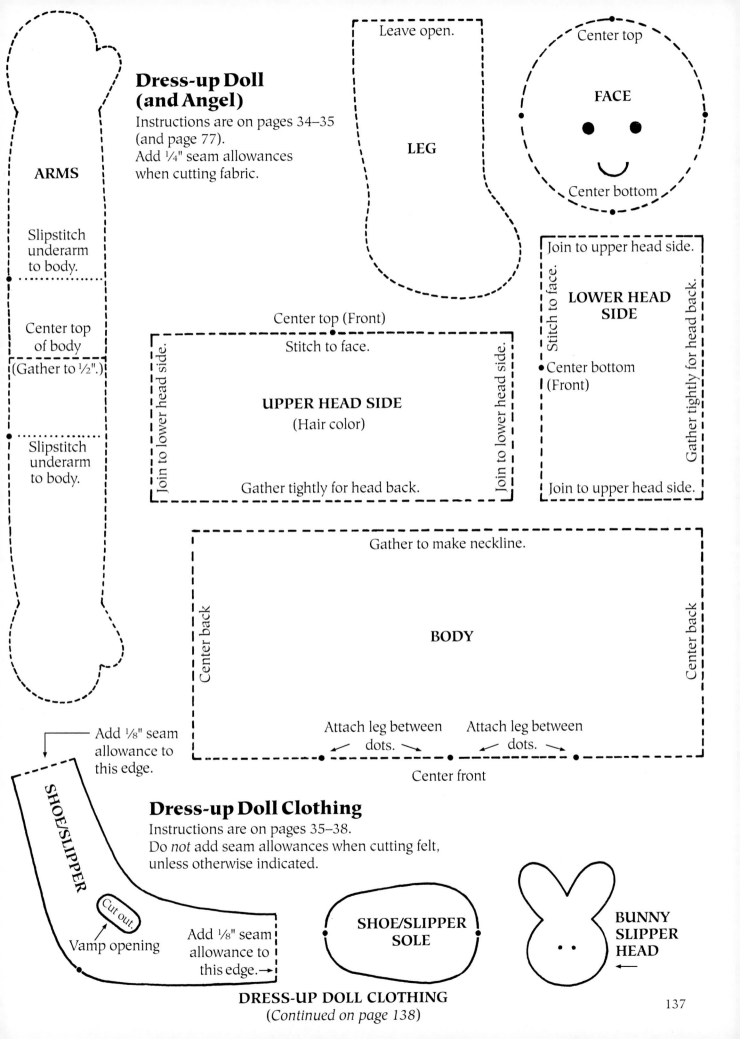

ARMS

Slipstitch underarm to body.

Center top of body
(Gather to ½".)

Slipstitch underarm to body.

Leave open.

LEG

Center top

FACE

Center bottom

Dress-up Doll (and Angel)

Instructions are on pages 34–35 (and page 77).
Add ¼" seam allowances when cutting fabric.

Center top (Front)
Stitch to face.

Join to lower head side.

UPPER HEAD SIDE
(Hair color)

Gather tightly for head back.

Join to lower head side.

Join to upper head side.

Stitch to face.

LOWER HEAD SIDE

Center bottom (Front)

Gather tightly for head back.

Join to upper head side.

Gather to make neckline.

Center back

BODY

Center back

Attach leg between dots.

Attach leg between dots.

Center front

Add ⅛" seam allowance to this edge.

SHOE/SLIPPER

Cut out.
Vamp opening

Add ⅛" seam allowance to this edge.→

Dress-up Doll Clothing

Instructions are on pages 35–38.
Do *not* add seam allowances when cutting felt, unless otherwise indicated.

SHOE/SLIPPER SOLE

BUNNY SLIPPER HEAD

DRESS-UP DOLL CLOTHING
(*Continued on page 138*)

137

DRESS-UP DOLL CLOTHING

(Continued from page 137)

Add ¼" seam allowance when cutting fabrics, unless otherwise indicated.

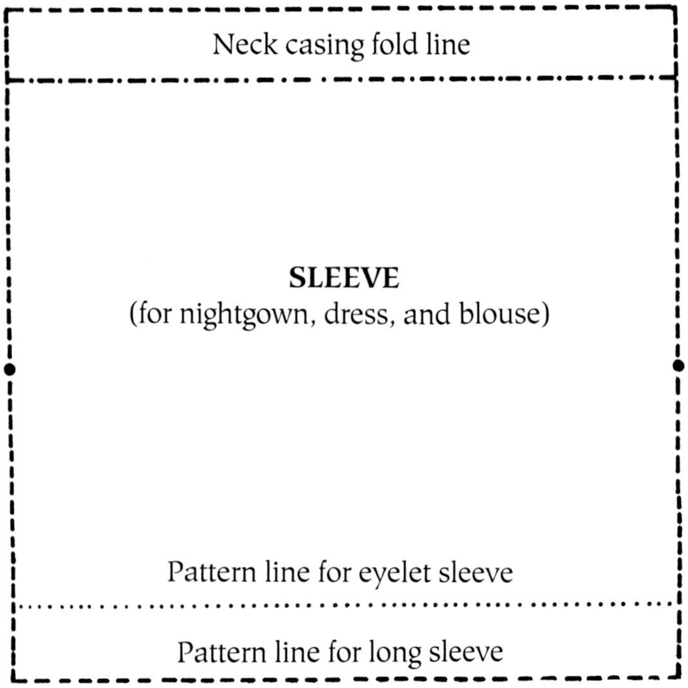

Waist casing fold line

Center front or
center back seam →

Place on fold of fabric.

PANTS

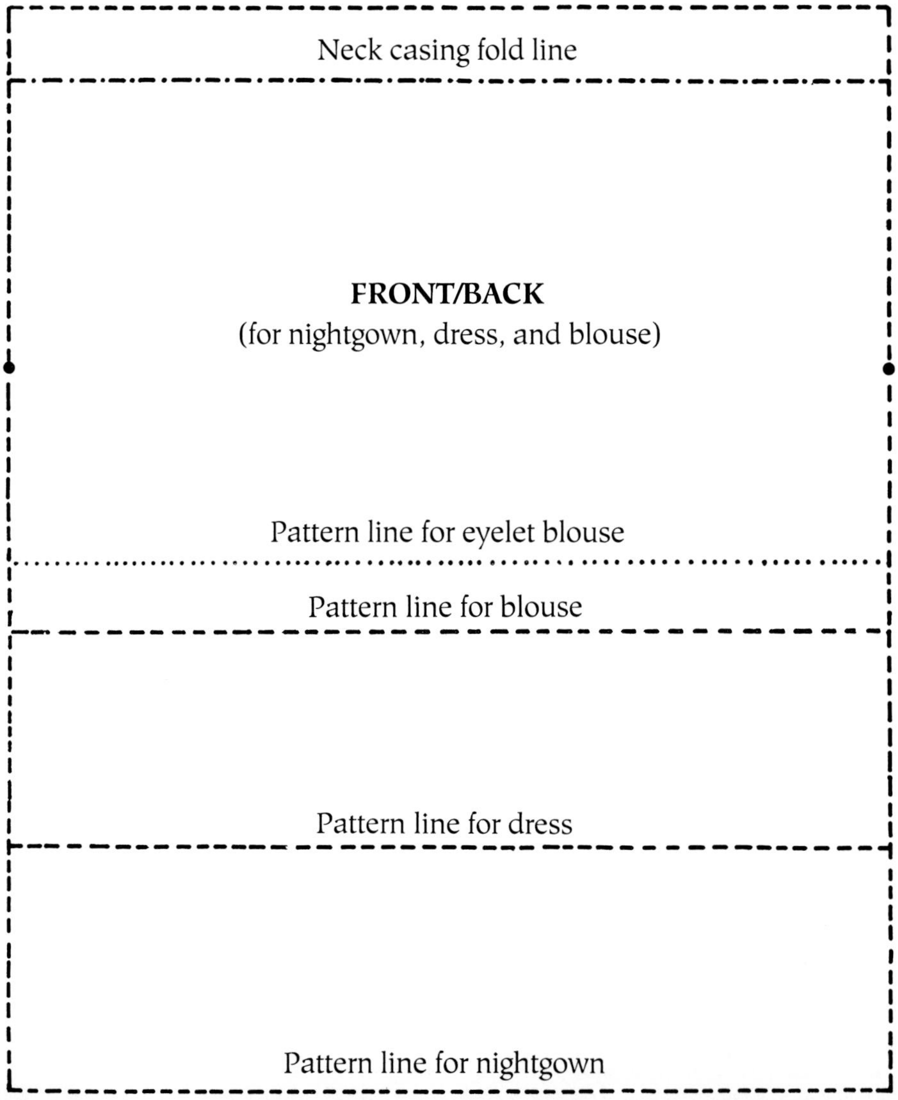

Neck casing fold line

SLEEVE
(for nightgown, dress, and blouse)

Pattern line for eyelet sleeve

Pattern line for long sleeve

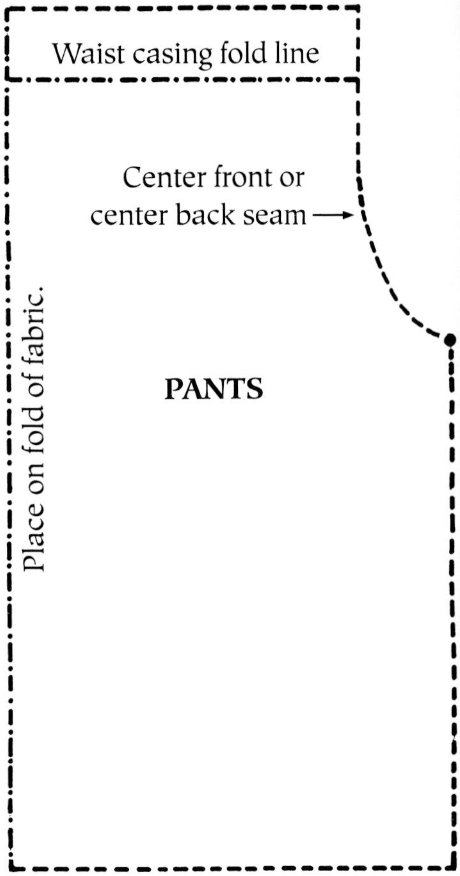

Neck casing fold line

FRONT/BACK
(for nightgown, dress, and blouse)

Pattern line for eyelet blouse

Pattern line for blouse

Pattern line for dress

Pattern line for nightgown

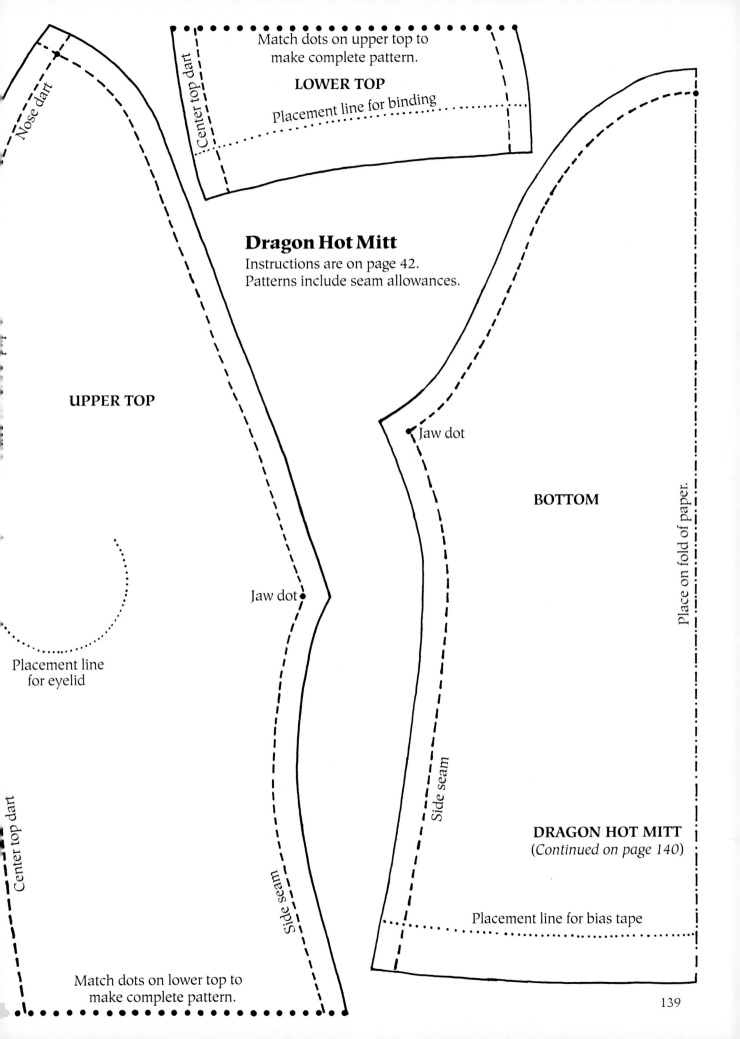

Match dots on upper top to make complete pattern.

Nose dart

Center top dart

LOWER TOP

Placement line for binding

Dragon Hot Mitt

Instructions are on page 42.
Patterns include seam allowances.

UPPER TOP

Jaw dot

BOTTOM

Place on fold of paper.

Placement line
for eyelid

Jaw dot

Side seam

Side seam

Center top dart

DRAGON HOT MITT
(*Continued on page 140*)

Placement line for bias tape

Match dots on lower top to
make complete pattern.

139

DRAGON HOT MITT
(Continued from page 139)

EYELID

Straight of grain

Placement line for rickrack
(and bias fold line)

Cut slit for turning.

POINT

Jaw dot

MOUTH
Lower portion

Place on fold of paper.

Upper portion

Place on fold of paper.

Align on seam.

Align on seam.

Heart Cluster Pot Holder
Instructions are on pages 42–43.
Add ¼" seam allowances when cutting fabrics.

POT HOLDER

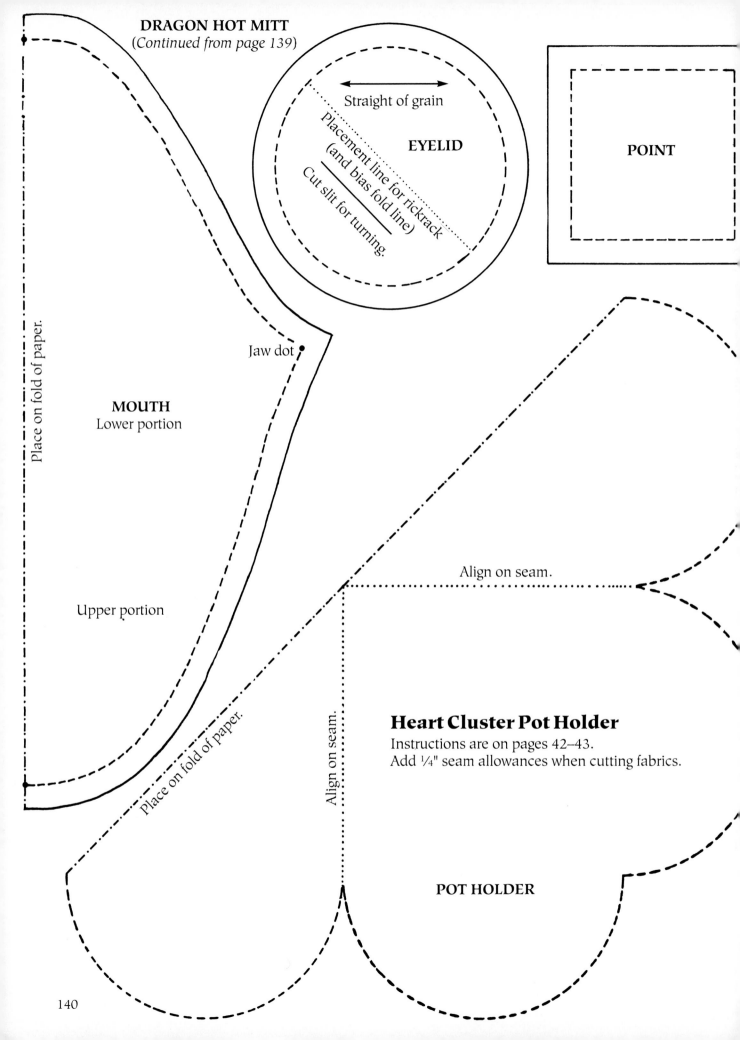

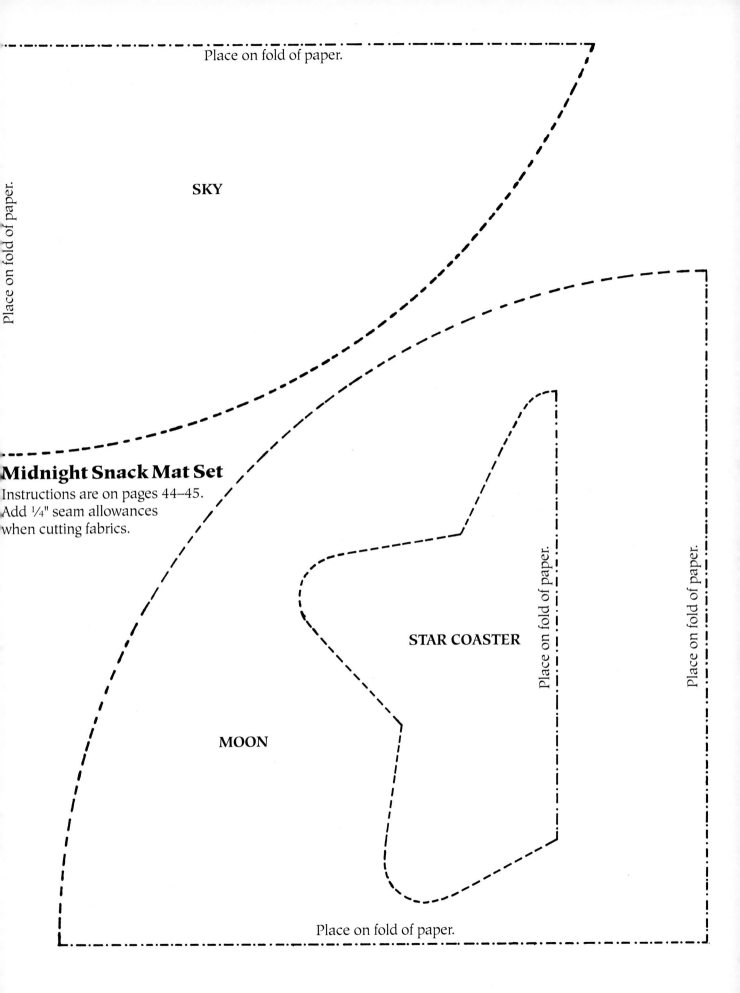

Place on fold of paper.

Place on fold of paper.

SKY

Midnight Snack Mat Set

Instructions are on pages 44–45.
Add ¼" seam allowances
when cutting fabrics.

STAR COASTER

Place on fold of paper.

Place on fold of paper.

MOON

Place on fold of paper.

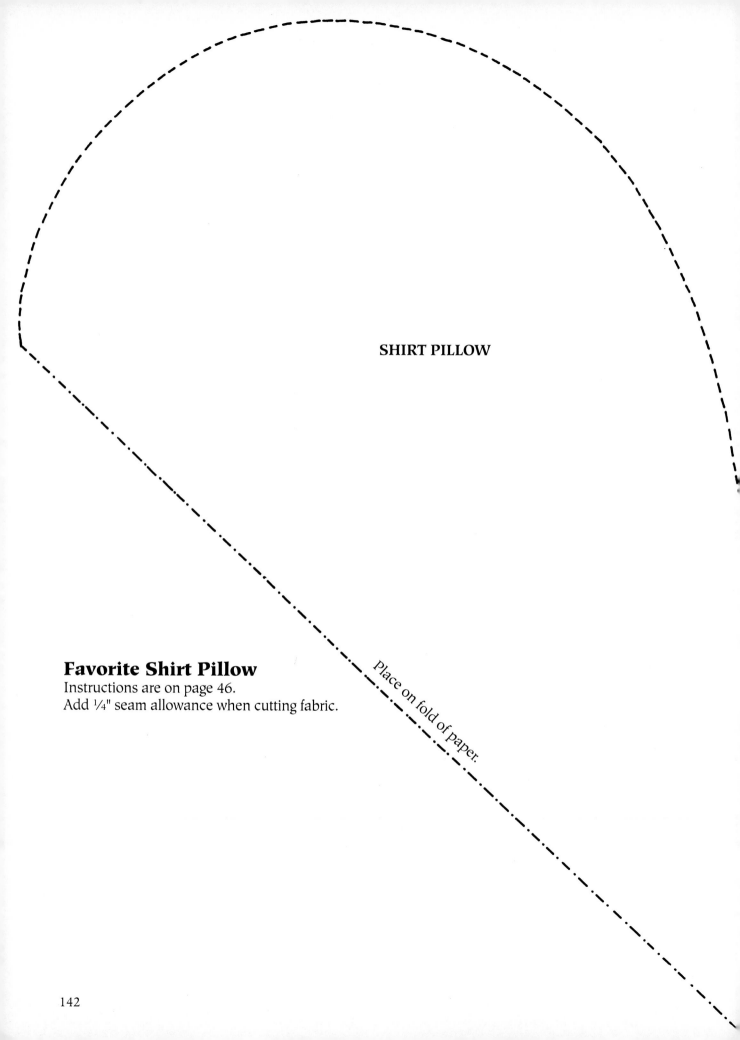

SHIRT PILLOW

Favorite Shirt Pillow
Instructions are on page 46.
Add ¼" seam allowance when cutting fabric.

Place on fold of paper.

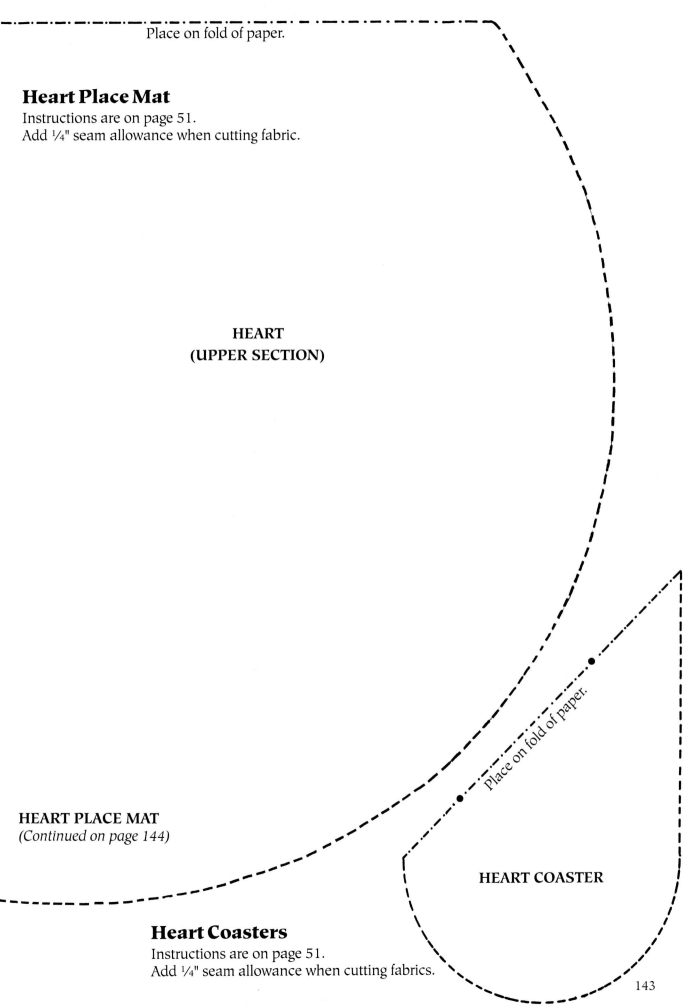

Place on fold of paper.

Heart Place Mat

Instructions are on page 51.
Add ¼" seam allowance when cutting fabric.

Join to lower pattern section along dots.

HEART
(UPPER SECTION)

HEART PLACE MAT
(Continued on page 144)

Place on fold of paper.

HEART COASTER

Heart Coasters

Instructions are on page 51.
Add ¼" seam allowance when cutting fabrics.

Place on fold of paper.

HEART PLACE MAT
(Continued from page 143)

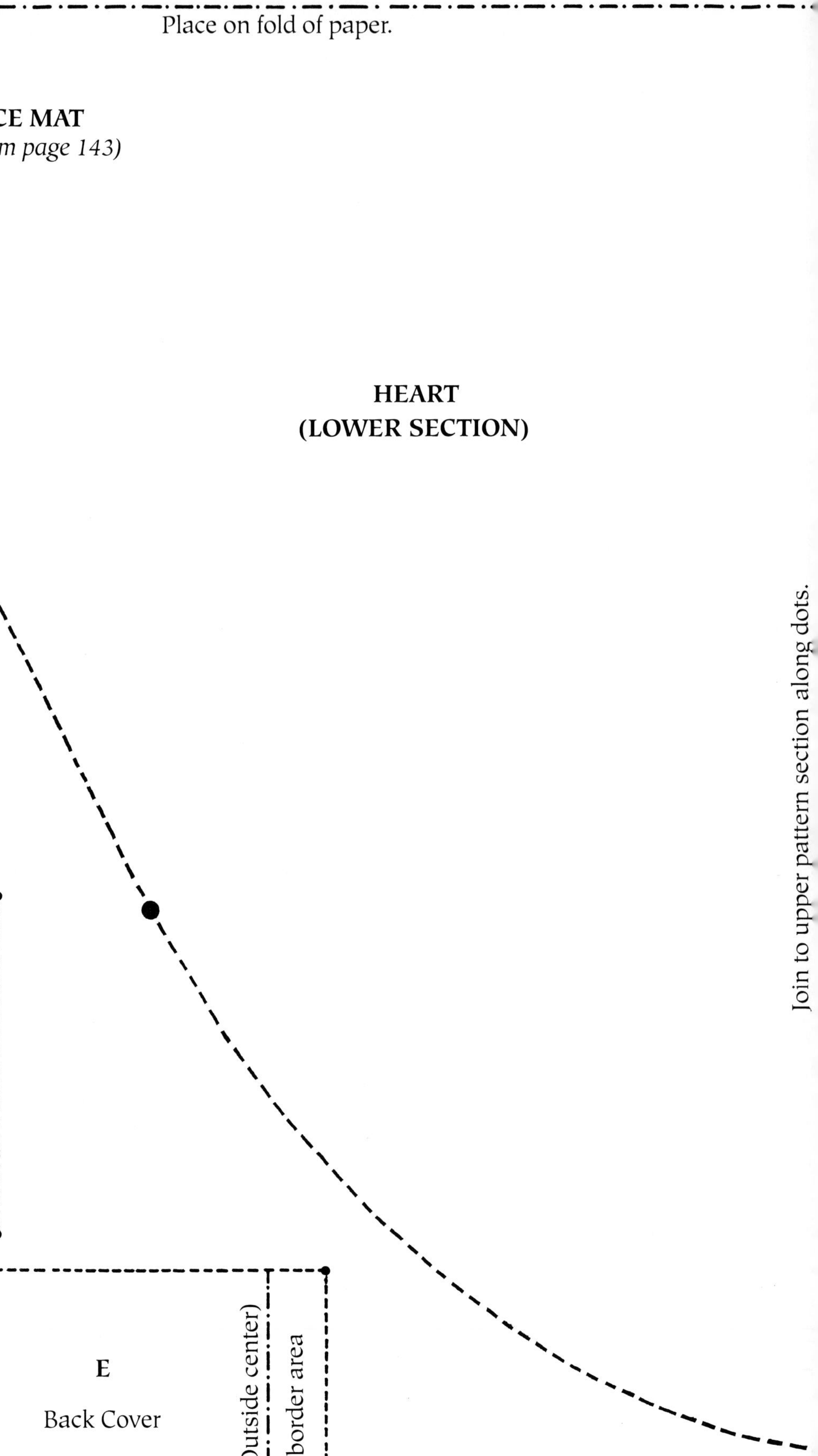

HEART
(LOWER SECTION)

Join to upper pattern section along dots.

Pieced Needle Books

Instructions are on pages 52–53. Add ¼" seam allowances when cutting fabrics.

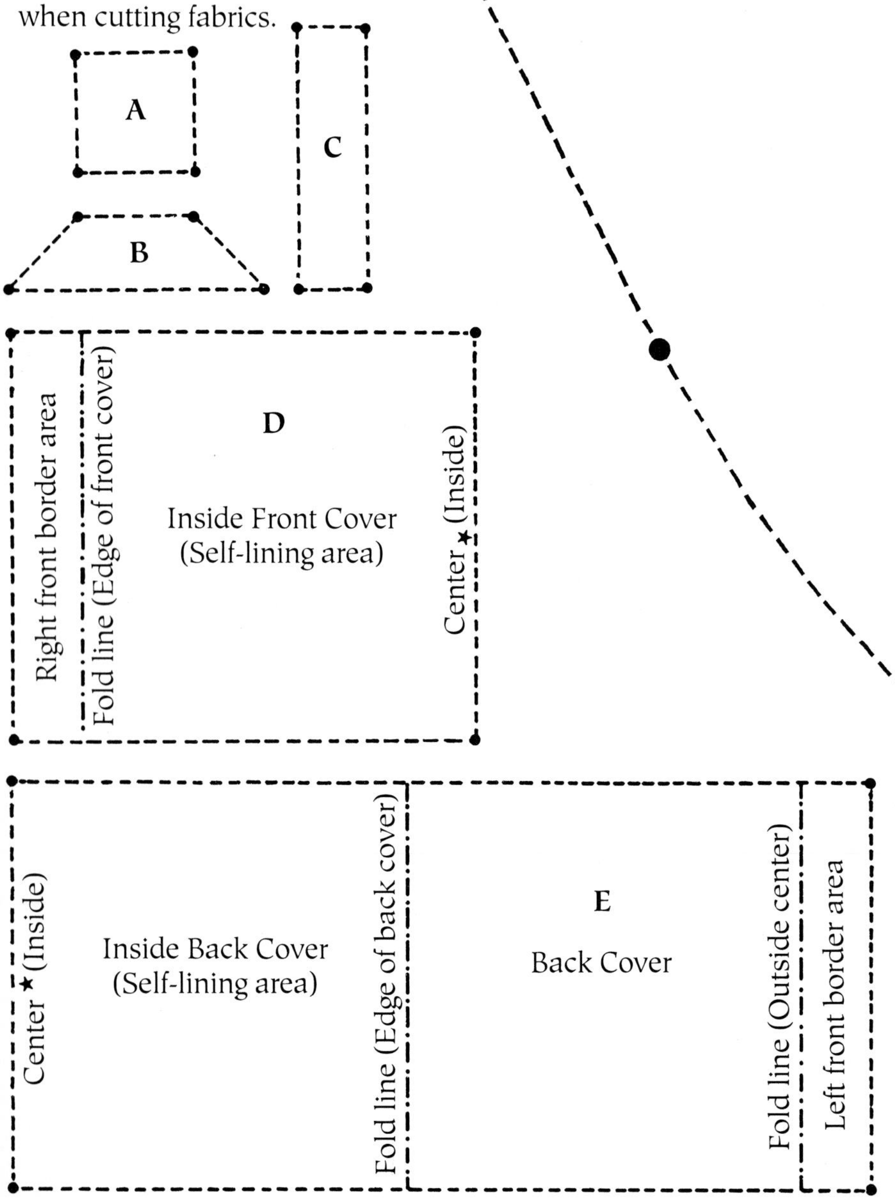

A

B

C

Right front border area

Fold line (Edge of front cover)

D

Inside Front Cover
(Self-lining area)

Center ★ (Inside)

Center ★ (Inside)

Inside Back Cover
(Self-lining area)

Fold line (Edge of back cover)

E

Back Cover

Fold line (Outside center)

Left front border area

Valentine Folder

Instructions are on page 57.

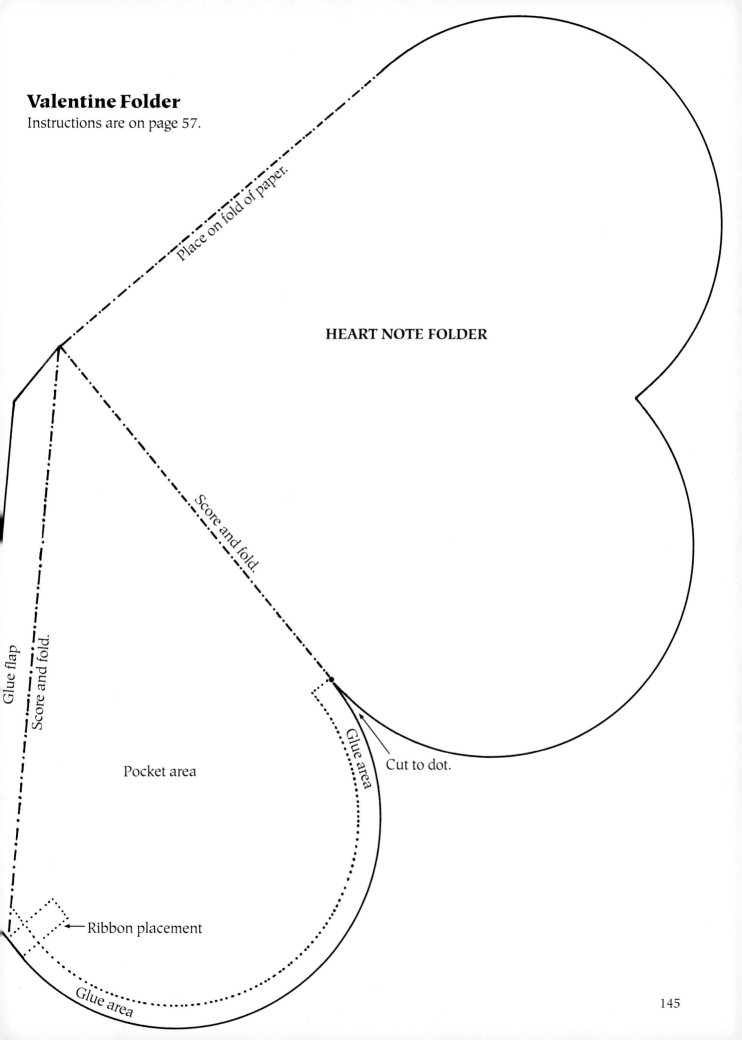

HEART NOTE FOLDER

Place on fold of paper.

Score and fold.

Glue flap

Score and fold.

Pocket area

Glue area

Cut to dot.

Ribbon placement

Glue area

Patriotic Heart

Instructions are on page 63.
Add ¼" seam allowances when cutting fabrics.

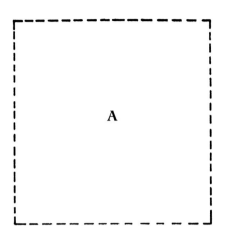

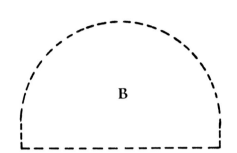

Jack-o'-lantern Lampshade

Instructions are on page 64.

Candy Corn Cup

Instructions are on page 66.

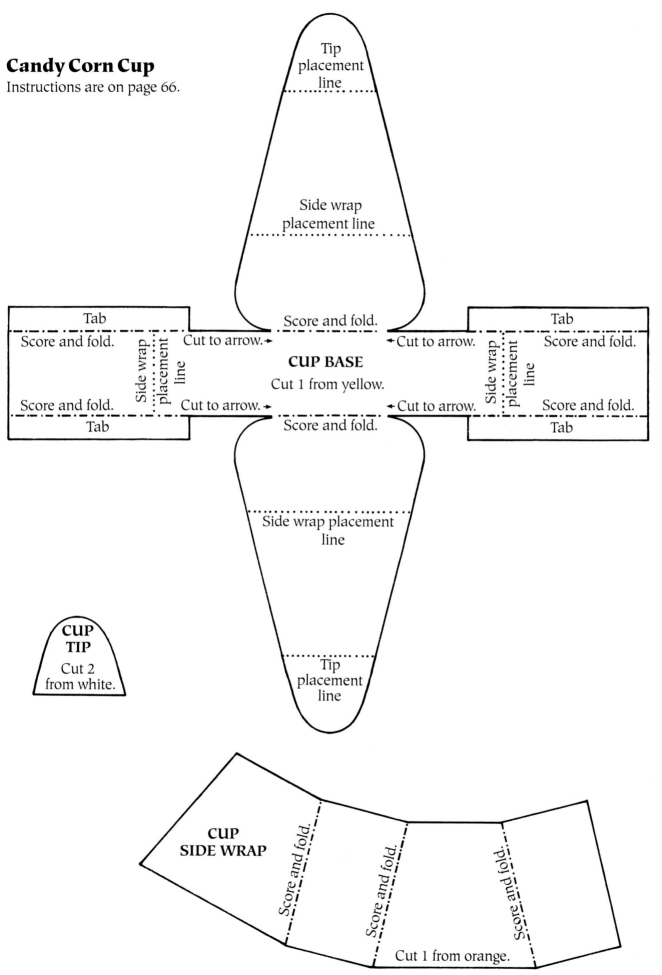

Tip placement line

Side wrap placement line

Tab

Score and fold.

Score and fold.

Side wrap placement line

Cut to arrow.

Cut to arrow.

CUP BASE

Cut 1 from yellow.

Cut to arrow.

Cut to arrow.

Score and fold.

Score and fold.

Tab

Score and fold.

Score and fold.

Side wrap placement line

Score and fold.

Score and fold.

Tab

Tab

CUP TIP

Cut 2 from white.

Side wrap placement line

Tip placement line

CUP SIDE WRAP

Score and fold.

Score and fold.

Score and fold.

Cut 1 from orange.

Paper Witch

Instructions are on page 66.

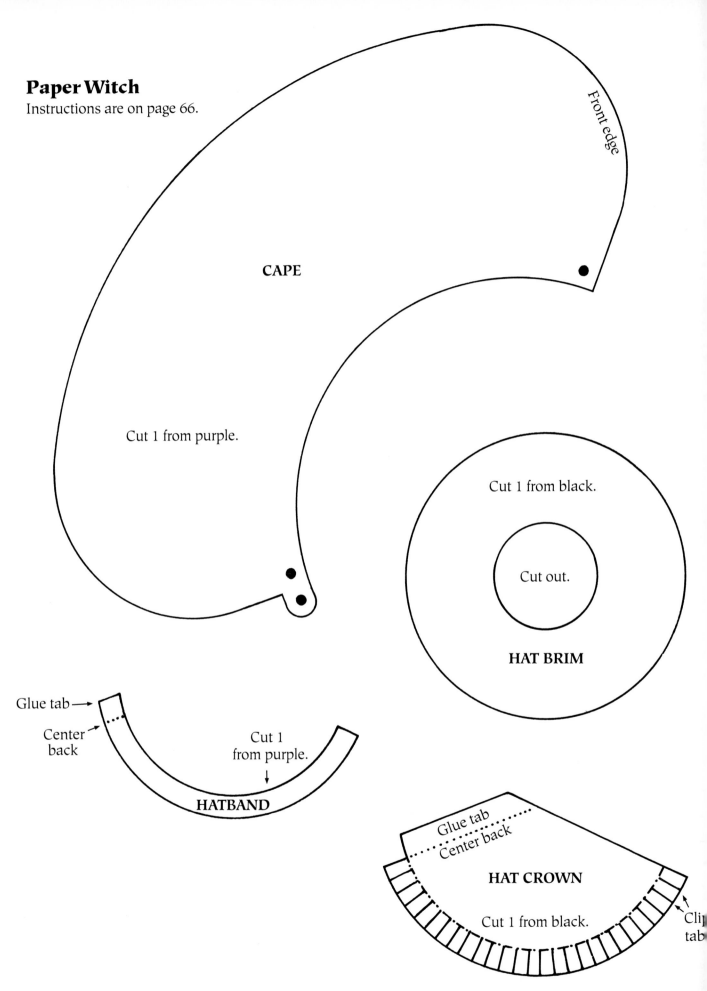

CAPE

Front edge

Cut 1 from purple.

Cut 1 from black.

Cut out.

HAT BRIM

Glue tab →

Center back →

Cut 1
from purple.

↓

HATBAND

Glue tab

Center back

HAT CROWN

Cut 1 from black.

Clip
tab

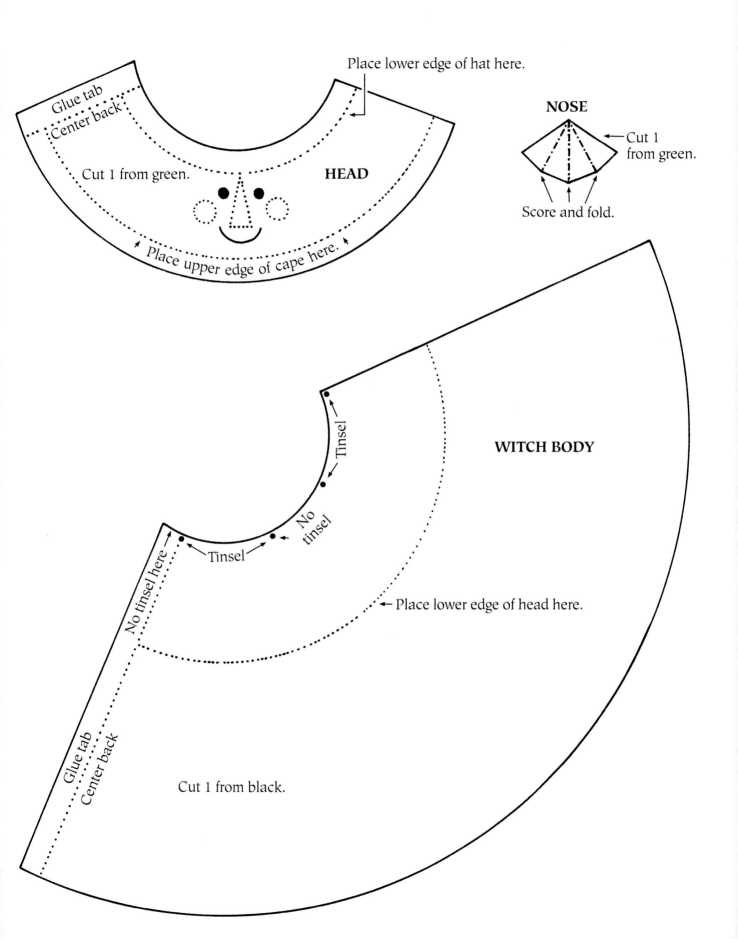

Place lower edge of hat here.

NOSE

Cut 1 from green.

Score and fold.

Glue tab

Center back

Cut 1 from green.

HEAD

Place upper edge of cape here.

Tinsel

No tinsel

WITCH BODY

No tinsel here

Tinsel

Place lower edge of head here.

Glue tab

Center back

Cut 1 from black.

Ghost Mittens

Instructions are on pages 68–69.
Add ¼" seam allowance when cutting fabric.

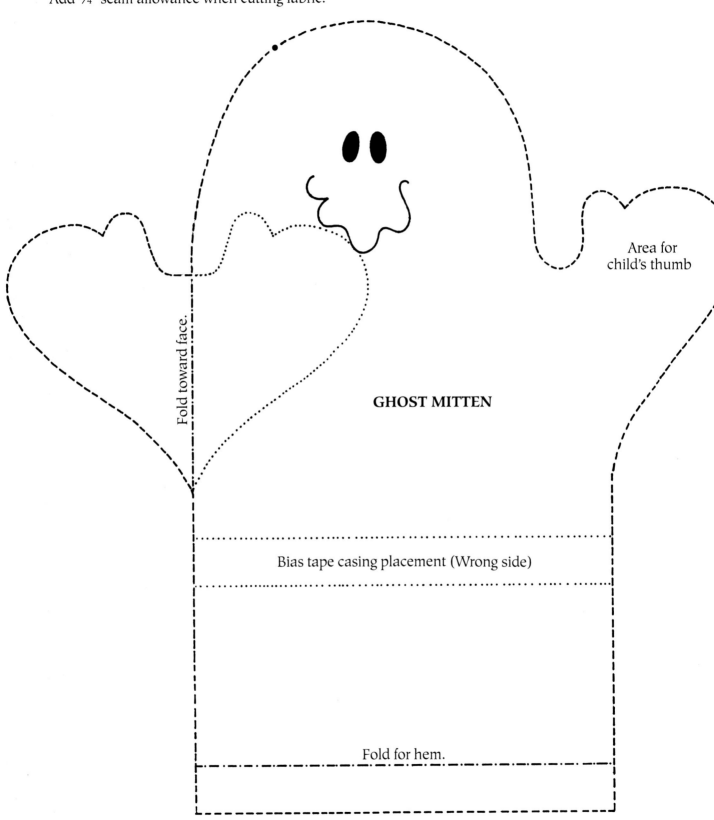

Area for child's thumb

Fold toward face.

GHOST MITTEN

Bias tape casing placement (Wrong side)

Fold for hem.

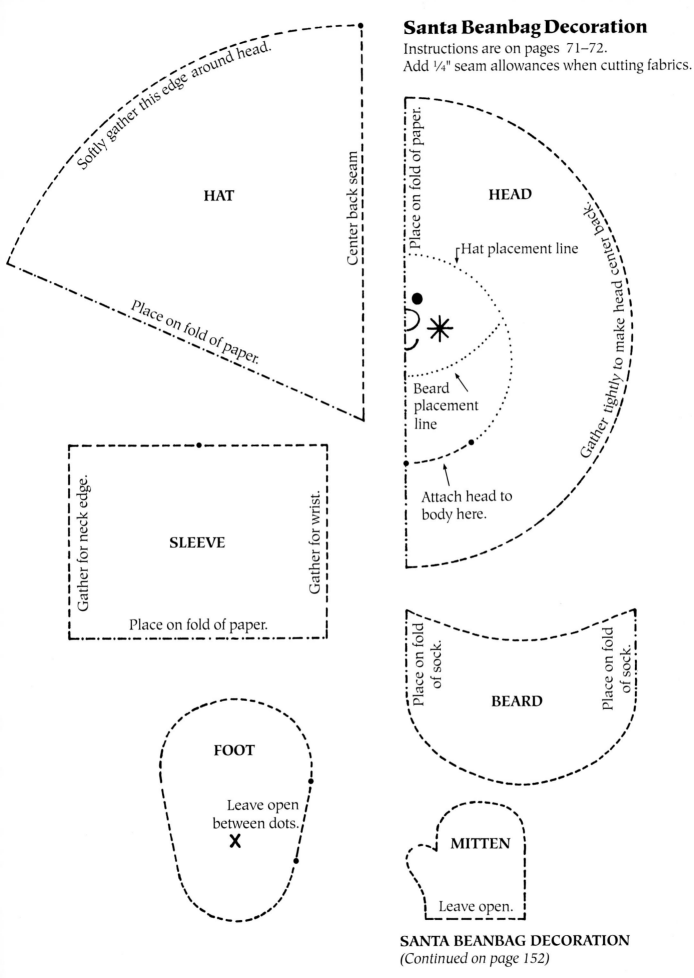

Santa Beanbag Decoration

Instructions are on pages 71–72.
Add ¼" seam allowances when cutting fabrics.

HAT

Softly gather this edge around head.

Place on fold of paper.

Center back seam

HEAD

Place on fold of paper.

Hat placement line

Beard placement line

Gather tightly to make head center back.

Attach head to body here.

SLEEVE

Gather for neck edge.

Gather for wrist.

Place on fold of paper.

BEARD

Place on fold of sock.

Place on fold of sock.

FOOT

Leave open between dots.

X

MITTEN

Leave open.

SANTA BEANBAG DECORATION
(Continued on page 152)

(Continued on page 152)

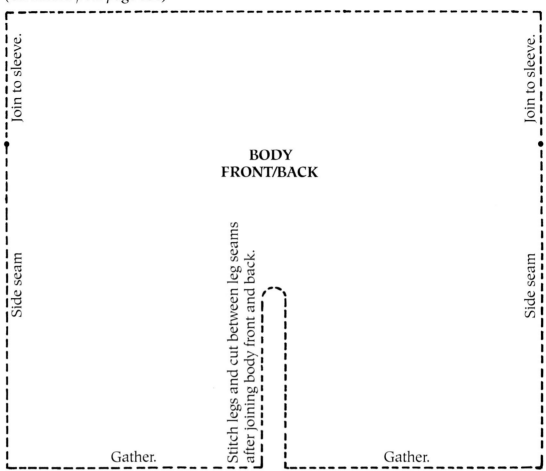

Join to sleeve.

Join to sleeve.

BODY FRONT/BACK

Side seam

Side seam

Stitch legs and cut between leg seams after joining body front and back.

Gather.

Gather.

Little Stocking Ornaments

Instructions are on pages 72–73.
Add ¼" seam allowances when cutting fabrics.

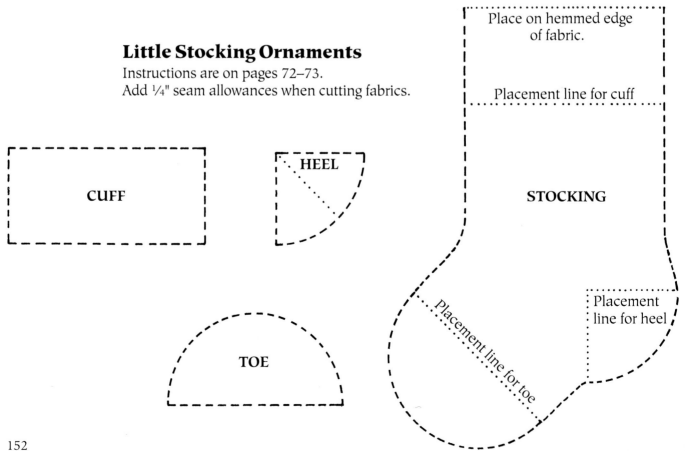

CUFF

HEEL

TOE

Place on hemmed edge of fabric.

Placement line for cuff

STOCKING

Placement line for toe

Placement line for heel

Folded Ribbon Stars

Instructions are on page 74.

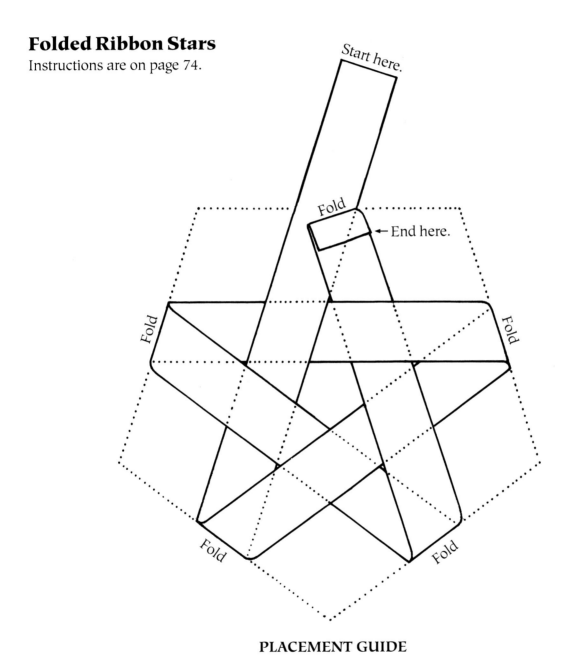

Start here.

Fold

← End here.

Fold

Fold

Fold

Fold

PLACEMENT GUIDE

Crocheted Stars

Instructions are on pages 74–75.
Add ¼" seam allowance
when cutting fabric.

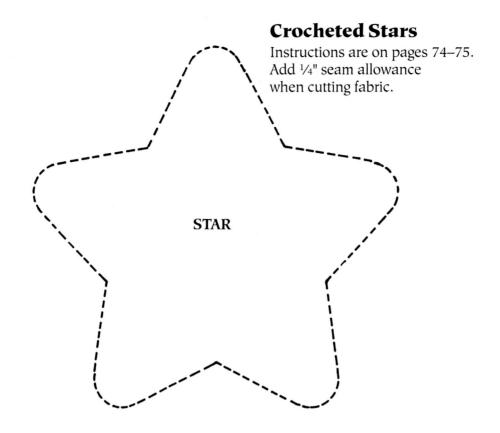

STAR

Miniature Mittens Ornament

Instructions are on page 75.
Add ¼" seam allowance when cutting fabric.

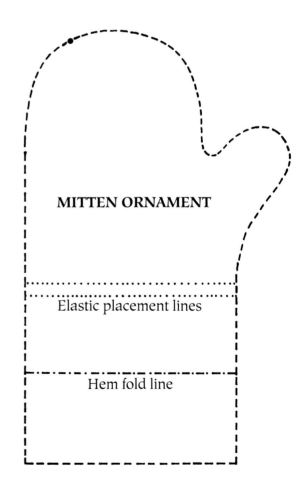

MITTEN ORNAMENT

Elastic placement lines

Hem fold line

Baby Jesus

Instructions are on pages 77–78.
Add ¼" seam allowances when cutting fabrics.

BABY
FACE

BABY
HAND

BABY HEAD SIDE

Fold this area inside cap.

Fold around face.

BABY CAP

Gather this edge for cap center back.

Center front
Gather for neck edge.

Center back

Center back

BABY BUNTING BODY

Bottom edge

BABY ARM UNIT
(Sleeves)

Gather for wrist.

Gather.

Gather.

Top fold line

Gather for wrist.

CANDY CANE ORNAMENT

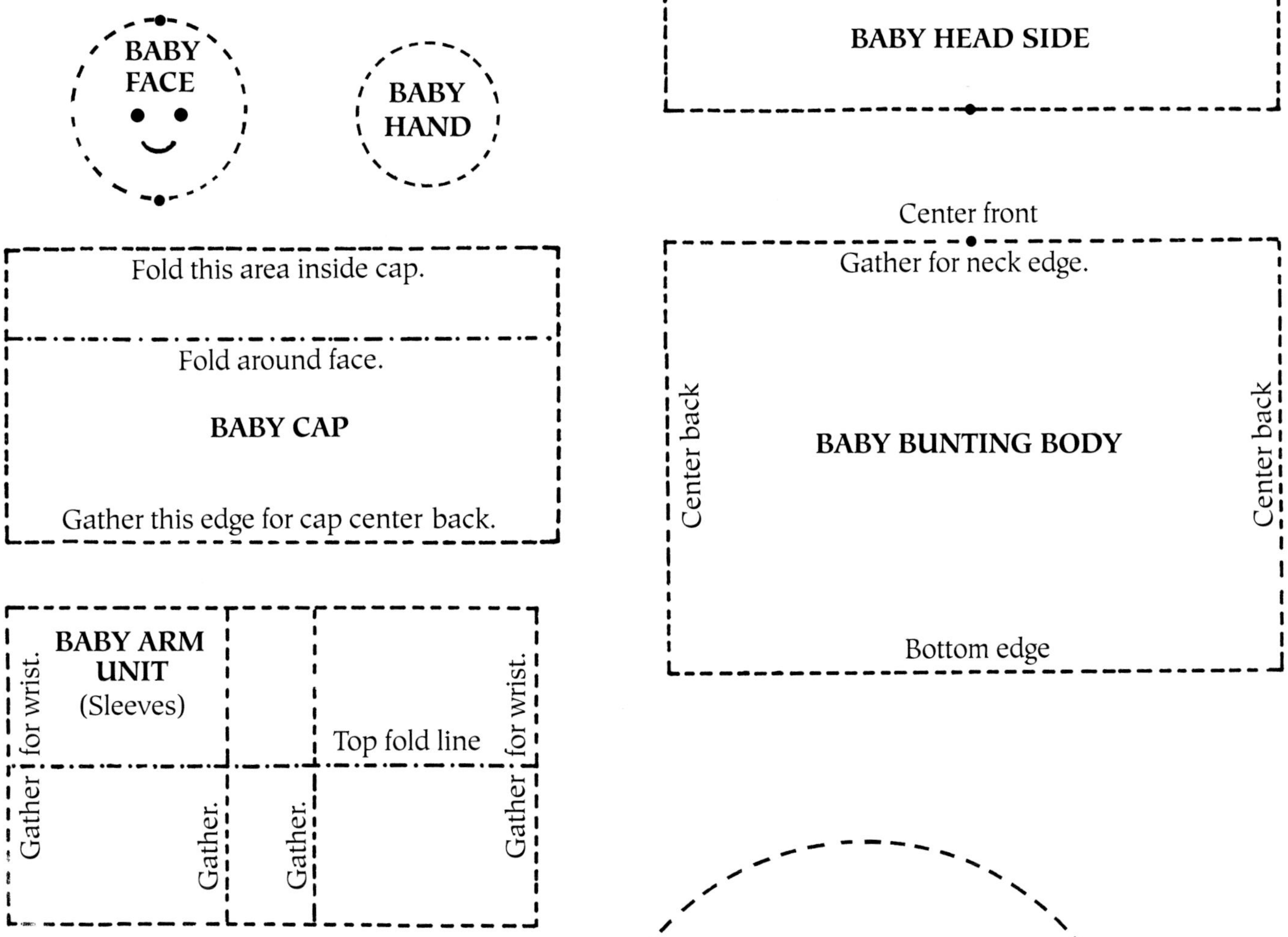

Candy Cane Heart Ornament

Instructions are on page 79.
Add ¼" seam allowances when cutting fabrics.

Leave open between dots.

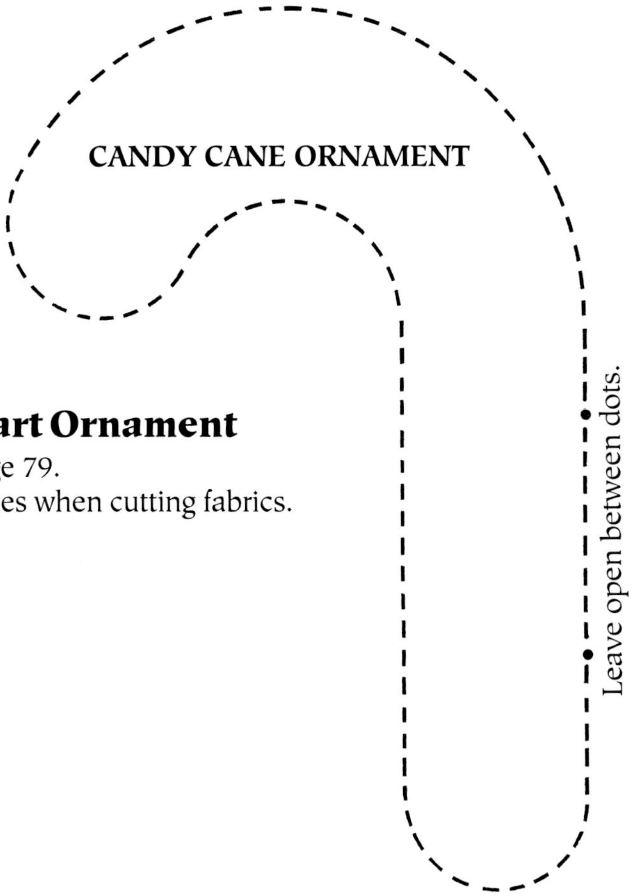

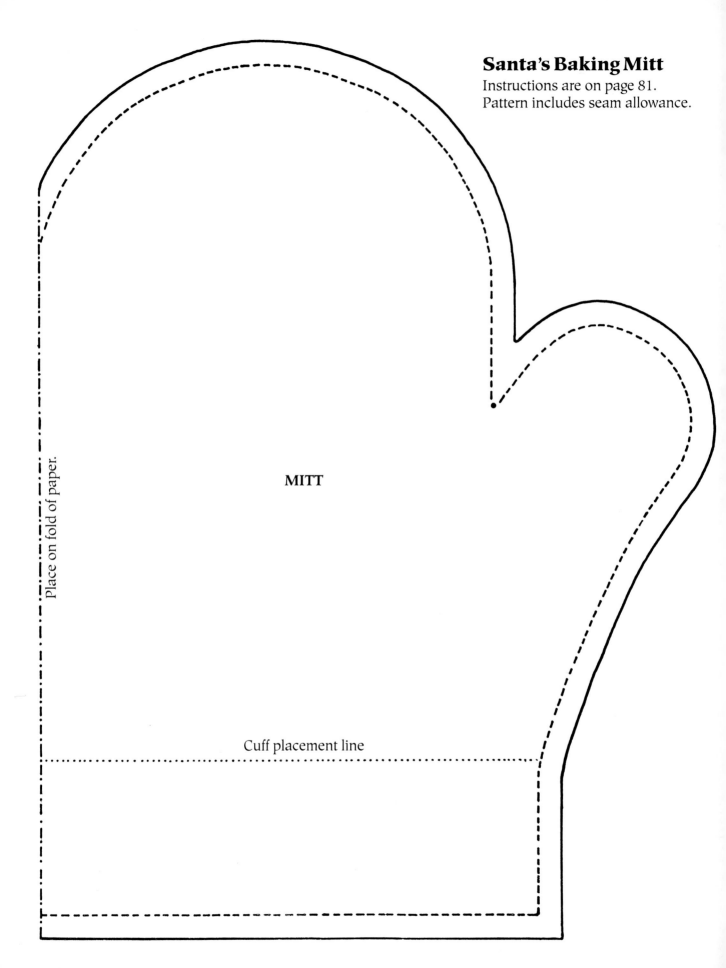

Santa's Baking Mitt

Instructions are on page 81.
Pattern includes seam allowance.

MITT

Place on fold of paper.

Cuff placement line

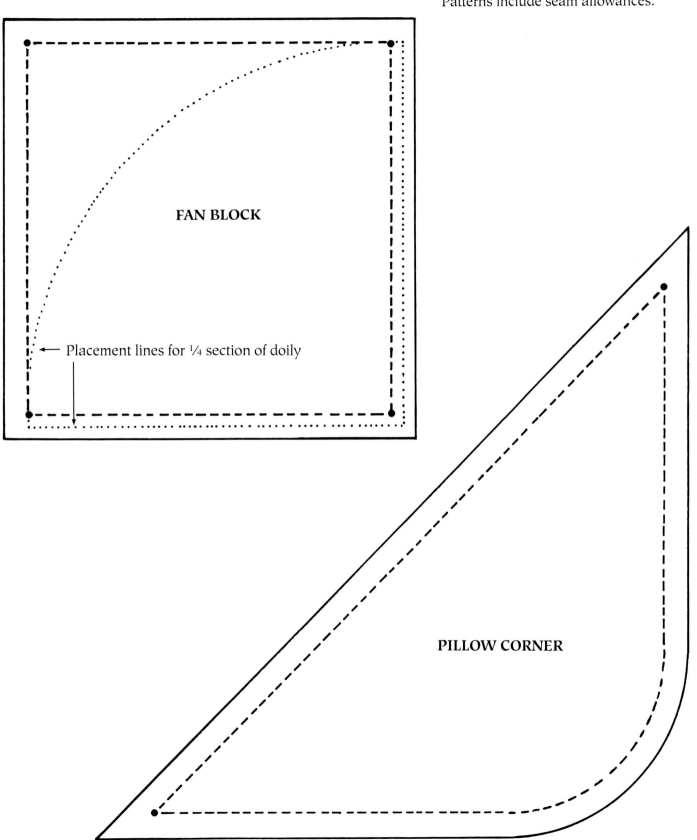

Lace Fan Pillow

Instructions are on page 85.
Patterns include seam allowances.

FAN BLOCK

← Placement lines for ¼ section of doily

PILLOW CORNER

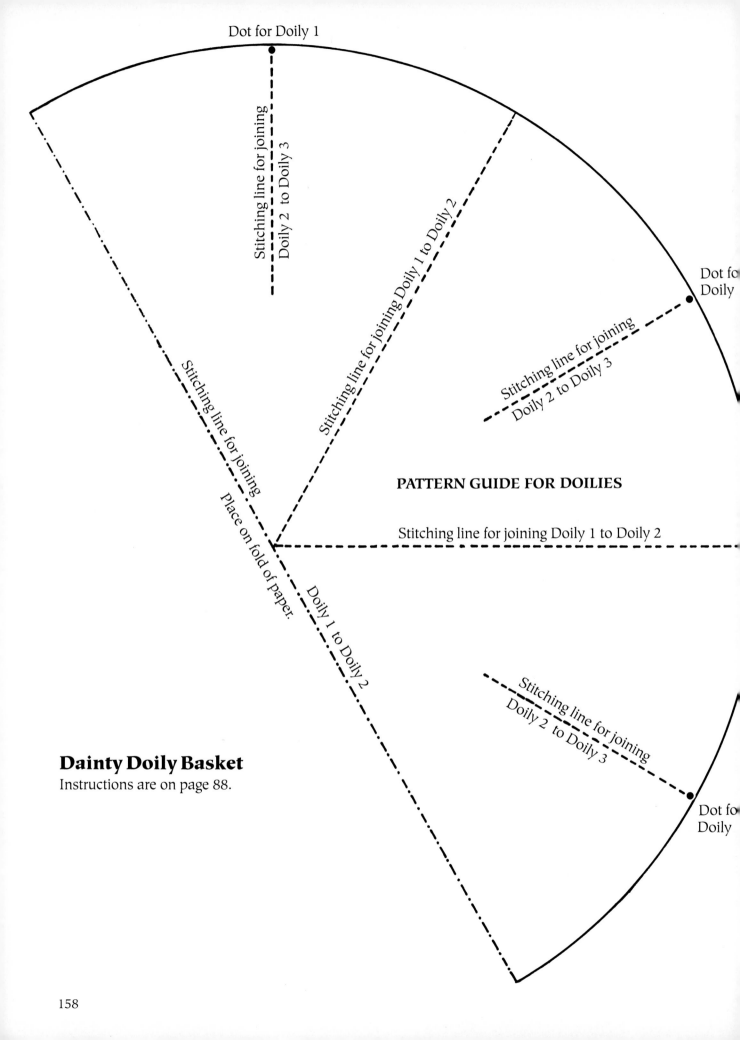

Dot for Doily 1

Stitching line for joining Doily 2 to Doily 3

Stitching line for joining Doily 1 to Doily 2

Dot for Doily

Stitching line for joining Doily 2 to Doily 3

PATTERN GUIDE FOR DOILIES

Stitching line for joining Doily 1 to Doily 2

Stitching line for joining

Place on fold of paper.

Doily 1 to Doily 2

Stitching line for joining Doily 2 to Doily 3

Dot fo Doily

Dainty Doily Basket
Instructions are on page 88.

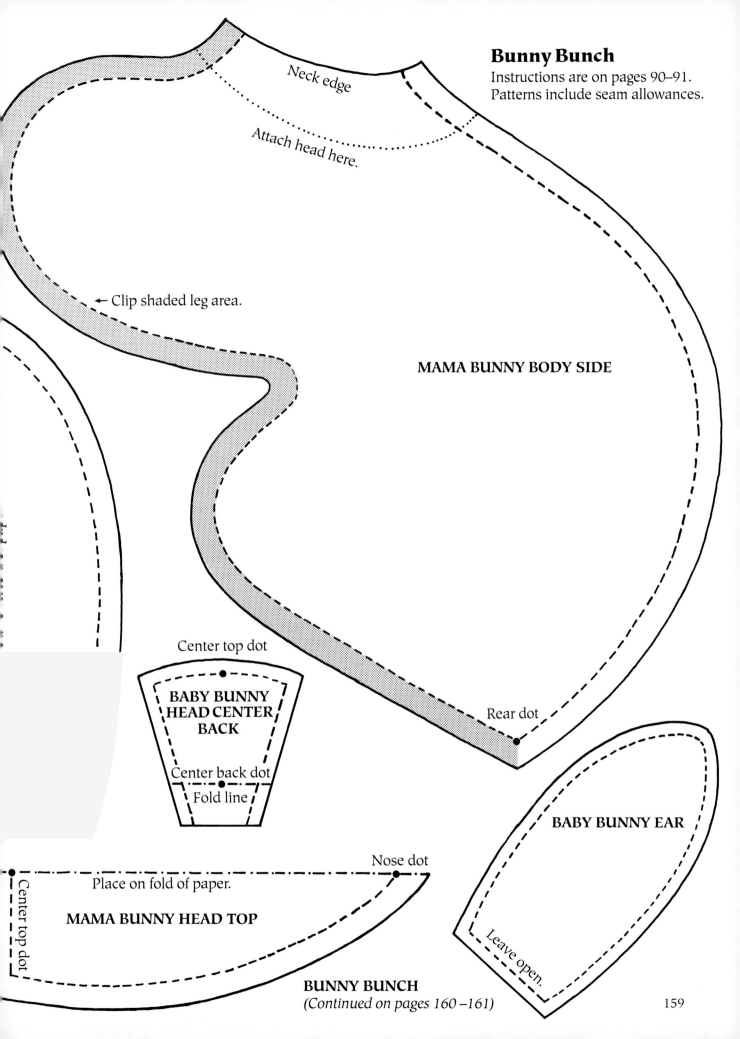

Bunny Bunch

Instructions are on pages 90–91.
Patterns include seam allowances.

Neck edge

Attach head here.

← Clip shaded leg area.

MAMA BUNNY BODY SIDE

Rear dot

Center top dot

**BABY BUNNY
HEAD CENTER
BACK**

Center back dot

Fold line

BABY BUNNY EAR

Leave open.

Nose dot

Place on fold of paper.

Center top dot

MAMA BUNNY HEAD TOP

BUNNY BUNCH
(Continued on pages 160–161)

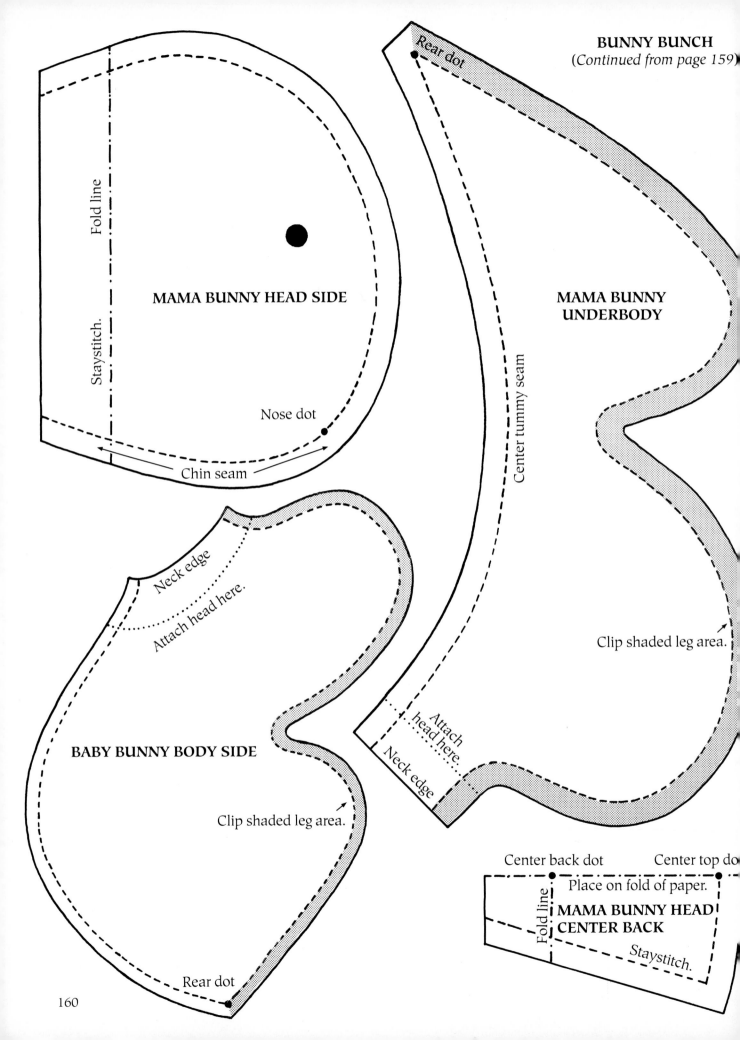

MAMA BUNNY HEAD SIDE

Fold line

Staystitch.

Nose dot

Chin seam

MAMA BUNNY
UNDERBODY

Center tummy seam

Rear dot

Clip shaded leg area.

Neck edge

Attach head here.

BABY BUNNY BODY SIDE

Clip shaded leg area.

Attach head here.

Neck edge

Rear dot

Center back dot

Center top dot

Place on fold of paper.

**MAMA BUNNY HEAD
CENTER BACK**

Fold line

Staystitch.

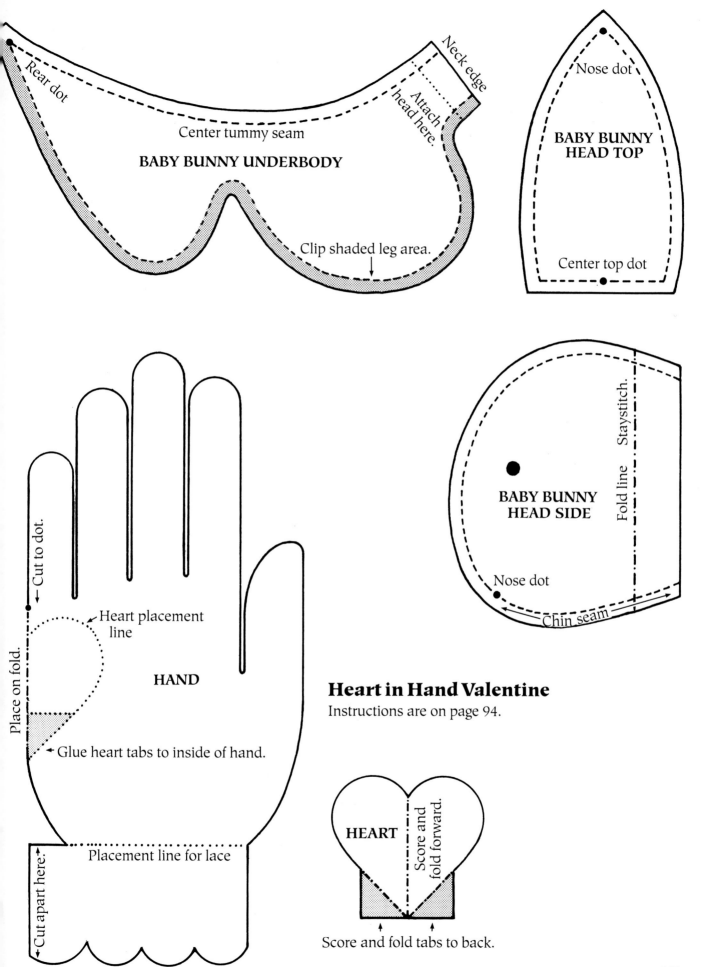

BABY BUNNY UNDERBODY

Rear dot

Center tummy seam

Neck edge

Attach head here.

Clip shaded leg area.

BABY BUNNY HEAD TOP

Nose dot

Center top dot

BABY BUNNY HEAD SIDE

Fold line

Staystitch

Nose dot

Chin seam

Cut to dot.

Heart placement line

Place on fold.

HAND

Glue heart tabs to inside of hand.

Placement line for lace

Cut apart here.

Heart in Hand Valentine

Instructions are on page 94.

HEART

Score and fold forward.

Score and fold tabs to back.

161

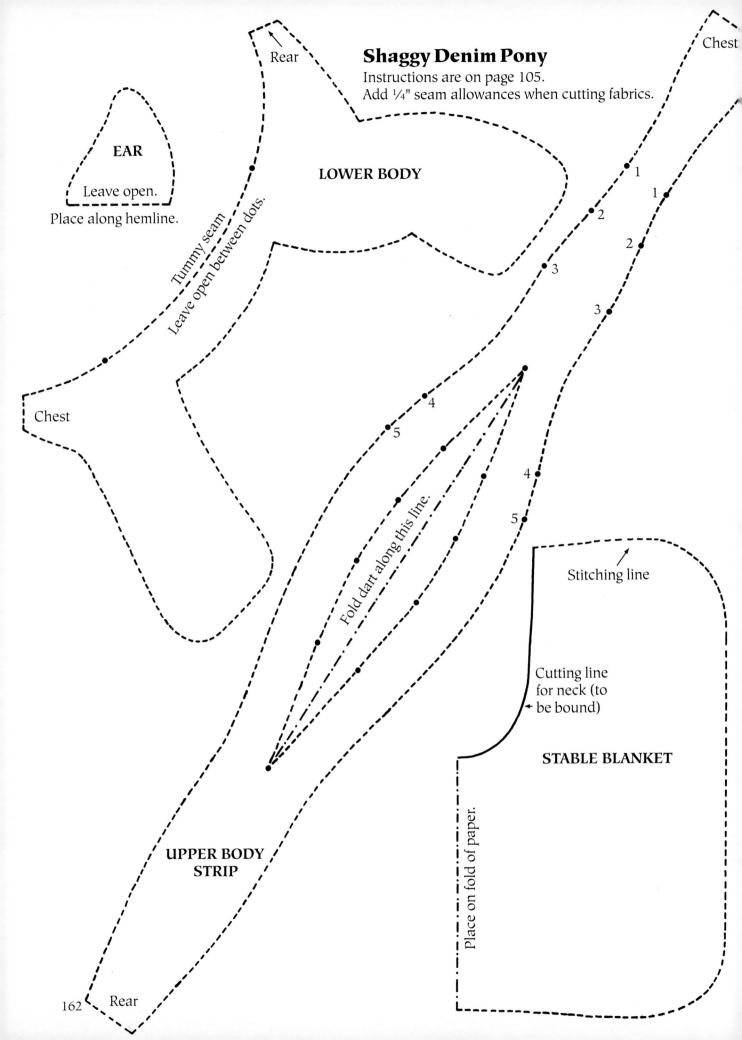

Shaggy Denim Pony

Instructions are on page 105.
Add ¼" seam allowances when cutting fabrics.

Rear

Chest

EAR

Leave open.

Place along hemline.

LOWER BODY

Tummy seam

Leave open between dots.

1

1

2

2

3

3

Chest

4

5

4

5

Fold dart along this line.

Stitching line

Cutting line
for neck (to
be bound)

STABLE BLANKET

Place on fold of paper.

**UPPER BODY
STRIP**

Rear

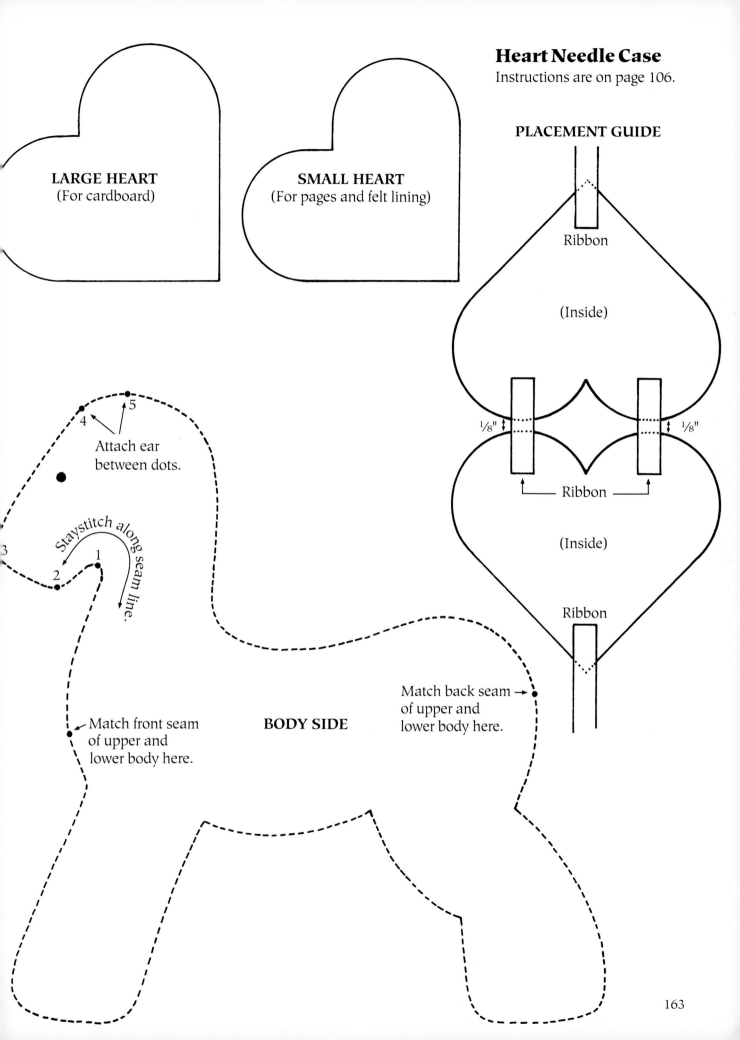

Heart Needle Case

Instructions are on page 106.

LARGE HEART
(For cardboard)

SMALL HEART
(For pages and felt lining)

PLACEMENT GUIDE

Ribbon

(Inside)

1/8"   1/8"

Ribbon

(Inside)

Ribbon

Attach ear
between dots.

Staystitch along seam line.

Match front seam
of upper and
lower body here.

BODY SIDE

Match back seam
of upper and
lower body here.

163

LARGE
WINDOW
AND
FRAME

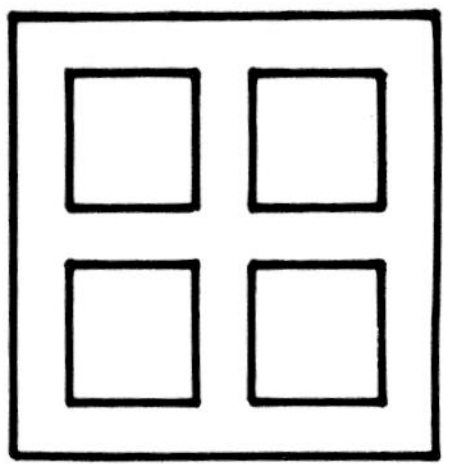

SMALL
WINDOW
AND
FRAME

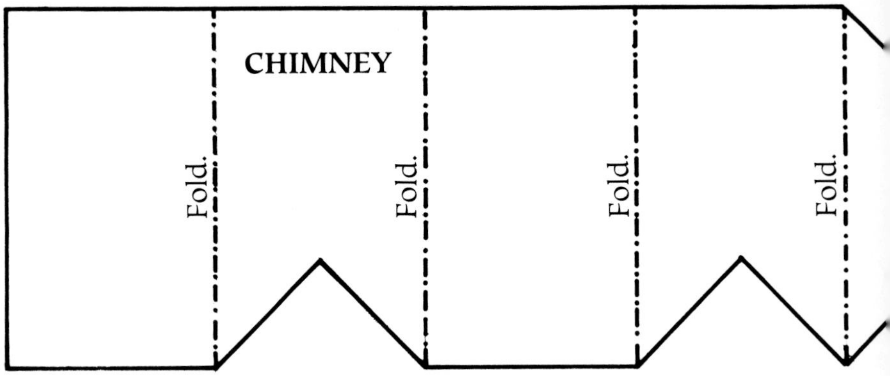

CHIMNEY

Fold. Fold. Fold. Fold.

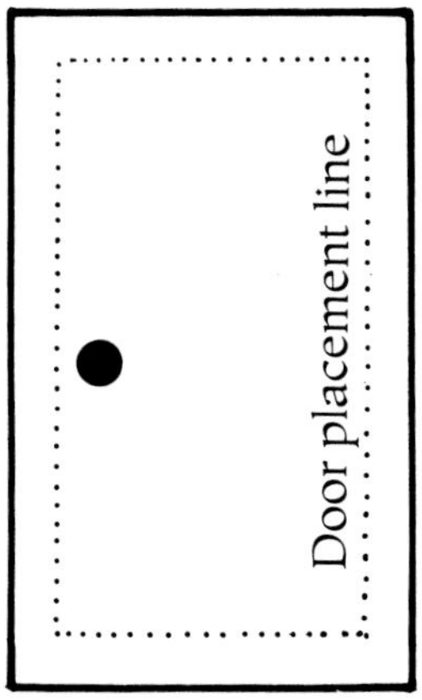

Door placement line

DOOR FRAME

Cozy Cottage Box

Instructions are on pages 108–109.

Miniature Sailboat Quilt

Instructions are on page 110.
Patterns include seam allowances.

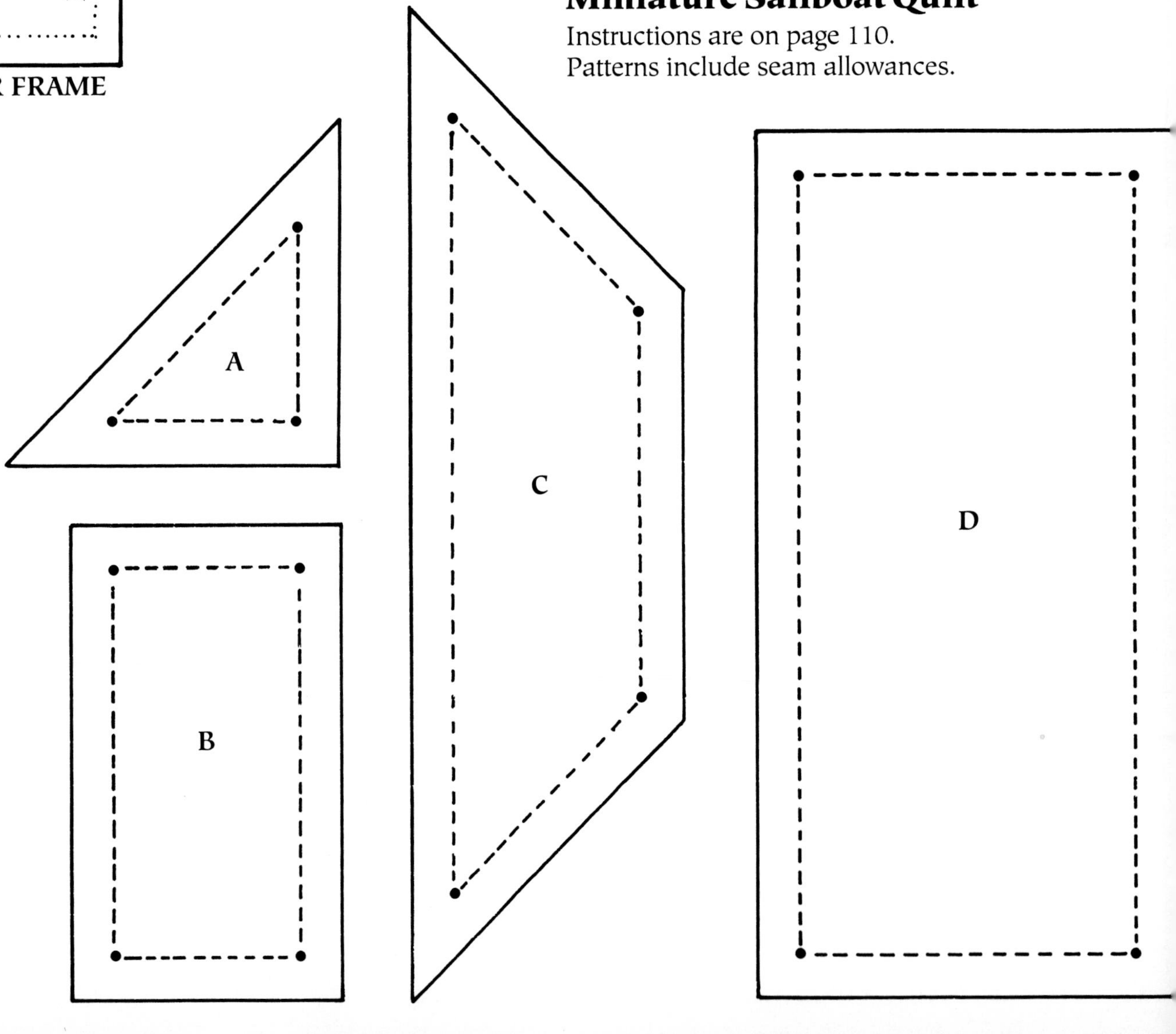

A

B

C

D

Pentagon Star Ball

Instructions are on pages 110–111.
Add ¼" hem allowance when cutting fabrics.

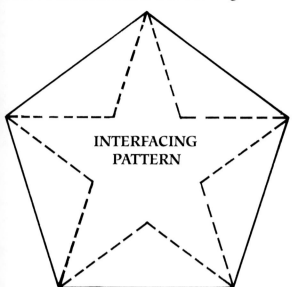

INTERFACING
PATTERN

Pentagon Basket

Instructions are on page 115.

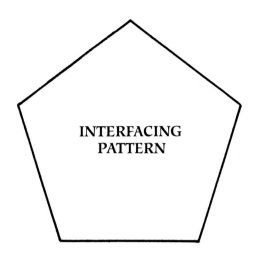

INTERFACING
PATTERN

E

Place on fold of paper.

F

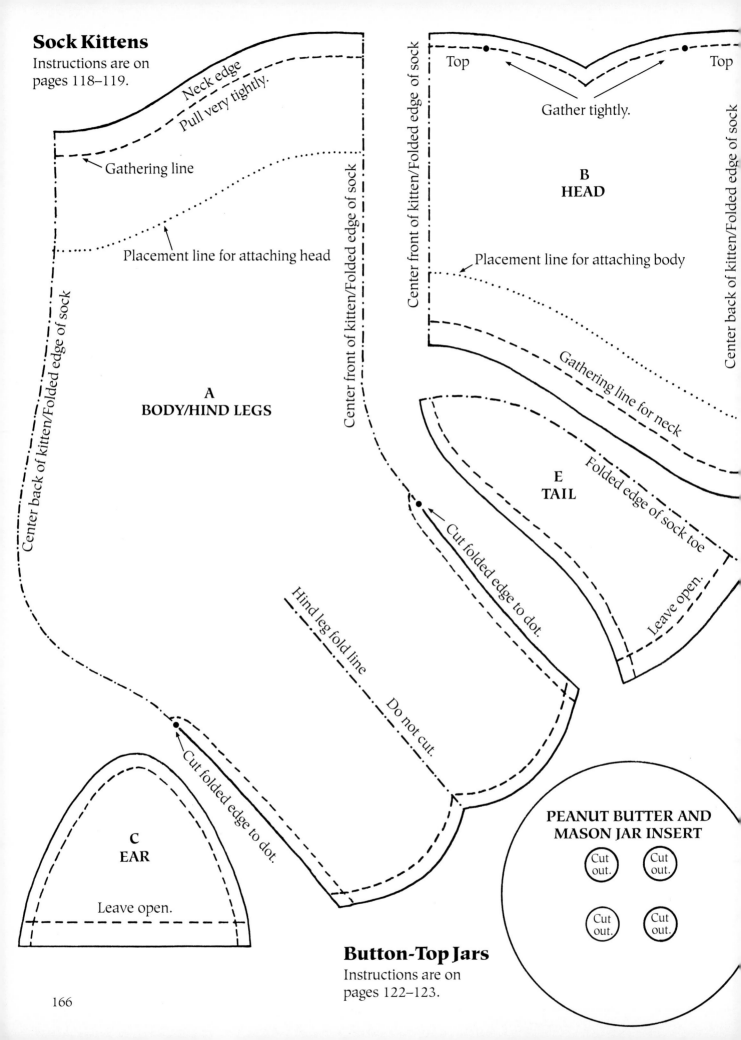

Sock Kittens

Instructions are on pages 118–119.

Neck edge

Pull very tightly.

Gathering line

Placement line for attaching head

Center back of kitten/Folded edge of sock

Center front of kitten/Folded edge of sock

**A
BODY/HIND LEGS**

Hind leg fold line

Do not cut.

Cut folded edge to dot.

**C
EAR**

Leave open.

Top   Top

Gather tightly.

**B
HEAD**

Center front of kitten/Folded edge of sock

Center back of kitten/Folded edge of sock

Placement line for attaching body

Gathering line for neck

**E
TAIL**

Folded edge of sock toe

Cut folded edge to dot.

Leave open.

**PEANUT BUTTER AND
MASON JAR INSERT**

Cut out.   Cut out.

Cut out.   Cut out.

Button-Top Jars

Instructions are on pages 122–123.

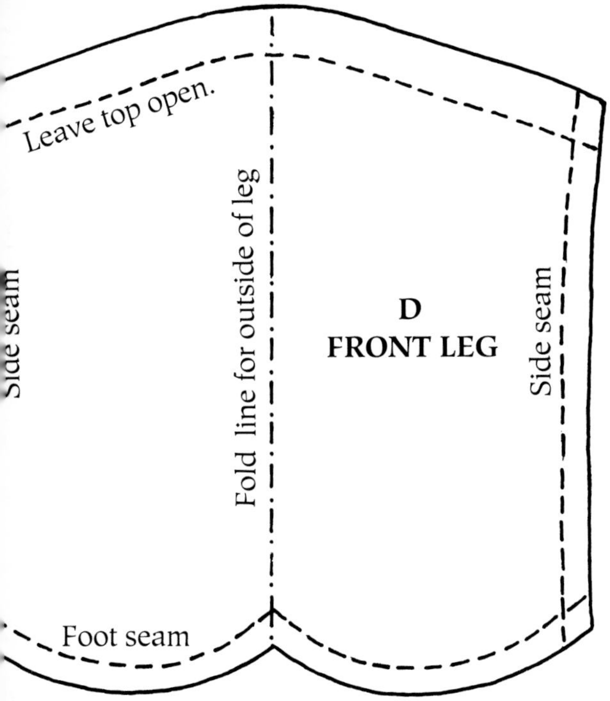

Leave top open.

Side seam

Fold line for outside of leg

**D
FRONT LEG**

Side seam

Foot seam

Sewing Basket Pincushion

Instructions are on pages 120–121.
Add ¼" seam allowances when cutting fabrics.

**A
BACKGROUND**

Cut 1 from floral print.
Cut 2 from star print.

Handle placement lines (Transfer to floral piece only.)

Cut 2 from star print.

**D
BASE**

**F
TABLETOP**

Cut 1 from check print.

**C
BASKET**

Cut 1 from star print.

**E
BASE**

Cut 1 from floral print. Reverse pattern and cut 1 from floral print.

B HANDLE

Cut 1 from star print.

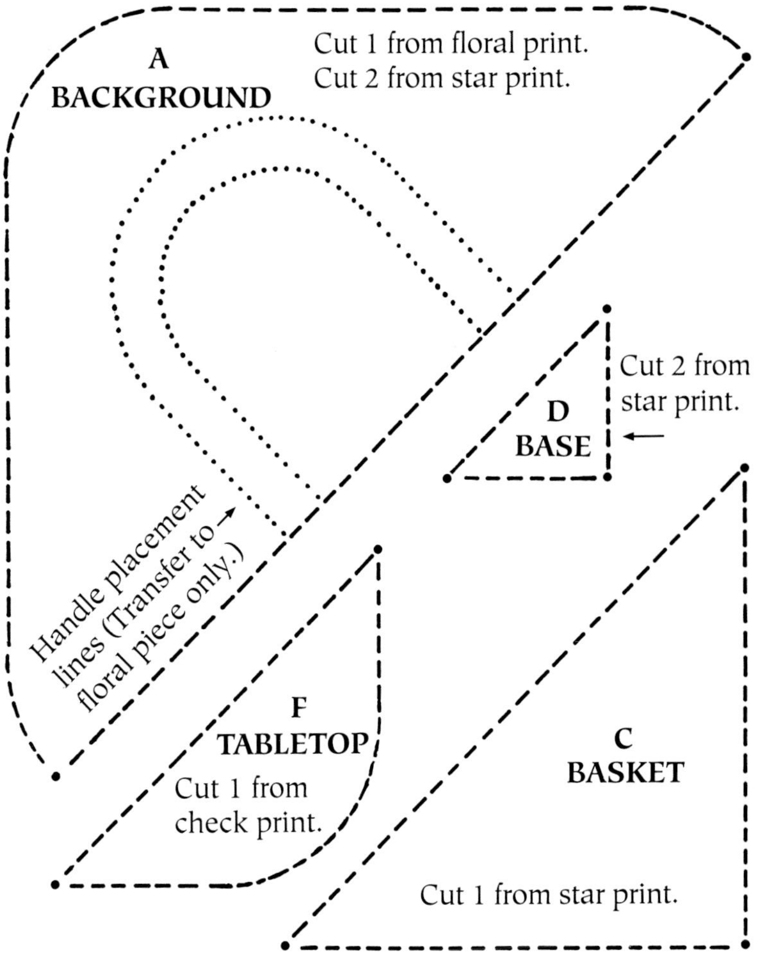

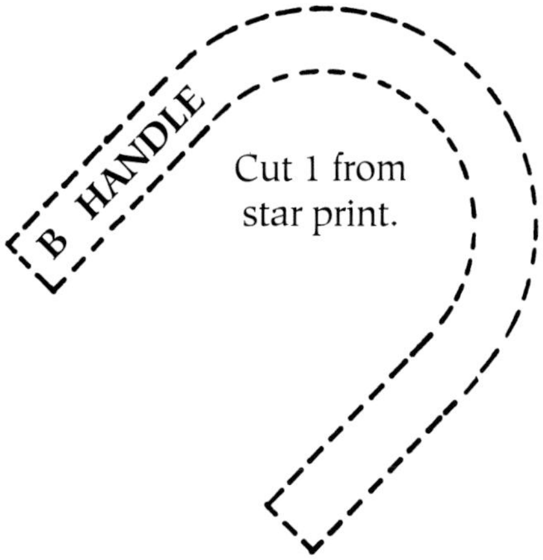

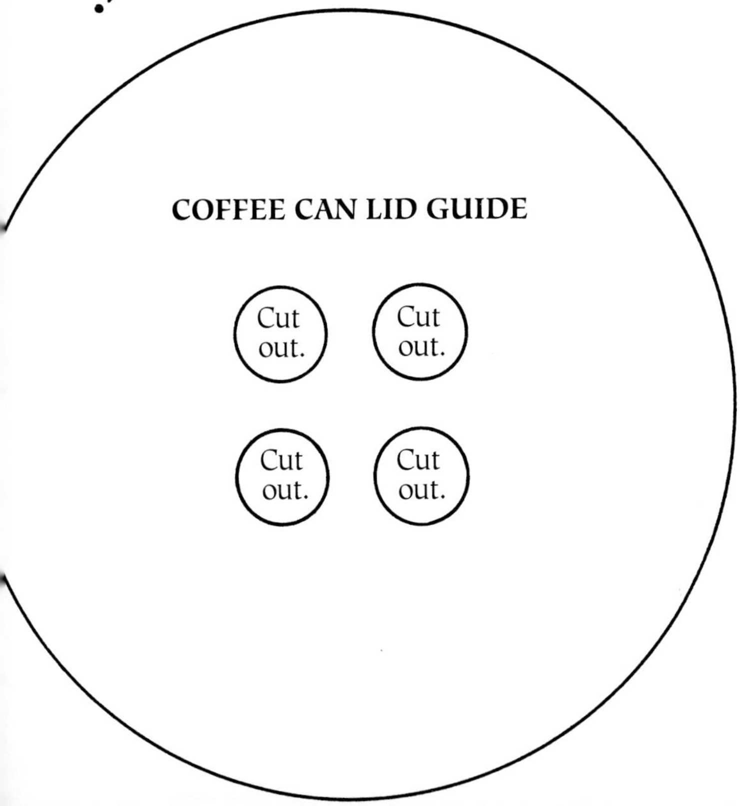

Ladybug Garden Gloves

Instructions are on page 122.
Add ¼" hem allowances when cutting fabrics.

HEAD

Cut 1 from black.

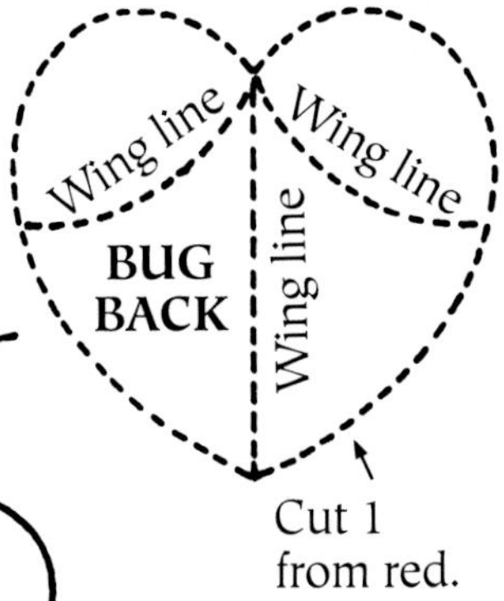

Wing line

Wing line

Wing line

BUG BACK

Cut 1 from red.

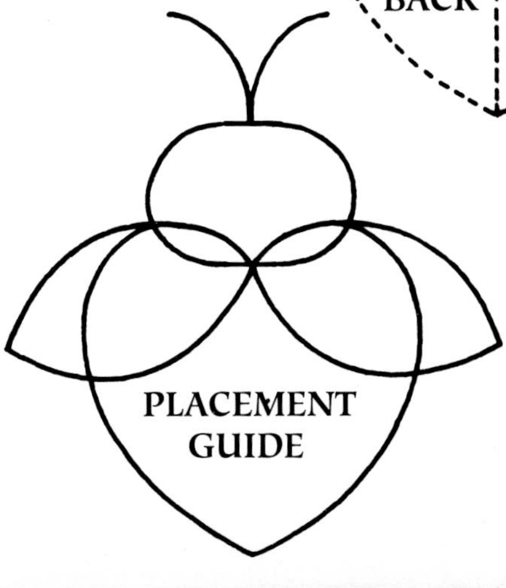

COFFEE CAN LID GUIDE

Cut out.

Cut out.

Cut out.

Cut out.

PLACEMENT GUIDE

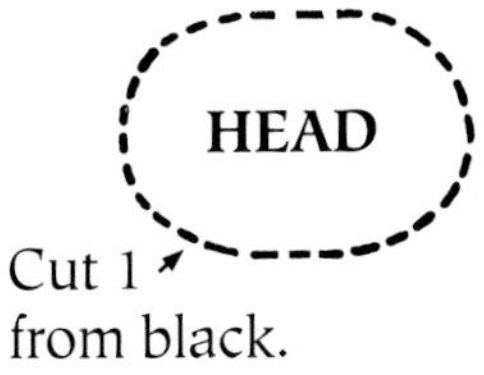

SUPPLIES & TECHNIQUES

Creative energy vanishes when you must stop and search the house for supplies. For safety and convenience, keep these items boxed together in a special hiding place.

Sewing Project Supplies

Scissors. Keep your sewing scissors sharp and don't use them to cut paper. For general cutting, use a pair of 5" sewing scissors. Embroidery scissors are perfect for trimming seam allowances and cutting out small pieces. You may also wish to have a pair of 7" or 8" lightweight sewing shears for larger projects. Pinking sheers are handy for simultaneously trimming and clipping narrow seam allowances.

Rotary cutter. As an occasional alternate to scissors, a rotary cutter in combination with a gridded self-healing mat and a straight-edge provides a fast way to cut multiple layers of fabric.

Craft knife. I prefer an X-acto® knife with a new #11 blade. I use it to cut patterns, and it's especially helpful for cutting out tiny details when making a template of a pattern. Practice using this tool, keeping the hand that is not holding the knife far away from the cutting line. Work slowly and carefully and do not use excessive pressure. Be sure to wrap old blades before discarding.

Pattern materials. You will use tracing paper to make most of the patterns. For making multiple projects, strengthen paper patterns by gluing them to thin cardboard or to the smooth side of fine sandpaper. The textured side of the sandpaper will prevent the pattern from slipping when placed on fabric.

Graph paper is great for making quick straight-sided patterns. Purchase a pad with ⅛" or ¼" squares for this purpose.

Special template plastic is sold in sheets at quilt shops and at many fabric stores. Acetate is also a good material for making patterns. It can be purchased in sheets from art supply stores or saved from the tops of gift and stationery boxes. The plastic lids from coffee cans also make sturdy pattern material.

Measuring tools. I prefer a 15"-wide transparent plastic sewing ruler (often referred to as "the sewer's T square") and a tape measure. Both of these can be purchased at fabric stores. Instead of a yardstick for making large patterns, I use a long metal ruler as a cutting edge along with the craft knife. These can be purchased from art supply stores.

Drawing tools. Use sharp #2 lead pencils on light fabric and white drawing pencils on dark fabric. Mechanical pencils are very helpful; because their points stay sharp, they're great for tracing around patterns and transferring markings.

Use a vanishing fabric marker when it will be necessary to remove pattern markings. It looks just like a felt-tip pen, but its ink usually fades within 48 hours and sometimes sooner. (Vanishing time varies according to the humidity. Fading takes especially long on some fabrics, such as felt.) Always test the pen on a swatch of your fabric to make sure the ink will completely vanish.

Seam ripper. You should have a seam ripper in your workbox. Here's a hint for using it: when you need to rip dark threads from dark fabric, trace the seam line with tailor's chalk to make the stitches more visible.

Tweezers. A pair of tweezers is especially handy for removing threads after you've ripped out seams. They can also help you thread the needle of your sewing machine.

Pins and needles. Rust- and corrosion-resistant pins are less likely to snag fabrics. I love extralong, super-strong quilting pins, but other sewers have different favorites.

I prefer fine, small needles, about 1½" long, for general sewing. But you'll need large-eyed embroidery needles when using multiple strands of embroidery floss. An assortment pack of sewing machine needles is important, too, although you'll use #11 and #14 most often.

When stitching by hand through sturdy fabrics, increase the needle power by first inserting the point into a bar of soap. Wearing a few cut-off fingers from an old rubber glove might help you pull the needle through thick or tough materials.

Pin keepers. Although magnetic pin dispensers are a bit expensive, they're convenient and spillproof, and they're also helpful in locating stray pins. I use several pincushions or dispensers at once, placing one at the cutting area, one at the sewing machine, and one at the ironing board. Another neat pin keeper is an adhesive-backed magnetic strip that will attach to the flat surface of your sewing machine. It attracts pins that wander too close to the needle or bobbin area.

Quilt batting. In most cases, use traditional-weight polyester batting. If necessary, you can substitute several thin layers for one thick layer. Purchase a crib-size piece for small projects and save the scraps for stuffing toys and pillows. If the batting is sold in a fat sausage shape, remove it from the plastic bag and unroll it at least a day before you plan to use it, letting the wrinkles relax. A tumble in a warm dryer will also help diminish wrinkles.

Pressing equipment. Pressing is very important for successful sewing, so place your ironing board near the sewing machine, if possible. Be sure to keep the iron's soleplate clean. (Check often, especially after using fusible web.)

A pressing cloth is a necessity, even if it's just a good-sized scrap of fabric. A small tailor's ham isn't a must, but it's helpful when pressing curved seams.

Other helpful tools. Embroidery hoops are useful when doing decorative hand stitchery. A 3"- or 4"-diameter hoop is handy for small projects.

For turning and stuffing small pieces, try a crochet hook or a blunt pencil (no lead showing). For larger work, use a wooden yardstick or a dowel. Once shapes are turned right side out, use a long, sturdy needle to pull out corners and curves (take care to avoid snagging the fabric). Washable fabric glue is a great time-saver, and the thicker its consistency, the less it will soak through the fabric. Always apply the glue sparingly. A glue stick is useful for quick basting jobs. Always test any glue on a fabric swatch before applying it to a final project. Allow the glue to dry thoroughly before you proceed with sewing.

Masking tape is another sewer's friend. When tracing patterns from this book, use it to anchor the tracing paper. (When you've finished tracing, the tape lifts off easily.) Masking tape can also be placed on the throat plate of your sewing machine to mark the seam allowance width. When you are machine-stitching a project that has a top layer of batting, the presser foot may often catch the top fibers. To avoid this nuisance, wrap the "toes" of the presser foot together with a single piece of tape.

Applying liquid ravel preventer or clear nail polish to cut ends of ribbons will prevent fraying.

Fabrics. When yardages are given, it should be assumed that the fabrics are at least 44" wide, unless otherwise specified. Lay all the pattern pieces as close to each other as possible, but maintain enough space for seam allowances if they need to be added.

Inspect fabrics carefully before purchasing and avoid those that fray easily. Use prewashed lightweight to medium-weight fabrics unless others are suggested. When the grain of the fabric is important to the design, grain lines are marked on the patterns. You should lay out patterns accordingly. Since felt isn't woven, it doesn't have a grain, so you can place patterns freely. Because the heat and moisture from an iron can cause felt to shrink, steam out wrinkles before marking and cutting felt. Most felt is not washable. There is a washable felt available, and for this type, I recommend gentle hand washing and line drying.

Sewing Project Techniques

Making patterns. Draw neat and accurate patterns, copying all the dots and embroidery and placement lines and labeling each piece. Or, to reproduce patterns quickly, use a photocopier. Though all the patterns in this book are protected by copyright, you may photocopy them to make the projects for your personal use.

Because of space limitations, occasionally only half or a quarter of a pattern is given. To make a complete pattern, trace the section on folded tracing paper and then transfer markings to full-sized pattern. The sectional patterns in this book are not meant to be placed on folded fabric unless indicated.

Before you begin tracing the patterns, read the directions for the project and determine whether the seam allowances are included or must be added when cutting the fabric. *Unless otherwise noted in the instructions, all seam allowances for these projects are ¼".*

Solid pattern lines indicate cutting lines for fabrics and felt, broken lines indicate stitching lines, fine dotted lines indicate placement lines, and alternating broken and dotted lines indicate fold lines.

I frequently cut quilt patterns from acetate and then, using nail polish, label them and paint a thin layer of color around the edges. This outlining makes it easier to center the transparent patterns on the fabric motifs. It also helps me locate the patterns quickly. Because of the painted label, I can also tell at a glance when the pattern is reversed.

Marking fabrics. Unless otherwise instructed, place each pattern piece facedown on the wrong side of the fabric, hold it or pin it in place, and trace around it with a sharp pencil.

When tracing small pattern pieces on fabrics, first place an 8½" x 11" piece of fine-textured sandpaper on your work surface. With this base, the fabric will not be pulled as much when you trace around the patterns.

Transferring markings. There are several ways to transfer markings to the right side of the fabric.
1. You can make a stencil of some markings on patterns, such as those for facial features, by cutting out the details. Center the pattern on the front of the cutout fabric shape and trace the details, using very light pencil strokes or a vanishing fabric marker. Or draw the details on

the back of the fabric and transfer them to the front with tiny basting stitches.
2. To transfer details using the rub-off technique, trace the details on the back of the patterns with a sharp #2 lead pencil. Center the pattern (marked side down) on the front of the fabric piece and then rub off the design with a flat wooden stick or a similar burnisher.
3. A sunny window can also be useful when transferring pattern details. Tape the pattern to the wrong side of a piece of fabric of manageable size and trace the pattern outline. Then tape the fabric and pattern to the window (pattern against the glass) and lightly trace the details onto the right side of the fabric.
4. When transferring details to felt, use the following method: Instead of making a template of the pattern, use a large needle to make holes along the pattern lines and details. Hold the pattern against the felt and carefully mark through the holes with a sharp pencil.
5. When I embroider facial details on a stuffed toy, I often trace the features with a vanishing fabric marker after the

head is stuffed. Since stuffing can distort the face considerably, I wait until after the head is formed to find the best position for the features.

Whichever method you use, trace lightly. Once you've marked the right side of the fabric, do not iron over the markings. (Heat may set the lines permanently, even those made with a vanishing marker.)

Stitching and trimming seams. Although shortcuts are tempting, it's best to pin and baste your fabric pieces together before stitching them. If there are dots to be matched, line up the pieces, with right sides facing and raw edges aligned, and push a pin straight down through both fabric layers at the dots. Then pin along the seam allowance (but not on the seam line), perpendicular to the edge. Baste, remove pins, and then machine-stitch the seams.

I don't advise sewing over pins. There is too much chance of injuring your machine or yourself!

Grading seam allowances. To make seams smooth on the right side of the fabric, bulky seam allowances (those involving batting or several layers of fabric) should be graded. Cut each layer of the seam allowance a different distance from the stitching line. For instance, if a seam allowance is ½" wide, trim the bottom layer to ⅜" and the top layer to ¼". Always cut across corners, trimming close to the stitching line. Make vertical clips in the seam allowance on curves, clipping almost to the stitching line.

Gathering. When making long machine stitches that will be gathered, two closely placed rows of stitches, 1/8" apart, are better than one. If you use different colors for the top and bobbin threads, it will be easy to identify the bobbin thread to pull for gathering.

Applying bias tape. Before binding an edge with bias tape, trim the seam allowance so that it is approximately 1/16" narrower than the bias tape. If the seam allowances are very thick, zigzag-stitch edges to flatten. Clip into any angles around the shape.

When using double-fold bias tape or quilt binding as a flat trim, use the following method: Open the center fold of the tape and trim one folded edge 1/8" or more from the center fold. Discard the trimming.

Mitering bias tape. Refer to the figures and the instructions in the Diagram to the right.

Quilting. When batting is sandwiched between two pieces of fabric, the layers must be pinned and basted together so that they won't shift. Work from the center to the outside of the piece, making 1" stitches horizontally, vertically, and diagonally across the piece. To quilt, use a short quilting needle and make uniform running stitches through all layers. Gather several stitches on your needle before pulling the thread through the fabric. Quilting stitches are usually placed 1/4" from the seam line, but I sometimes quilt right on the seam line or "in the ditch." For machine-quilting, use long straight stitches.

Adding appliqué. If you plan to handstitch an appliqué, the piece must be cut with a hem allowance. For the best results, make tiny basting stitches along the outline of the appliqué shape to create a precise folding edge for the hem. To make the hemming of small pieces easier, cut them out with pinking shears or clip hem allowances at close intervals. Turn under the hem allowance and baste. Pin and baste the shape in place and appliqué it invisibly with slipstitches or blanket-stitch the shape's edges.

If you intend to attach an appliqué with machine zigzag stitches, it need not be cut with a hem allowance. To secure the appliqué before stitching, use fusible web to attach it to the fabric and then stitch with very close zigzag stitches.

Stuffing and such. Polyester stuffing is easiest to work with. Keep it clean and free of thread and fabric clippings.

It's best to add stuffing in small quantities. When filling a doll or an animal, start with the smaller parts, such as the arms, the legs, and the head. To stuff firmly, use a crochet hook, a blunt pencil, or a wooden spoon handle. (Have an extra bag of stuffing on hand. You'll almost always need more than you expect.) Most projects will need to be stuffed firmly, although occasionally a project will require a flat, softly stuffed appearance. Mold the item with your hands as you stuff it.

Some words of caution. Please don't add buttons, bells, pom-poms, or similar embellishments to gifts that will go to households with very young children. Heed my advice if I suggest that a certain design is not intended to be a plaything. There are lots of gifts for little ones in this book, so choose the safe ones, use pre-washed materials, and stitch items securely.

Diagram: Mitering Bias Tape Used as a Binding

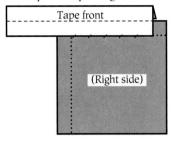
Figure A: Open center fold of tape and place one edge of tape along placement line. Slipstitch tape to right side of fabric.

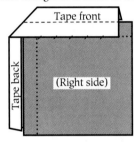
Figure B: At corner, fold loose end of tape toward wrong side of fabric at 45° angle.

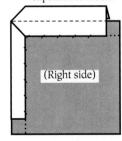
Figure C: Turn work over and pin tape along placement line as shown.

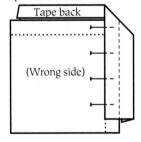
Figure D: Turn work to right side. Fold flap of pinned tape toward right side and slipstitch to fabric.

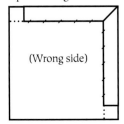
Figure E: Turn work to wrong side, fold down remaining tape, and pin in position. Slipstitch tape to wrong side of fabric.

Paper Project Supplies

Paper. To assure best results, use sturdy, high-quality paper, such as Canson or Crescent, when making the paper projects in this book. These richly hued papers can be found in art supply stores. Or consider colored paper used for pastel drawings and watercolors. Some large photocopy stores offer beautifully colored heavyweight paper for sale by the sheet. Don't be tempted to substitute construction paper. It often splits when scored and folded.

Cutting tools. You'll need a cutting board or a piece of heavy cardboard (not corrugated) to protect your work surface. I prefer an X-acto® knife with a new #11 blade for cutting and scoring. Dull blades make ragged, inaccurate cuts, so keep an extra supply of blades on hand. Standard ¼" and ⅛" paper punches are sometimes used for paper projects in this book.

Paper Project Techniques

Making patterns. Accuracy is essential when drawing and cutting patterns for paper projects. A photocopier is the most efficient way to reproduce paper project patterns. Photocopy the pattern directly from the book, glue the photocopy to lightweight cardboard or acetate, if desired, and then cut out the pattern.

If no photocopier is available, trace the pattern and markings onto tracing paper, glue the tracing paper to cardboard or acetate, and cut out the pattern.

Marking paper. Transfer patterns to art paper with a sharp #2 lead pencil. Score fold lines by lightly drawing the sharp end of a craft knife blade over the fold line.

Other hints. To increase the art paper's flexibility on pieces that will be curved, such as cone shapes and basket handles, gently pull the piece over a table edge or a scissors blade. The paper will curl slightly, making it easier to bend into shape.

To keep your hands free for other tasks, hold glued areas of paper projects together with paper clips or clothespins until dry.

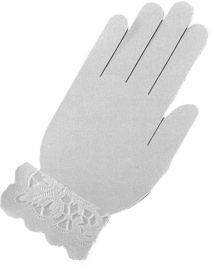

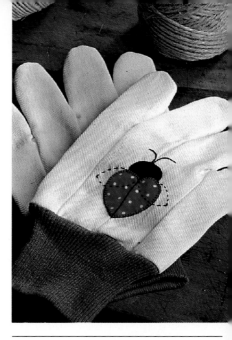

Embroidery Stitches

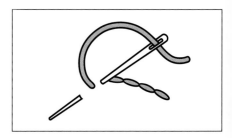

Backstitch. Working from right to left, or top to bottom, bring the needle up on the guideline. Take a stitch backward and bring the needle up an equal distance ahead of the first hole made by the thread. Repeat, taking the needle back to the beginning of the previous stitch.

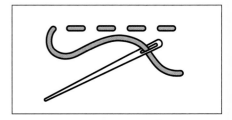

Running stitch. Working from right to left, make evenly spaced stitches of the same size. Use running stitches for quilting, gathering several stitches on the needle before pulling the thread through the fabric.

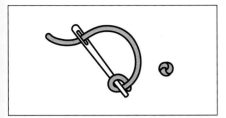

French knot. Bring the needle up where you want an embroidered knot. Wrap the thread several times around the point of the needle. Insert the needle again as close as possible to the spot where the thread emerged. Holding the wrapped thread in place, pull the thread to the wrong side.

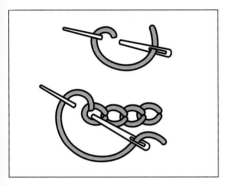

Chain stitch. Working from right to left, or top to bottom, bring the needle up and make a loop with the thread. Holding the loop against the fabric, insert the needle again as close as possible to where the thread last emerged. Take a short stitch over the final thread to anchor it.

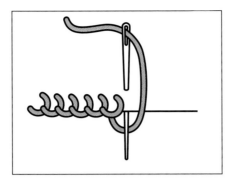

Blanket stitch. This is a decorative stitch for finishing edges. Bring the needle out along the edge of the fabric. Insert the needle above and to the right of the starting point and bring it out in line with the last stitch on the fabric edge, keeping the thread behind the needle point. Continue working from left to right and top to bottom.

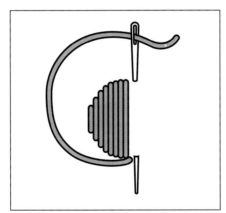

Satin stitch. Working from one end of traced detail to the other, bring the needle up on one edge of shape and insert it on the opposite edge. Carrying the thread behind the work, repeat from edge to edge, keeping the stitches parallel, smooth, and close together.

RESOURCES

You will find most of the supplies and materials for the projects in this book at your local stores. If these items are not available in your area, please write to the following companies to receive product and catalog information:

Stuffing Pellets
UNIEK, Inc.
805 Uniek Drive
P.O. Box 457
Waunakee, WI 53597-0457
(608) 849-9999

Doilies, Poly Boning, Lace, Tiny Buttons, Squeaker
Home-Sew
P.O. Box 4099
Department LG
Bethlehem, PA 18018-0099
(610) 867-3833
Call for free catalog.

Balsam Fir Tips
Maine Balsam Fir Products
P.O. Box 9
West Paris, ME 04289
(800) 5-BALSAM
(Please enclose a self-addressed, stamped envelope.)

Lavender, Potpourri
The Rosemary House
120 South Market Street
Mechanicsburg, PA 17055
(Catalog $2.00)

INDEX

Acknowledgments

Special thanks to the following:

C. M. Offray & Sons, Inc., for
supplying ribbons

Mary Reilley, Philadelphia, Pennsylvania,
for her updated design of the
Crocheted Stars on page 74

Photographers

Photographs by John O'Hagan,
except for the following:
Ralph Anderson, 56, 108, 116 (girl), 122
Sylvia Martin, 13, 43, 44, 49, 50, 55, 57, 62,
65, 69, 70, 76, 80